Essays and Studies 2000

Series Editor: Gordon Campbell
Associate Editor: Helen Lucas

The English Association

The objects of the English Association are to promote the knowledge and appreciation of the English language and its literature, and to foster good practice in its teaching and learning at all levels.

The Association pursues these aims by creating opportunities of co-operation among all those interested in English; by furthering the recognition of English as essential in education; by discussing methods of English teaching; by holding lectures, conferences, and other meetings; by publishing journals, books, and leaflets; and by forming local branches.

Publications

The Year's Work in English Studies. An annual bibliography. Published by Blackwell.

The Year's Work in Critical and Cultural Theory. An annual bibliography. Published by Blackwell.

Essays and Studies. An annual volume of essays by various scholars assembled by the collector covering usually a wide range of subjects and authors from the medieval to the modern. Published by D.S. Brewer.

English. A journal of the Association, *English* is published three times a year by the Association.

The Use of English. A journal of the Association, *The Use of English* is published three times a year by the Association.

Newsletter. A *Newsletter* is published three times a year giving information about forthcoming publications, conferences, and other matters of interest.

Benefits of Membership

Institutional Membership

Full members receive copies of *The Year's Work in English Studies*, *Essays and Studies*, *English* (3 issues) and three *Newsletters*.

Ordinary Membership covers *English* (3 issues) and three *Newsletters*.

Schools Membership includes copies of each issue of *English* and *The Use of English*, one copy of *Essays and Studies*, three *Newsletters*, and preferential booking and rates for various conferences held by the Association.

Individual Membership

Individuals take out Basic Membership, which entitles them to buy all regular publications of the English Association at a discounted price, and attend Association gatherings.

For further details write to The Secretary, The English Association, The University of Leicester, University Road, Leicester, LE1 7RH.

Essays and Studies 2000

Reading the 'New' Literatures in a Postcolonial Era

Edited by
Susheila Nasta

for the English Association

D. S. BREWER

ESSAYS AND STUDIES 2000
IS VOLUME FIFTY-THREE IN THE NEW SERIES
OF ESSAYS AND STUDIES COLLECTED ON BEHALF OF
THE ENGLISH ASSOCIATION
ISSN 0071–1357

First published 2000
D. S. Brewer, Cambridge

D. S. Brewer is an imprint of Boydell & Brewer Ltd
PO Box 9, Woodbridge, Suffolk IP12 3DF, UK
and of Boydell & Brewer Inc.
PO Box 41026, Rochester NY 14604–4126, USA
website: http://www.boydell.co.uk

ISBN 0 85991 601 4

A catalogue record for this title is available
from the British Library

The Library of Congress has cataloged this serial publication:
Catalog card number 36–8431

This book is printed on acid-free paper

Printed in Great Britain by
St Edmundsbury Press Limited, Bury St Edmunds, Suffolk

Contents

Introduction: Stepping out. Reading the 'New' Literatures in a Postcolonial Era

SUSHEILA NASTA

> the new Englishes do not form one English . . . they do not derive simply from one source . . . they are unlikely to form a unified whole for which a single theory could suffice. We are on the verge of something new, trying to rethink our assumptions at the same time as we rethink the boundaries of our work, the nature of our subject and the nature of ourselves as subjects and the objects of our studies
> (Diana Brydon 1989, 13)

> The great essays on storytelling are done in stories themselves
> (Ben Okri 1997, 123)

> An important question for the English critic, is not what the West Indian novel has brought to English writing. It would be more correct to ask what the West Indian novelists have contributed to English [ways of] reading   (George Lamming 1960, 50)

> My own awareness as a writer reaches back to x-thousand B.C., at the end of which measureless time the British came, and stayed, and left. And now they're gone, and their residue is simply one more layer added to the layer upon layer of Indian consciousness. Just one more
> (Nayantara Sahgal 1992, 30)

THE TURN OF THE CENTURY seems a suitable point for both envisioning the possibilities of change and marking a moment for a reassessment of the past. How we remember, read and see the past is as important as how we move into and imagine the future. The 'new' literatures have most commonly been seen as being a part of the 'past' history of the current 'postcolonial' era – a staging post en route to the supposedly radical revisioning of dominant and hegemonic cultural hierarchies that has been the postcolonial challenge.[1] Yet, the 'new' literatures and the diverse

---

1   Common formulations are described as follows: 'The label "Commonwealth" slowly gave way to looser designations such as "New Literatures in English" . . . Postcolonial criticism . . . makes claims to transcend the academic nexus which generated' earlier categories (Moore-Gilbert 1997, 39); in 'Reading for Resistance in Post-Colonial Literature', Slemon draws the reader's attention to the MLA convention in 1988 which places the 'new literatures' as 'English literature

subjects and cultural histories which they represent are older than post-colonial readings of them. They are sometimes remembered and sometimes forgotten. Ben Okri recently redefined the subjects of the new literatures as voices of the 'newly ascendant spirit';[2] not necessarily coming after in the sense of the 'post' in postcolonial or existing before such a temporal division was so defined, the implication being that the 'new' literatures co-habit alongside – before and after – in stories of the past, present and future. As many of the contributors to this volume attest, the 'new' literatures – like many other similar nomenclatures, or attempts to label, define and name a vastly different and multi-layered range of writing stemming from a variety of different cultural contexts and geographical locations – can both liberate as well as confine. Whilst the term poses the inevitable difficulties of false containment and exclusion, reduction and misreading that all such generalized namings involve, these literatures may also 'be thought of as new' in the 'prominence they give to the politics of the present' for 'our lives are not just inextricably bound up with signs and texts, but with signs and texts of power' (Walder, 149). Moreover, as Walder also suggests, literature can claim its own spaces and exists between and across current preoccupations with philosophy and cultural theory. It *evokes*, in other words, 'the literary dimension of cultural activity' without forcing us to adopt an overtly 'theoretical posture' although such concerns are embedded in any analysis of it (Walder, 151).

One might hope that in the 'global' future, the various namings for 'other' literatures created by the West for those not of the West (which have ranged over time from 'Commonwealth', to 'World Literatures Written in English', to 'Third World Literatures', to 'New' and 'Postcolonial') will no longer need to exist as part of the institutional pedagogies of 'otherness' in Western academies or their commodification in the marketing strategies of metropolitan publishing lists.[3] That is, we may move beyond the need for such sweeping and apparently (un)comfortable definitions, demarcations which often mistakenly create an over-emphasis on superficial comparisons (due to a shared colonial history),

---

other than British or American'. The emphasis here is on 'other' as a means of displacing the oppositional force of the literature under signs of 'secondariness. Derivation, simulacrum, or mimicry' (Maes-Jelinek, Peterson, Rutherford eds, 1989, 100).

[2] 'The Marvellous Responsibility of the Unseen', Arthur Ravenscroft Memorial Lecture, University of Leeds (1994).

[3] This is also suggested as a possible development (Boehmer 1995, 249) in the final chapter 'Postcolonialism and Beyond'.

rather than articulating the depth of the subtle nuances of the differences engendered by the specific contexts which the individual literatures address and which exist, both conceptually and theoretically, in excess of their postcolonial affiliations. This is not to reiterate once again the margin-centre or nativist-cosmopolitan arguments elegantly summarised elsewhere as being symptomatic of the difficulties of being either an excluding 'insider by virtue of method' or an excluding 'insider by virtue of experience'[4] but it is often forgotten, or simply not commented upon, that whilst much postcolonial literature is linked due to a shared experience of imperialism and colonial rule, it is born out of a more complex reality written, read and produced in different historical contexts – whether temporal or spatial. Significantly too, the reading of such texts may also involve a coming to terms with their difficulty, their untranslatability into the now familiar postcolonial literary strategies of counter-discourse, hybridity, mimicry, ambivalence, collusion or resistance. For such writings may often be initially inaccessible to an ill-informed Western readership; their intertextual commentaries local rather than centrifugal to the familiar signs of a dominant canon. Yet, as the Swiss poet Ramuz observed as early as 1906, one can be all the more international for being thoroughly local, grounded in one's own language traditions and ethnicity.[5] As many of the essays here testify, the literature of decolonization was also the literature of nationalism and the evolution of parallel if less easily recognizable modernities. In addition, the realities of specific histories and individual struggles for independence were never as 'fully pervaded by [European] colonialism as the authorities might have desired' (Boehmer 1995, 245). As Gurnah suggests in his contribution to this volume, 'Imagining the Postcolonial Writer' – an essay which exposes some of the complex layers of history and language in Zanzibar – 'postcolonial theory' is at times a 'triumph of the imagination over a more problematic reality, and the postcolonial writer, shed of her or his complicating difference, comes into being' (Gurnah, 85).

Importantly too, as both Gikandi and de Caires Narain make clear, the 'real' thing may not be what it seems. We do not need to only consider whether or not the *subaltern can speak*, or whether previously silenced

---

4   Diana Brydon is referring here to Said's distinction in making a larger point about how dominant discourses repeat themselves in 'Commonwealth or Common Poverty?:The New Literatures in English and the New Discourse of Marginality', eds Slemon and Tiffin 1989, 10.
5   I am paraphrasing a point made by the writer Han Suyin in her 'Foreword' to *Mirror to the Sun* (Hussein 1993, ii).

voices can be *heard*, but also need to examine more closely who is doing the speaking and to whom that speaking is addressed. 'We hear about the natives but we still don't hear them' suggests de Caires Narain quoting the Caribbean poet, Kamau Brathwaite, for, '*voice* is as crucial to discussions in postcolonial critical discourse as it is to those *about* "post-colonial" literary texts' (de Caires Narain, 113). As Gikandi elaborates, in his discussion of African literature and the writing of modernity, whilst the imaginary is frequently treated as 'both the source and end of the act of narrativity', little attention has been paid 'to the referent that was the subject of figuration in the first place' (Gikandi, 97). Thus, as a quick glance at many reading lists on university literature courses will reveal, current pedagogies and reading practices reconfirm the repetitive canonization of certain texts above others. And such texts, like Jean Rhys's now famous novel *Wide Sargasso Sea* (1966), speak to a far wider constituency of Caribbean women writers than some *a priori* theories of counter-discourse or the current need to make audible the 'authenticity' of the subaltern voice will allow.

And, in only looking for 'newness' as defined by predominant orthodoxies, we may miss what is already present, fail to see or hear the unsettling mediations of writers previously assigned to different 'minority' contexts *within* Europe itself. As Cheyette reveals, in his exposure of the literary history of Venice as a 'liminal' racialized space, now suggestively redrawn by writers such as Caryl Phillips and Anita Desai, the 'Jewish diaspora' has seldom been allowed a space for articulation within 'postcolonial narratives'. For the current confinement of discussions of 'otherness' and/or 'difference' to certain predictable theoretical boundaries can also act as an 'impediment' to productive readings denying 'the existence of more than one time frame or more than one kind of Europe' (Cheyette, 60). Innes makes a similar point in her examination of the history of the literary reception of two eighteenth-century writers, Ignatius Sancho and Seek Dean Mahomed. Illustrating that audience reactions, even at this time, were determined primarily by racial expectations, Innes shows how both Sancho's and Mahomed's deliberately ambivalent locations as 'exotic' outsiders and Asian and Black Englishmen have clouded literary responses to their work – both then and now. It is perhaps not surprising that many texts and potentially illuminating comparisons can go missing as a result of such 'one-eyed' readings and may deprive subsequent readers of the fullness of discovering less restricted modes of perception, modes that may enable a partial understanding at the very least of discursive economies that attempt to analyse these ' "other" worlds in their own terms' (Gikandi, 89).

It is 'time' then, as one of the contributors points out, to 'historicize' both beyond and before 'the postcolonial moment' and in so doing acknowledge the complex literary antecedents and diverse local traditions of the text itself. In many ways, the previous volume of essays in this series on 'Postcolonial Criticism and Theory' sought to do just this. Jointly edited by Laura Chrisman and Benita Parry, its main purpose was to 'ground the analysis of aesthetic culture in the historical, social and political realities of its production'.[6] This volume, in contrast, with the title 'Reading the "New" Literatures in a Post colonial Era', might be seen by some to be set up in opposition to the materialist theoretical nexus of the Chrisman/Parry essays. However, there are, as many readers will perceive, a number of convergences between the two despite their different emphases. Whilst the focus here is primarily on the literary, on the voices of the writers and the need to re-place the text and its referents as a prime object for analysis, it also seeks like the previous volume to expose some of the material gaps and faultlines which the recent explosion of interest in 'postcolonial theory' rather than the subjects of postcolonial histories, has subsumed.

One strategic use of the term 'new' as opposed to 'postcolonial literatures' despite its more unfortunate associations with the patronizing and paternalistic idea of 'emergent' or 'nouveau', is its ability to sit both inside and outside contemporary postcolonial discontents. These literatures do not fit neatly into either the humanist and sometimes dangerously universalist tonalities of some Commonwealth criticism, nor do they only gain life through the blinkered readings of some essentially neo-orientalist postcolonial criticism. And there are of course many other possible models we could add to the continuum.[7] All of the contributions to this volume are, of course, informed by recent debates – and indeed critique many of them – but the general aim of the essays is to attempt to discover a genuine eclecticism in approaches to reading, to permeate current analyses with a creolised methodology and a critical ambidextrousness which both draws on the insights and limitations of theories (whether Western or indigenous) to elucidate their particular subjects. In so doing, many of the essays seek to extend the relevance of the new literatures in the context of postcolonial readings of them and variously

---

6   Chrisman, L. and Parry, B., eds, 2000. *Essays & Studies: Postcolonial Theory and Criticism*, Cambridge: D.S. Brewer.
7   In *Postcolonial Theory: Contexts, Practices, Politics* (Moore-Gilbert 1997, 152–185) we are offered an extensive history of how these literatures have been theorised and read in the past.

indicate the extent to which the supposed 'newness' of many now familiar postcolonial concepts can be seen to have been anticipated from within indigenous contexts and the voices of the writers themselves.

This is not a particularly new observation. Critics such as Barbara Christian, Helen Tiffin and Carole Boyce Davies have frequently asked readers in different ways not to forget how the literary text itself engenders not only its own politics but its own theories and methodologies. As Barbara Christian once said in 'The Race for Theory':

> people of color have always theorized – but in forms quite different from the Western form of abstract logic. And I am inclined to say that our theorizing . . . is often in narrative forms, in the stories we tell . . . in the play with language, because dynamic rather than fixed ideas seem more to our liking.   (Christian 1988, 68)

Yet, in a critical climate which has been dominated by poststructuralist dogmas, where to quote Derrida, *'il n'y a pas de hors-texte'*,[8] it is imperative to remember not to forget that despite fixations on the 'text' as object for analysis in much contemporary criticism, the subjects of the texts have ironically disappeared. Not only have the writers' voices become eclipsed by the authoritative tone of much critical exegesis but the very categories that are refuted in the reluctance to accept any concrete definition of 'truth' or 'meaning' in certain poststructuralist readings often minimize the pressing political contexts from which many of the 'new' literatures derive. Most significantly perhaps, contributors to this volume all agree that the discontinuities addressed in 'postcolonial' writings are generated as much from fragmentations within as they are by those imposed from outside.

In her examination of the inception of the 'new' literatures in nineteenth-century Bengal, Firdous Azim makes this clear. As she says, 'the creation of a notion of Bengali literature echoed many of the motives that the creation of a field such as English literature served in the colonial sphere. Thus cultural superiority was a notion that could be applied to

---

[8]   Derrida makes the point in *Of Grammatology*, trans. Gayatri Spivak (1967, 1974, 158–9), that there has never been anything but writing. In their introduction to *After Europe*, Slemon and Tiffin illustrate the extent to which the loss of the 'referent in the literary sign and the "crisis of representation" that has followed in its wake has effected . . . a wholesale retreat from geography and history into a domain of "pure textuality" in which the principle of indeterminacy smothers the possibility of social or "political" significance' (Slemon and Tiffin eds, 1989, x).

both Bengali and English, as both devised a literary history for itself' (Azim, 41). A similar point is made in Abdulrazak Gurnah's Booker prize short-listed novel, *Paradise* (1994), where he provides a creative exploration of some of the critical issues problematised in his essay. *Paradise*, which is set on the East Coast of Africa in the early years of the twentieth century, unravels a complicated and multi-layered history of many colonialisms, whether of the Arab or European, many 'savageries' and many versions of the 'civilised'. Constructions of 'otherness' are always represented in their full complexity – never just white or black – as are the cultural differences between the various coast and inland communities and their languages, whether Arabic, Kiswahili, the unnamed 'dialects' of the interior, German or English. Throughout the novel and the interweaving of the many different stories which it enacts, the 'European' is as much the potential source for exoticisation as is the 'native' and the notion of 'civilisation', whether of Arab or Muslim, Christian or the mercantile traders, is constantly deconstructed. The novel demonstrates the potentiality of the creative work in liberating the 'reader into seeing affiliated networks of knowledge and meaning',[9] networks that need constant negotiation and understanding.

This collection does not seek to enter into the already well-rehearsed and amply documented debates that have been characteristic of the various branches of 'postcolonial' criticism and theory in the past twenty or so years and longer still if we go back in history to the move *From Commonwealth to Postcolonial*.[10] Nor is it attempting to argue a case to valorize one term as being more ideologically sound or inferior to another, to get caught up, in other words, in the tortuous 'culture wars' that have been characteristic of the wrangles of late twentieth-century literary studies and which have focussed in particular on the uneven politics of the postcolonial 'playing' field. But it is one of the objects of this volume to stress the pressing need to widen the angle of our vision, to 'open' as Rushdie once said, the 'universe a little more'[11] and to make an intervention into the need for a criticism which is not only controlled and

9   In her review of this novel in *Wasafiri* no. 24, 1996, Liz Maslem draws us to many of these points and quotes Gurnah's essay on the fiction of Ngugi wa Thiong'o from which this quotation derives (Gurnah 1993, 156–7).
10   This was the title of a pivotal book edited by Anna Rutherford from the proceedings of the Silver Jubilee Conference of the Association for Commonwealth Literature and Language Studies which was held in 1989, in which quoting John Berger as an epigraph makes the point that 'Never again will a single story be told as though it were the only one' (Rutherford 1992).
11   *Imaginary Homelands* (Rushdie 1991, 21).

propelled by the myopic adoption of fashionable orthodoxies – however seductive they may be to either the metropolitan critic or the native informant. It attempts in short, to evolve a reading practice which may seize upon resonant spaces often written over in conventional and now 'canonical' readings of the new/postcolonial literatures thus allowing more 'room for maneuver'.[12] The evolution of such a poetics of reading may, if we are lucky, 'lift the sentence'[13] of prescribed reading formations and affect some changes in the range of our vision. As Ross Chambers has argued elsewhere, 'literary discourse . . . foregrounds the practice of reading that produces authority, and on which the whole system depends. That is why literature can provide such fertile ground for speculation on the nature of the system itself' (Chambers 1991, xix). He emphasises the ways in which reading can effect shifts in desire, shifts which may ulti-mately, as George Lamming hoped in his early discussion of the West Indian novel in *The Pleasures of Exile* (1960), create changes in our ways of seeing, thus reopening a space for dialogue and discussion which may in time perhaps better instruct us as to how to hear. This is not to suggest a reactive or oppositional turning away from some of the more positive effects of postcolonial 'theory' – which has been crucial in its political project and opened up spaces for new voices to be heard in literature departments all over the world – nor is it a plea to return to models of reading lacking in methodological rigour (which was one of the predomi-nant if rather dismissive criticisms by postcolonial critics of Common-wealth Literary Studies as an 'expansionist epigone'),[14] but to propose a more profound analysis and acceptance of alternatively conceived para-digms, a willingness to engage with epistemologies, languages and concept metaphors that may be unfamiliar and at times only partially understood.

This volume focuses then on processes of *reading* and *remembering*. Convergences and contradictions in the 'field' are illuminated by indi-vidual essays which, covering a number of different regional and historical contexts, do not seek to make a case for special pleading –

---

[12] I am drawing here on the title of an excellent study of the methodologies of reading as an oppositional practice by Ross Chambers entitled *Room for Maneuver: Reading Oppositional Narrative* (1991, xix).

[13] Robert Fraser's forthcoming book, *Lifting the Sentence: A Poetics of Postcolonial Fiction*, to be published by Manchester University Press in 2000, raises a number of these questions in detail.

[14] Bhabha, Homi (1985) dismissed Commonwealth Literature in these terms in 'Signs Taken For Wonders: Questions of Ambivalence and Authority under a Tree Outside Delhi, May 1817', *Critical Inquiry* 13, 190.

begging us to read those who have supposedly been placed as 'marginal' –
but wish instead to draw attention to the ambivalences and difficulties
that have always been present (if not always visible) in the construction
and reception of both European and non-European literary discourses.
Theory is only useful in so far as it enables us to ask informed questions
about our reading and, of course, different theories ask different questions. In addition, literature can sometimes travel where theory cannot
go; moreover, the best literary works are challenging precisely because
they take us to the limits of what we can or must say in forms which cross
and have always crossed difficult boundaries. As Hanif Kureishi once
suggested, the discursive worlds of fiction, poetry or drama constantly
renew and are renewed precisely because they often point to those spaces
where language itself cannot yet go but where imagination and desire
would like to reside.[15]

   To be fair to recently published post colonial work however, there has
been a move to begin to stress the convergences as well as the potentiality
of a cross-cultural dialogue between apparently Western derived postcolonial theories and the literary objects of its desire. This is particularly
apparent in one of Homi Bhabha's frequently cited essays, 'How *Newness*
[my italics] Enters the World' (1994), which examines Salman Rushdie's
earlier posing of the very same question in his now infamous novel *The
Satanic Verses* (1988). There is an obvious irony however in the nature of
the question posed by both Rushdie and Bhabha in the context of this
volume particularly as the articulation of the dilemma comes from the
mouths of two of the most prominent voices in postcolonial studies.
Nevertheless, my point here is that Bhabha's exploration of the concept
of 'newness' in the milieu largely of cosmopolitan migrant writing is
instructive not so much for his examination of ideas which, despite his
overt intentions, suggest paradoxically a questionable telos – such as the
implied positive in the development from a position of 'in-betweenness'
to 'hybridity' to the 'third space'[16] – but because of the ways in which this
essay points to the fact that the very foundations of some of his fundamental theoretical concepts were clearly anticipated by a much less well-
known Caribbean critical source, the writer Wilson Harris. In Bhabha's
earlier work, little acknowledgment is given to the influence of Carib-

15 Lecture delivered at the School of Oriental and African Studies, 1996.
16 The difficulties with some of these concepts were debated in a dialogue
between Homi Bhabha, Rasheed Areen and Susheila Nasta, first broadcast on
BBC Radio 3, *Nightwaves*, 1997 and later published as a forum in *Wasafiri* 29,
1999, 37–44.

bean criticism on the development of his theories.[17] However, in this essay, and an earlier piece 'The Commitment to Theory' (1988), Bhabha draws explicitly on Harris's early critical work *Tradition, the Writer and Society* in which Harris, like Bhabha much later, attempts to articulate a cross-cultural space for survival and the articulation of cultural difference. Whilst Harris does not name the space – referring to it as a 'certain void' attending 'every assimilation of contraries' (Harris 1965, 62) – clear links can be drawn between Harris's early plea to critics to move away from realism and attempt to 'consume their own biases' and the development of Bhabha's later naming of 'the third space'. I do not intend here to score points between Caribbean criticism and post colonial theory but merely to highlight the extent to which ideas have always permeated in both directions, although few students of 'postcolonial literatures' may be aware of Harris's essay today or its seminal influence on Bhabha's ideas.[18]

Moreover, Bhabha's essay on 'How Newness Enters the World' can be (mis)read deliberately in the light of this volume as a parody on the ambivalent location of the 'new literatures' themselves. Describing the location of migrant discourses within a metropolitan context Bhabha has said that their 'newness' has to be 'discovered in *medias res*'; for it is 'a newness that is not part of the "progressivist" division between past and present, or the archaic and the modern; nor is it a "newness" that can be contained in the mimesis of "original and copy" ' (Bhabha 1994, 227). Whilst I am being unfair to the subtlety of Bhabha's complex attempt to locate the slippery hybridity of migrant writings, these points surely also reflect outwards and ironically on the literatures that were in many ways the antecedents of some of these very same works. Thus in future we may discover that we are focussing as much on the migration of discourse as the discourse of migration.[19]

As Wood suggests in 'Shamanism in Oceania', which focuses on Pacific writing and the poetry of Albert Wendt, 'shamanism redefines the hegemonically determined terms of colonization by re-contextualising them' (Wood, 134). As in Harris's concept of the 'womb of space', Albert Wendt has 'mobilised' the Samoan concept of *va* into literary discourse, a

[17] Bart Moore-Gilbert has suggested a similar line of approach in *Postcolonial Theory: Contexts, Practices, Politics*, 183–4.
[18] In fact Bhabha explicitly acknowledges Caribbean writing as the 'diversionary, exilic route that ied me to the historical themes and theoretical questions that were to form the core of my thinking' (Bhabha 2000, 140).
[19] A similar point is made in a recent editorial to *Wasafiri*, 31, 2000, a special issue on 'Migrant Writing in Europe'.

'concept that facilitates the description of existence and identity not simply as either/or, but as a mediated and transitional state, a crossing' (Wood, 133). As with the relative invisibility of Harris's early ideas as formative in the development of postcolonial concept metaphors, Pacific writing and more 'indigenous models of reading and writing' have yet to register their impact on the 'binary structures' of European and American debates (Wood, 129).

The seriousness of the consequences of the ways in which we read is explored in a number of the essays. The effects of a narrow reading – whether of the 'liberal' West or the apparently 'fundamentalist' Islamic traditionalists – has nowhere been more profoundly illustrated than in the damaging consequences of the imposition of the *fatwa* on Salman Rushdie for the publication of *The Satanic Verses* in 1988. As history has told us before readings of literature can have appalling political consequences and, as was only too clearly apparent in that particular war, the issues at stake cost lives. Whether or not such misunderstandings are the case of Lyotard's postmodernist *differend*, where two languages cannot ever seem to speak to each other because they are drawing on epistemological and philosophical bases that will always be a variance, is another matter. What has emerged from the *fatwa* is the urgent need to look more carefully at how such positionalities can result in such apparently intractable oppositions. And there have been other versions since, less overtly political in that they have been conducted through the forum of literary essays, but significant nevertheless.

One such version, which is taken up by de Caires Narain's essay in this volume, was the dispute between Kamau Brathwaite (a major Caribbean poet/critic) and Peter Hulme (a well-known metropolitan postcolonial critic) rehearsed in the pages of *Wasafiri*, a literary magazine, on the location of Jean Rhys's novel *Wide Sargasso Sea*. It is not possible here to go into all the various ramifications of the conflict that ensued in attempting to establish a dialogue between what Hulme called at one stage the 'West Indian yard' and 'the English garden' but one question that was crucial was the attempt to not only define to whom the text supposedly belonged – whether to 'postcolonial' critics of the past ten or so years (who were given prominence in the Hulme piece) or the earlier West Indian critics who had long debated its history since its publication in 1966 – but how it should be read and how those readings should be expressed.[20] As de Caires Narain subtly argues 'the contestation over the reception' of Rhys

---

[20] This debate was published in *Wasafiri* 20, Autumn 1994, 5–11; *Wasafiri*, 21, Spring 1995, 69–78; *Wasafiri*, 23, Spring 1996; *Wasafiri*, 28, Autumn 1998, 33–8.

might best 'be seen to cohere around the . . . meanings' invested in the
word 'Creole' (Narain, 111–12) for 'post-colonial discourse has tended to
be less interested in the Creole speaker than in the hybridity and oppositionality which Creole symbolizes' (Narain, 109) in the Caribbean
context. Whilst Gayatri Spivak, for instance, argues as de Caires Narain
suggests 'that Rhys cannot *make the subaltern* [Christophine] *speak*', the
denial of voice which she ascribes to Rhys's white West Indian background is 'too categorical, and . . . denies the possibility of strategic
constructions – and deconstructions – of subjectivities and voices' (110).
De Caires Narain complicates both Brathwaite's and Hulme's antagonistic readings of Rhys and attempts to place her work in a context
outside the 'authoritative' voices of post-colonial critics who have not
only 'canonized' this particular text but also failed to read it, or Rhys's
other writings, alongside other Caribbean 'Creole' voices such as Merle
Hodge, Erna Brodber and Olive Senior. This is not to set up a local
ranking in order of how successful these writers are in using the Creole
voice but to stress the dangers in automatically reading the 'oral' as a
signal of native resistance and authenticity when it is clear that Rhys, like
many of the Caribbean women writers who followed her (whether white
or black), was clearly manipulating the language for 'strategic literary
ends' (Narain, 125). Rhys is, of course, a perfect example of a writer whose
texts have been reduced to wearing the uncomfortable clothes of contemporary postcolonial agendas. Rhys herself perhaps anticipated such developments in her early story 'Let Them Call It Jazz' (1968) where the
protagonist, Selena's, 'Holloway Song' is appropriated by a male jazz
musician at a London party and ceases to be a song she had ever heard.
And Jean Rhys's own history as a writer – she moved from a position of
almost total invisibility in the early 1970s to becoming one of the most
frequently discussed authors on university 'English' courses – also reflects
this.

Within any dedicated history of an individual region or a close study of
the layered evolution of its literatures, one can see similar reductions and
exclusions. If, for example, we look at African literatures (which of course
represent the different countries, languages and histories of an entire
continent), we can also see, as Gikandi and Gurnah both illustrate, the
need for problematising the ways in which postcoloniality is to be read
through fictional texts. It is no accident, argues Gikandi, that the texts
which 'dominate the discourse of postcolonialism' are most often the
ones which repeat strategies that fit in to 'reading formations' predetermined by Western universities, whereas, in the 'countries themselves, the
texts that have been at the center of the discussion . . . are works which

only a few specialists in the European and American academies have read or written on' (Gikandi, 89). Taking examples from Ahmadou Kourouma, Sol Plaatje, Dambudzo Marechera, Flora Nwapa and Tsitsi Dangarembga, Gikandi stresses the need to develop what he calls new 'protocols of reading' (92), a methodology open to examining the intertextual referents *within* African writing and history that can move beyond narrow 'contrapuntal' readings whose terms of reference repeatedly reflect back on Western canonical discourse. This is particularly important given that the promise as well as the limits of African modernity existed in excess of European colonialism and relate to 'real' not 'imaginary' conditions. Azim makes a similar point, albeit in the very different context of nineteenth-century Bengal, when she demonstrates that whilst, as Gauri Viswanathan has shown, English literary studies were established in India before Britain as part of Macaulay's colonial dictum, they were not just 'thrust' on to 'native subjects' but were 'an enterprise in which the native elites participated directly' (Azim, 40). This is evidenced in her interesting discussion of Vdyasagar's 'Notes on the Sanskrit College' which demonstrates the mixed nature of the modernising process.

The ways in which we are instructed to read in the present also often determine our perceptions of the past. In 'Eighteenth-Century Men of Letters: Ignatius Sancho and Sake Dean Mahomed', Innes unravels how old our concepts of the 'new' still are and how imposed critical agendas continue to distort the reception of texts. Unlike Equiano, whose work – *The Interesting Narrative of the Life of Olaudah Equiano, or Gustavus Vassa, the African* – slots more easily into conventional expectations of an oppositional slave narrative, neither Sancho or Mohamed's epistolary and travel narratives can be placed so neatly. As Innes says, 'Sancho has been most consistently read . . . as a "black" author' but 'how has the reading of "blackness" changed in the past two hundred years and what do such readings exclude' (Innes, 18)? This is particularly significant, as both Sancho and Mahomed deliberately situate themselves as straddling both a self-constructed 'Englishness' at the same time as highlighting their racial differences. Remaining alert to the ways in which the past reception of certain texts has affected our current readings of them is perhaps a way of avoiding the common error of essentialising the identities of these writers into reductive categories which place them as 'either black or Asian or white, African or Indian or English, victims of or participants in empire' (Innes, 34).

In 'Venetian Spaces: Old-New Literatures and the Ambivalent Uses of Jewish History', Cheyette argues for a similar problematisation of critical categories which distort rather than clarify thus preventing productive comparisons. As in Innes, Cheyette examines the ambivalent histories of minorities written over[21] *within* Europe and draws belated links between the Jewish, black and Asian diasporas. He reveals the extent to which the conventional portrait of Jews as either 'archetypal victims' or 'exemplary Europeans' is not as clear-cut as it seems. Moving beyond the 'spatial' to the temporal uncertainties of history, Cheyette's comparison between Caryl Phillips and Anita Desai exposes the need for a comparative reading of diaspora which will not only lead in time to the deconstruction of a narrow identity politics but also points, like Gikandi's essay earlier, to the need for a more nuanced reading of contemporary modernities.

The 'pleasures of reading' may only be 'enhanced once texts are made to speak from all the sites they occupy and with all the voices that resonate through them' (Azim, 51). If this is the case, then we must also be aware of the significance of memory as a crucial marker of the politics of both the past and the present. Walder's essay on the role of theatre as a dynamic force for change is a salutary reminder of the potentially powerful force that literature can play and has played in our writings of the future and our rememberings of the past. In his discussion of the South African play *Ubu and the Truth Commission* and Ariel Dorfman's *Death and the Maiden*, Walder, echoing Nietzsche, foregrounds the need to always confront the 'necessity of error' not only in our memories (whether *real* as participants in violent and ongoing contemporary histories, or *received* as audiences) but also in the ways in which we continue to read and live the present.

It will be apparent that I have been circumnavigating the term 'new literatures'. This is not because it no longer has a potent validity but due to the fact that it is well nigh impossible to disentangle it entirely from its previous and sometimes less suggestive designations. Terminologies are less important than critical practices and the 'new literatures' require a more broadly informed pedagogy than current 'postcolonial' readings have allowed. It is no longer sufficient within literature department courses to include a few nominal postcolonial texts nor is it sensible to follow a policy of indiscriminate accretion. Changes need to occur at a structural and epistemological level in terms of how courses are organised, books are read, subjects for discussion are valued and far more atten-

[21] I am using the idea of writing over in the sense originally suggested by one of my Ph.D. students, Tony Ilona, in his doctoral thesis 'Writing Over the Past: Historical Self-Determination and Caribbean Literature', QMW, University of London, 1999.

tion should be focused, as Gurnah suggests, on the translations of non-Anglophone voices.

This volume was initially commissioned around the idea of 'new literatures' and the millennium. We must therefore ask ourselves how far have we come, if there is indeed a destination. One of the major events of 'English Studies' in the last thirty years has been the transformation of Departments of English to a broader nomenclature which acknowledges the fact that we can no longer easily study only a narrowly defined canon of 'English Literature' but must study in an area much more broadly defined by Literatures in English. But how far have we come? Despite certain strategic continuities between the 'new literatures' and post-colonial critics in their common aim to shift the dominance of Western universalisms, one wonders whether the literary playing field still remains an unequal one and how far the inner sanctums of academic institutions and reviewing practices have been transformed by the voices of the 'new'. The names of winners of literary prizes in the West would certainly seem to suggest so but from other contexts such changes can look like window dressing. As we approach and pass through the eye of the millennium (I am writing this by my study window which looks out over the dome at Greenwich) one cannot but speculate on what the recipes for change will be both in our methods of reading and importantly too in our pedagogical practices. What seems to be developing is a slow acknowledgment that the new/postcolonial literatures are here to stay and that their varied and creolising voices may cast a different light on how to move beyond the narrow parochialism of certain ways of seeing and reading the world. Even if the playing of the national anthem to calypso rhythms may be seen as a potentially tokenistic gesture on millennium Eve in Britain, it still points to the possibility of change, the acknowledgment of histories that have always been present but frequently rendered absent and which may, to quote a line from Bob Dylan, 'change our way of thinking'. There is not much point, whatever the political impact of recent postcolonial interventions, in simply incorporating disparity[22] into what remains still an essentially dominant discourse. Instead, we must face the challenge and accept, as Chinua Achebe warned us in 1958,[23] that things fell apart a long time ago and that the only way we can see anew is to accept the errors and misdemeanours of our mutual pasts.

---

[22] Brydon, D. 1989. 'New Approaches to the New Literatures in English: Are We in Danger of Incorporating Disparity' in *A Shaping of Connections*.
[23] Achebe's first novel was entitled *Things Fall Apart*. The title derives from W.B. Yeats' poem 'The Second Coming'.

Works Cited

Achebe, C. 1958. *Things Fall Apart*, London: Heinemann.

Bhabha, H. 1985. 'Signs Taken For Wonders: Questions of Ambivalence and Authority under a Tree Outside Delhi, May 1817', *Critical Inquiry* 13, 190.

—— 1988. 'The Commitment to Theory', *Questions of Third Cinema*, London: British Film Institute.

—— 1994. *The Location of Culture*, London: Routledge.

—— 2000. 'The Vernacular Cosmopolitan', in Dennis and Khan, eds, *Voices of the Crossing: The Impact of Britain on Writers from Asia, the Caribbean and Africa*, London: Serpent's Tail.

Boehmer, E. 1995. *Colonial & Post-colonial Literature*, Oxford: Oxford University Press.

Brydon, D. 1989. 'Commonwealth or Common Poverty?: The New Literatures in English and the New Discourse of Marginality', in Slemon and Tiffin eds, *After Europe*, Denmark: Dangaroo, 1–17.

Brydon, D. 1989. 'New Approaches to the New Literatures in English: Are We in Danger of Incorporating Disparity', in Maes-Jelinkek et al., eds, 89–100.

Chambers, R. 1991. *Room for Maneuver: Reading Oppositional Narrative*, Chicago: University of Chicago Press.

Chrisman, L. and Parry, B., eds, 2000. *Postcolonial Criticism and Theory, Essays and Studies* 52, Cambridge: D.S. Brewer.

Christian, B. 1988. 'The Race for Theory', *Feminist Studies*, 14, No. 1, 67–79.

Derrida, J. 1967. *Of Grammatology*, trans. G. Spivak, 1974, Baltimore: Johns Hopkins University Press.

Gurnah, A. 1993. *Essays on African Writing: A Re-evaluation 1*, Oxford: Heinemann.

—— 1994. *Paradise*, London: Hamish Hamilton.

Harris, W. 1965. *Tradition, the Writer and Society*, London: New Beacon.

Hussein, A. 1993. *Mirror to the Sun*, London: Mantra.

Lamming, G. 1960. *The Pleasures of Exile*, London: Michael Joseph.

Maes-Jelinkek H., Holst Petersen K., Rutherford A., eds, 1989. *A Shaping of Connections*, Sydney: Dangaroo.

Maslem, L. 1996. 'Stories, Constructions and Deconstructions: Abdulrazak Gurnah's *Paradise*', *Wasafiri*, 24, 53–57.

Moore-Gilbert, B. 1997. *Postcolonial Theory: Contexts, Practices, Politics*, London: Verso.

——, and Stanton, Maley, eds, 1997. *Postcolonial Criticism*, Harlow: Longman.

Okri, B. 1999. *A Way of Being Free*, London: Phoenix House.

Rhys, J. 1966. *Wide Sargasso Sea*, London: Penguin.

—— 1968. 'Let Them Call It Jazz', in *Tigers are Better Looking*, London: Andre Deutsch.

Rushdie, S. 1988. *The Satanic Verses*, London: Viking.

—— 1991. *Imaginary Homelands*, London: Granta.

Rutherford, A. ed. 1992. *From Commonwealth to Post-Colonial*, Aarhus: Dangaroo.

Sahgal, N. 1992. 'The Schizophrenic Imagination', in Rutherford ed.

Slemon S. and Tiffin H., eds, 1989. *After Europe*, Aarhus: Dangaroo, 30–36.

Eighteenth-Century Men of Letters:
Ignatius Sancho and Sake Dean Mahomed

LYN INNES

THE STUDY OF TEXTS by eighteenth-century African and Asian writers in Britain and Ireland raises questions about many of the categories which have become current in contemporary critical discourse. Do labels such as 'postcolonial' or 'New Literatures in English', used to refer to the profuse creative activity which during the last 50 years has emanated from areas previously colonised by England, apply to writers such as Ignatius Sancho and Sake Dean Mahomed, whose writings were first published more than 200 years ago, who identified with the English and Anglo-Irish, and were at times themselves involved in imperial enterprises, or Olaudah Equiano, who was both an abolitionist and himself at one point a slave owner? How do their writings and their 'positioning' compare with current assumptions about what will categorise the work of 'Black British' authors? The dictated narratives of Gronniosaw and Mary Prince, the use and re-contextualisation by Equiano and Dean Mahomed of passages from previous writers, the mingling of travel, anthropology, and autobiography by these two writers, the intersection of private and public concerns in the writing and publication of Sancho's letters, all complicate and subvert generalisations about genre, authenticity and the boundaries between oral and literary composition – generalisations which for many years have been taken for granted in our literary text-books and classrooms.

This essay will concentrate on two eighteenth-century writers, Ignatius Sancho who identified himself as African, and Sake Dean Mahomed who identified himself as Indian, although both also frequently identified themselves *with* the British. Each writer used the epistolary genre in very different ways, and each sought to draw upon and respond to English and Anglo-Irish perceptions and literary traditions in order to create contexts for new attitudes and perceptions. Until recently, the letters of Ignatius Sancho have been given a narrow and often censorious press, while *The Travels of Dean Mahomet* has been almost completely ignored. In both cases, I suggest, the genre in which they write and the personas they adopted have perhaps led critics to see them as writers who fail to fit the dominant tradition of the slave narrative or autobiography, into which

Equiano could be more easily inserted, and therefore failing to fulfil the reader's expectations of 'black' writers. The strength of 'black studies' emanating from the United States and the Caribbean, with an emphasis on African origins and continuities, has also led to the marginalisation of early South Asian writers or Afro-British writers who did not foreground an identity in the terms marked out by African-American and Caribbean scholars and writers. The discussion which follows will read these two writers against Equiano's text, and against the expectations and conventions critics have set up for 'black' literature in relation to *The Interesting Narrative of the Life of Olaudah Equiano, or Gustavus Vassa, the African*.

There is a moment in Mark Twain's *Huckleberry Finn* when Jim suddenly steps outside the circumscribed role he has been assigned by his society, by Huck, and by the author. This is not the famous passage where he berates Huck for pretending to have drowned, but the part where he tells Huck about his discovery of his little daughter's deafness – how he commanded her to shut the door, how he struck her for not doing so, and how he suddenly realised she had not been able to hear him. For an instant that anecdote takes Jim out of the frame through which he has been insistently viewed by author, characters, *and* readers – as a black man, as a slave, as a black man who is always viewed in his relationship to white people and white society. Suddenly that framework becomes irrelevant or is superseded by his identity as a father in relationship to his own children – and at that moment, and perhaps only briefly, Jim ceases to be in the reader's mind a black 'boy' whose crucial relationship is with a white boy, and becomes a man.

Charles Ignatius Sancho, it seems to me, has suffered something of the same fate as Jim, and perhaps it is impossible that it should be otherwise. From the very first publication of his letters, he has been 'framed' in 'the castle of his skin' – to use George Lamming's phrase –, but I would suggest that for Sancho more than almost any other Afro-British writer of his time or later, the aphorism that 'an Englishman's home is his castle' was appropriate. Sancho has been consistently read, and we continue to read him, as a 'black' author, but what does that mean? How has the reading of 'blackness' changed? And what do such readings leave out of the picture? Is it ever possible, or indeed desirable, to read him now as his implicit reader – or readers, for Sancho adopts numerous voices in relation to his numerous contemporary readers, for some of whom his colour mattered, for others to whom it seemingly was relatively unimportant?

The first publication of the letters was framed by his editor and correspondent, Mrs Crewe, who declared her motives as 'the desire of shewing that an untutored African may possess abilities equal to an European; and the still superior motive, of wishing to serve his worthy family' (Carretta 1998, 4). The frontispiece identifies him as 'An African' and is accompanied by a mezzotint of Gainsborough's portrait of him, to ensure that we cannot miss the fact of his colour. The first and subsequent editions were also framed by a 'Life of Ignatius Sancho' written by Joseph Jekyll, which identifies Sancho first of all as 'this extraordinary Negro' (Carretta 1998, 5).

Jekyll's phrase sums up the double bind which haunted all black writers of this period and for many years afterwards: as a Negro he was to be read as a representative of his race, as a Negro *writer*, he is read as 'extraordinary'. His extraordinariness is in proving himself 'the equal of an European'; his representativeness derives not only from the assumption that he speaks for all black people, but also from his 'faults'. Referring to Sancho's loss of money at gambling, Jekyll informs us that '[f]reedom, riches, and leisure, naturally led a disposition of African texture into indulgences', and goes on to cite a French writer who relates 'that in the kingdoms of Abdrah, Whydah, and Benin, a Negro will stake at play his fortune, his children, and his liberty' (Carretta 1998, 6–7). Later (nineteenth-century) editions of the *Letters* include a very long footnote quoting the German scientist Johann Friedrich Blumenbach's 'Observations on Bodily Conformation and Mental Capacity of the Negroes' (Edwards and Rewt 1994, 25–9).

Given these framing apparatus, then, it is not surprising that the first reviewers of Sancho's letters all note the colour or race of the writer first, and view the content and merit of his letters in relation to that aspect. Every review published between 1782 and 1784 foregrounds Sancho's identity as a 'black of the Duke of Montague's' (*A New Review*, August, 1782, cited in Caretta, 1998, xv) and as a Negro who writes no better than 'many other Negroes, we suppose, could, with the same advantages, have written' (*Gentleman's Magazine*, September 1782, xv). The *Monthly Review*, December 1783 refers to Sancho as 'this very honest and very ingenious African' and 'this amiable Black' (cited in Carretta 1998, xvi). Thomas Jefferson in his *Notes on the State of Virginia* (1787) names both Phyllis Wheatley and Ignatius Sancho as proof of the limits of black achievement, placing them at the top of Negro attainment, but at 'the bottom of the column' if listed with their white comperes (Carretta 1998, xx). Like a number of other reviewers, Jefferson deplores the Sternian qualities in the letters, noting their fanciful and extravagant style, their lack of order and restraint, 'his substitution of sentiment for demonstration', which are seen implicitly as characteristic of his racial inheritance;

like his gambling, they are the indulgences to which 'a disposition of African texture' is all too prone.

Interestingly, it is a French scholar, the Abbé Gregoire, who in his *De la litterature des negres*, having summarised the life of Sancho as given by Jekyll, concentrates on his qualities as a writer, and compares him to other writers of letters such as Mme de Sevigny and Sterne. The passages he cites illustrate Sancho's style, and especially his range of tone, concerns and sentiments, rather than his views on race or slavery. Gregoire comments on Sancho's wit, grace, wisdom, and seeks to refute the 'severity' of Jefferson's judgement (Gregoire 1808, 252–60). Sancho's relationship with Sterne is evidently the criterion which places him as the only British 'Negro writer' in the late nineteenth-century edition of the *Dictionary of National Biography*.

Apart from that entry in the *DNB*, Sancho's name drops out of consideration for a good 150 years till the revival of interest in earlier black writers in the 1970s, and following facsimile editions of the *Letters*, Equiano's *Narrative*, and Cugoana's *Sentiments*, by Paul Edwards in 1968. So by the time attention began to turn to Sancho again, Equiano had also been rediscovered, and it is against Equiano and the tradition of the slave narrative that Sancho is tested, rather than against his European contemporaries. Equiano more easily slotted into the category of forceful black spokesman, most powerfully represented by Frederick Douglass, and later Malcolm X. In the backwash of the 1960s and early 1970s and the rhetoric of Black Power and Black pride, Equiano was read as a true representative of black manhood, Sancho as an 'Uncle Tom'. Both readings were not only ahistorical but also remarkably one-sided, ignoring a great deal of contrary evidence within the writings themselves. Nevertheless they have had a strong influence even to the present, when Norma Myer's 1996 study of Blacks in Britain between 1780 and 1830 refers to Sancho as 'apologetic, complaisant' and 'self-debasing', a British form of the 'Sambo' stereotype (Myers 1996, 133). Myers is merely reiterating James Walvin's earlier description of Sancho as 'the most obsequious of eighteenth-century blacks' just as she repeats many of the factual errors regarding Sancho's life and *Letters* to be found in Walvin's books (Walvin 1973, 61). Paul Edwards' judgement that 'Sancho's letters point clearly to his almost complete assimilation into eighteenth-century English society' (Edwards 1968, xv) is disputed by both the black historian Folarin Shyllon and the Nigerian critic S.E. Ogude. To refute the charge of assimilation Shyllon cites in particular Sancho's letter to Julius Soubise and his anger at 'those very wretches who roll in affluence from *our* labours' (Shyllon 1977, 193, author's emphasis). Ogude, on the other hand, is more inclined to see Sancho as a man divided, suffering from what Ogude deems the impossibility of being both black and English:

> The letters show that Sancho was emotionally attached to Tory ideals although he was always conscious of his African origin. His is the sad case of what we now call the divided-self – for he was that uncomfortable phenomenon – the black Englishman. One does not realise how much the racial problem plagued a very sensitive nature like Sancho until one has read these letters.   (Ogude 1983, 101)

Although Ogude goes on to demonstrate the inadequacy of Jefferson's assessment, and to illustrate the richness and variety of subject and tone, the often brilliant mastery of English and the genre of the letter-writing, he also comments on what he terms 'the charming naivete' and 'passionate simplicity' of the letters. He concludes by almost endorsing the binary oppositions implied or asserted by Jekyll, Jefferson, and others:

> His was a divided-self; divided between the cultural world of the decent aristocratic society of London and the dark brooding consciousness of a heritage denied of its warmth and its intense sensibility. His reading lists show how closely his intellectual life was linked to the English tradition; but his occasional urge to identify with his primitive-origins [sic] is an expression of his emotional tie with his African heritage. In a word Sancho experienced what none of his black contemporaries experienced – a tragic sense of the black predicament.   (Ogude 1983, 116)

In a different way, the assumption that one must choose between being 'black' or 'African' and being 'English' or 'British' underlies most discussion of Sancho, and encourages critics to place Equiano on one side of the divide, and Sancho on the other. The possibility of a hybrid identity is either not contemplated or condemned, and is also undermined by the conventions of literary critical discourse which encourage sorting writers into clear categories. Thus Keith Sandiford's *Measuring the Moment*, along with Ogude's study one of the first attempts since the Abbe Gregoire's to assess and understand the contribution of early Black writers, affirms Equiano as a truly 'black' writer, but like Ogude laments the 'double identity' expressed in Sancho's letters: 'what seems to emerge, then, is that as Sancho approached middle age, he felt more keenly the affliction of his double identity, . . . [and] found it increasingly difficult to sustain the old posture of the compliant, assimilated Black'. But where Ogude saw

Sancho's playfulness as 'charming naivete', Sandiford views the 'charm' not as naivete but as a deliberate masking and concealment:

> Sancho expressed this self-awareness in apologetic, complaisant terms, concealing the trenchant possibilities of his style and clothing himself in a garb of meekness and self-mockery. Thus he won that immunity which a society will typically allow an outsider whom it perceives as unthreatening to its way of life.   (Sandiford 1988, 150)

Sandiford contrasts Sancho with the 'more combative' temperaments of Cugoano and Equiano, both seen as writers who affirm their African identities and forcefully attack the assumptions and evils of the slave traders and owners.

These responses to Sancho have been summarised and dismissed succinctly and wittily by Sukhdev Sandhu in a recent essay on 'Ignatius Sancho and Laurence Sterne'. Parodying the standard contrast between Sancho as 'Uncle Tom' and Equiano as a Malcolm X precursor, Sandhu writes:

> Sancho, one infers, is an inauthentic black Englishman. How, the assumption runs, can he be 'real' if, unlike most of his fellow Negroes in the capital, he managed to escape a life of hard maritime, plantation, or domestic drudgery by acquiring an aristocratic cicerone in the form of the Duke of Montagu? How can he have known suffering when Gainsborough's portrait shows him not only to be amply girthed, but, heaven forfend!, smiling? What chance have we of hearing the slave's primal scream when Sancho wrote so plummily, so polysyllabically? In contrast, we are often led to believe, Oloudah Equiano [whose *Interesting Narrative* was published in 1789] was the real deal: he was lean, necessarily mean, an activist who travelled the length and breadth of the United Kingdom hawking copies of his autobiography and promoting Abolitionism. In today's academic parlance, he was palpably a 'cultural worker'.   (Sandhu 1998, 89)

Such judgements of Sancho have also been questioned by Vincent Carretta, in his notes and his 'Introduction' to his richly annotated edition of the *Letters*. Both Sandhu and Carretta castigate earlier ahistorical critiques and seek to place Sancho in a more complex literary, cultural and historical perspective.

Sandhu's 1997 and 1998 essays make a significant break with previous traditions of reading Sancho by allowing us to see him in different contexts. They place him in relation to Sterne, not as his black shadow, but as a writer and artist, a man of letters, who chose and adapted Sterne's techniques for reasons of temperament, philosophy, morality and aesthetics. He cites the narrator of *Tristram Shandy* regarding the moral point of Sterne's narrative technique, and refusal of linearity, citing Sterne's comment in *Tristram Shandy* ('my work is digressive, and it is progressive too, – and at the same time'), and also Sterne's sermon on the Good Samaritan, which praises him for his willingness to deviate from the straight line (Sandhu 1998, 92–3). And later in the essay (94) he tellingly quotes Sancho's letter about Phyllis Wheatley, casting a jaundiced eye on those who praised and certified her genius without releasing her from bondage: 'These great good folks – all know – and perhaps admired – nay, praised genius in bondage – and then, like the Priests and Levites in sacred writ, passed by – not one good Samaritan among them'.

Sandhu and Carretta both bring into the picture the importance of acknowledging the genre of letter writing and the rhetorical strategies which Sancho, as a self-conscious (rather than 'charmingly naive') man of letters employed. They have pointed the way for further work which would lead to more precise identification of his strategies with regard to individual readers, the first recipients, of his letters, and how these differ from reader to reader and letter to letter. Such a study would lead, I believe, to a better understanding of Sancho's writing and identity not in terms of his relationship to a collective 'black' identity, but in terms of what Stuart Hall has termed a cultural identity of 'positioning' (Hall 1993). Although Hall's essay is directed towards the differences of positioning (between African, European and American 'presences') of various Caribbean groups, his discussion can also be made relevant not only to the general cultural positioning of Ignatius Sancho with regard to his society and his readers then and now, but also in regard to different readers. For whereas the writing of Cugoano and Equiano seeks to position the author more single-mindedly as an African and ex-slave addressing a generalised public audience, Sancho writes from a multiplicity of positions to a variety of audiences, the play between author and reader marked by differences or similarities in gender, class, status, age and colour. And yet, what Hall says with regard to the difference between Martinique and Jamaica, and Martinique and France is also relevant. He comments:

> One trivial example is the way Martinique both *is* and *is not* 'French'. It is, of course, a *department* of France, and this is reflected in its standard and style of life: Fort de France is a much richer, more 'fashionable' place than Kingston, – which is not only visibly poorer, but itself at a point of transition between being 'in fashion' in an Anglo-African and

Afro-American way – for those who can afford to be in any sort of fashion at all. Yet, what is distinctively 'Martiniquais' can only be described in terms of that special and peculiar supplement which the black and mulatto skin adds to the 'refinement' and sophistication of a Parisian-derived *haute couture*; that is, a sophistication which, because it is black, is always transgressive.   (Hall 1993, 396–7)

One might replace 'Martinique' with the name of Ignatius Sancho, and 'Jamaica' with that larger group of black labourers, sailors and escaped slaves who lived in eighteenth-century England. It seems to me that the Derridean notion of the supplementary, and of meaning in relation to positioning becomes a useful one to allow us to move away from judging Sancho only in relation to some imagined and static collective black identity to seeing him as a man inventing himself, and doing so with particular flair, wit and compassion, at a particular moment in history.

Reading back into their historical and social context, one might see the *Letters* in the spirit of the 'conversation pieces' painted and popularised by Hogarth and other artists earlier in the century. As Jenny Uglow puts it, 'Art that resembled conversation was both intimate and public' and every social or group conversation involved the assuming of a persona for the occasion. As Uglow goes on to say, 'The conversation piece was civilized but informal, fanciful and new, and . . . radically different to baroque decoration, classical solemnity, or even to the sympathetically straightforward portraits' (Uglow 1997, 159–60). My point is that the age did not demand or expect an essential self to be revealed, nor did it use the criteria of authenticity and sincerity, and it is as post-Romantic critics that we judge by such criteria. Sancho's readers, many of them like him great addicts of the theatre, would have appreciated his skill at role-playing, and his ability to perform the right role for each occasion and each reader. His awareness of the varied letter writing modes is made clear in his November 1777 letter to Mrs Cocksedge:

Now, whether to address – according to the distant, reserved, cold, mechanical forms of high-breeding – where polished manners, like a horse from the manage, prances fantastic – and, shackled with the rules of art – proudly despises simple nature; – or shall I, like the patient, honest, sober, long-ear'd animal – take plain nature's path – and address you according to my feelings? – My dear friend – you wanted to know the reason I had never addressed a line to you; – the plain and honest truth is, I thought writing at – was better than writing to you – that's one reason; – now a second reason is – I know my own weakness too well to encounter with your little friend – whom I fear as a critic – and envy as a writer.   (Carretta 1998, 105)

And yet, this performing of roles was not the same as 'playing up to' or placating the white folks. An attentive reading of the letters, it seems to me, sees Sancho playfully pretending to accept certain labels and roles precisely so that his readers will reject them. The obvious example is in the famous letter to Sterne, where he identifies himself as 'one of those whom the vulgar and illiberal call '*Negurs*' – thus making it impossible for Sterne or any other reader to affirm such an identification and its connotations. But I would argue that a similar strategy runs through a great many of the letters, where the reader is placed in the position of hearing and rejecting the simple reduction of the writer to such identities as 'a blackamoor', 'a black Falstaff', an outcast from Noah's ark. It is interesting to note the exception where he willingly assumes and affirms the persona of an African is in his public letters, many of which are signed 'Africanus'.

Sancho's device of offering labels and stereotypes for his readers to refuse is also part and parcel of his technique as a letter writer, a conversationalist, who actively engages with his readers, and demands their involvement. In other words he 'writes to, rather than at' his readers. This engagement with his readers, and within the letters the frequent references to other friends and members of the family, has a further function – that of establishing a *community* of letter readers, or rather communities within communities (widening out to the readers of all the letters and readers over the centuries), at which Sancho rather than being at the margins is at the very centre! It is a community in part created and orchestrated by him, responding to him, and finally responding to one another in relation to him.

Unlike Equiano and Sancho, Sake Dean Mahomed,[1] the first Indian author to take up residence in Britain, left his native land of his own free will, choosing to journey from India to Europe and then to remain there. Born in 1759 in Patna, and related to the family which governed Bengal and Bihar, Dean Mahomed followed in his father's footsteps as a petty officer in the ranks of the East India Army, before travelling with a Protestant Anglo-Irish army officer, Captain Godfrey Evan Baker, to Ireland, where he married an Irishwoman and remained for over 20 years. In 1794 he published *The Travels of Dean Mahomet*, written as a series of letters to an unnamed and fictitious friend. In 1807 he and his family left Ireland to

---

[1]   During the second half of his life, he consistently spelled his name 'Mahomed', although 'Mahomet' is used for the publication of the *Travels*. The spelling 'Mahomed' will be used in this essay, except when directly referring to the title of his book.

live in England, first in London and then in Brighton, where he gained
some fame as a practitioner of oriental medicine, patronised by wealthy
and aristocratic Englishmen and women, including the royal family, and
wrote *Shampooing, or, Benefits resulting from the Use of the Indian Medicated
vapour Bath* (1822). He died in Brighton in 1851.

Dean Mahomed uses the epistolary genre in a very different manner
from Ignatius Sancho, and combines it with the genre of the travel narrative. He could have been influenced by the success of Equiano's *Narrative*,
which like Dean Mahomed's work interweaves autobiography, writing
about military action, and observation of scenes and peoples in other
lands. It is possible that the Indian author met Equiano when the latter
visited Cork to promote his work when it was published in Ireland in
1791. Yet another influence may have been travel books such as Arthur
Young's *Travels in Ireland* (1780) and Tobias Smollett's *Travels Through
France and Italy* (1766), which was also written in the form of a series of
letters to imaginary correspondents, or the anonymous epistolary novel
Hartley House Calcutta (1789) which contains many observations about
the relative merits of Hindus and Muslims, generally weighted in favour
of the former. But while we can guess at the possible influences on Dean
Mahomed's *Travels*, it is more difficult to gauge the reception of his works.
Unlike Sancho and Equiano, he appeared to receive no reviews or
biographical notices for this particular work, and indeed when he wrote
Shampooing, he omitted all reference to his Irish sojourn and publications
from his biography. And even more than Sancho, Dean Mahomed failed
to fit into the 'Black British' model Sukhdev Sandhu describes with
regard to Equiano.

Despite the differences in circumstances and aims, there are some
similarities in the ways in which Equiano and Dean Mahomed represent
themselves. In each case the frontispiece shows the author in the dress of
an English or Anglo-Irish gentleman, although their facial features are by
no means Europeanised, and in each case the title page emphasises that
the book is 'written by himself'. Arguably this assertion by Dean
Mahomed is more concerned with investing his work with authenticity,
and distinguishing it from the numerous travels written by Englishmen
and women such as William Hodges (*Travels in India . . . 1780 . . . 1783*),
Jemima Kindersley (*Letters from the Island of Teneriffe . . . and the East
Indies*), and John Henry Grose's *Voyage to the East Indies*, than with
asserting the author's humanity through his ability to write. As Michael
Fisher (1996 and 1997) demonstrates, Dean Mahomed drew on the writings of Grose and Kindersley, reorienting their words for his own purpose.

Like Equiano, Dean Mahomed begins by setting up a contrast between his utopian native land and a more artificial and less moral Europe. Beginning by asserting his sense of the strangeness of Ireland when he first arrived from India, and how it contrasted with 'those *striking scenes* in India which we are wont to survey with a kind of sublime delight' (his italics), Dean Mahomed goes on to portray the natural bounty of India and goodwill of its inhabitants:

> The people of India, in general, are peculiarly favoured by Providence in the possession of all that can cheer the mind and allure the eye, and tho' the situation of Eden is only traced in the Poet's creative fancy, the traveller beholds with admiration the face of this delightful country, on which he discovers tracts that resemble those so finely drawn by the animated pencil of Milton. You will here behold the generous soil crowned with various plenty; the garden flowers diffusing their fragrance on the bosom of the air; and the very bowels of the earth enriched with inestimable mines of gold and diamonds.
>
> Possessed of all that is enviable in life, we are still more happy in the exercise of benevolence and good-will to each other, devoid of every species of fraud or low cunning. In our convivial enjoyments, we are never without our neighbours; as it is usual for an individual, when he gives an entertainment, to invite all those of his own profession to partake of it. That profligacy of manners too conspicuous in other parts of the world, meets here with public indignation, and our women, though not so accomplished as those of Europe, are still very engaging for many virtues that exalt the sex.   (Fisher 1997, 34–5)

Despite their shared emphasis on the natural bounty of their native lands, the generous and uncorrupted character of its inhabitants, and the virtue of its women, these opening comments suggest the divergences between Equiano's and Dean Mahomed's works. Whereas Equiano has a distinct moral and polemical purpose, and presents a persona who speaks plainly, even naively at times, Dean Mahomed begins by appealing to the aesthetic tastes and the curiosity of his readers, for whom he will 'describe the manners of [his] countrymen', who, he proudly maintains, 'have still more of the innocence of our ancestors, than some of the boasting philosophers of Europe'. Within the first letter he establishes himself as a cultivated man of letters, whose allusions to Milton and whose ready use of literary language demonstrate his credentials as a writer, not only as a witness. It is perhaps indicative of the differences that when Equiano cites Milton, it is in reference to descriptions of hell which he compares to the condition of slavery in the West Indies; Dean Mahomed cites Milton in the passage above and later in *Travels* with reference to descriptions of

Paradise, in order to evoke, and in the later citation to authorise, the natural beauty and bounty of India.

Unlike Equiano, Dean Mahomed does not seek to recreate the narrative from the point of view of a child, except briefly when he tells of his fascination with the military and his determination to become attached to the English army. Apart from some mention of his mother's grief at losing him and 'resigning her child to the care of Europeans' (Fisher 1997, 42) the reader may easily forget that it is an 11-year-old boy who apparently accompanies the English officers to the lavish entertainments at the Raja's palace near Patna, and observes the dancing girls 'displaying such loose and fascinating attitudes in their various dances as would warm the bosom of an Anchoret' (Fisher 1997, 37). Nor are we encouraged to speculate how such a young boy could have absorbed and retained such detailed knowledge of the lay-out of military camps and officers' houses at various places, or come to know such precise details as the kind of cloth used as an undergarment by the Nawab of Bengal on ceremonial occasions and the fact that his turban contained 44 yards of fine white muslin, 'which quantity, from its exceeding fineness, could not weigh more than a pound and a half' (Fisher 1997, 61). Not only does Dean Mahomed erase differences of age between himself and his patron, Baker, and other Englishmen, he also frequently erases differences of rank, race, and culture. Once he has separated himself from his mother and allied himself with Godfrey Baker (at the beginning of Letter III) he replaces the first person plural with a generalised 'we' when writing about army movements and events: 'Notwithstanding all her vigilance, I found means to join my new master, with whom I went early the next morning to Bankeepore, leaving my mother to lament my departure. As Bankeepore is but a few miles from Patna, we shortly arrived there, that morning' (Fisher 1997, 39). In Letter IV, he writes how 'we lay in Bankeepore about six months, when we received orders from Col. Leslie to march to Denapore, where we arrived in the year 1770, and found the remaining companies of the Europeans and Seapoys,[2] that were quartered here for some time before. Our camp here, consisted of eight regiments' (Fisher 1997, 43). This passage is typical of those in which he writes about the army's movements. Such merging of his identity with that of the army, and particularly the English officers within it with whom he visits other officers and wealthy administrators in the East India Company, is almost total. It compares with those scenes in Equiano's *Narrative* when he is a member of

[2] 'Seapoys' (or Sepoys) were Indian soldiers enlisted to serve the East India Company army and given Europeanised uniforms.

the naval crews involved in the Seven Years War or later as a member of the expedition to Greenland in search of a Northwest passage, although in Equiano's account there is almost always the presence of his distinctive individual experience within that collective identity. Only in the final nine letters of the 38 in the volume does Dean Mahomed sometimes surface as an individual actor, with a distinctive role and perspective. Thus in Letter XXX, concerning his activities when he would then have reached the age of 20, he describes vividly the taking of Fort William, and how afterwards:

> From one of the apartments of the Imperial palace, built by Akbar, within the fort, I looked down, and beheld, as it were from the clouds, the town, four hundred feet below me: such an awful scene forms a subject for the pen of the most sublime artist.   (Fisher 1997, 113)

Here Dean Mahomed presents himself as a mature and authoritative viewer, who perceives and orders the world around him with the sensibility of an eighteenth-century European artist. In the subsequent letter, he writes not as a spectator, but as a participant with an active role, enabled by his appointment as a Subidar (or ensign) in charge of a Sepoy detachment. His description of his encounter with a group of angry peasants, his struggle for survival and near drowning as he swims across the Ganges, and his rescue by other peasants, is reminiscent, in its partly self-ironic presentation, of Equiano's mode of presenting himself as not so much a hero as one who gets into scrapes, and one who owes his survival to Providence rather than traditional heroic feats. Such feats belong, in Dean Mahomed's book, to his 'superiors', both British and Indian.

Equiano had also made much of the barrier created by language, his inability to understand his captors, and his struggle to acquire English and to learn to read and write. Dean Mahomed entirely suppresses the issue of language; he does not tell us how he learned English, or whether he possessed any understanding of it when he first followed Mr Baker. We do not know how or in what language Baker ascertained that Dean Mahomed 'would like living with the Europeans', nor in what language the 11-year-old Dean Mahomed 'told him with eager joy, how happy he could make me, by taking me with him' (38), nor in what 'language of supplication' his mother entreated that he might be returned to her (42). Nowhere is there any indication that the languages spoken by English administrators and traders, by Mogul rulers and other Muslims, by Hindu princes and soldiers, by the Marathas and by mountain peoples such as the Pahareas, might differ from one another, or indeed be incomprehensible from one group to the next. One effect of this erasure is the tension it creates between the conventions of literature of sensibility and the insistence on Dean Mahomed's own agency. As Kate Teltscher points out, the scene in which Dean Mahomed describes his parting with his mother and her anguished plea for his return is replete with 'the language and even the punctuation of the literature of sensibility':[3]

> I would not go, I told her – I would stay in the camp; her disappointment smote my soul – she stood silent – yet I could perceive some tears succeed each other, stealing down her cheeks – my heart was wrung – at length, seeing my resolution fixed as fate, she dragged herself away, and returned home in a state of mind beyond my power to describe. Mr Baker was much affected.   (Fisher 1997, 42)

The tears, the anguish, the 'state of mind beyond my power to describe' are all reminiscent of those scenes where mothers are parted from their children in narratives of slavery and abolitionist poems. The style is also reminiscent of many of Sancho's letters. But as Kate Teltscher also points out, Dean Mahomed is emphatic that he willingly chooses to go with Baker, and indeed has engineered the invitation by persistently placing himself in Baker's presence and seeking to attract his attention. Dean Mahomed is both seduced and seducer, both sufferer and inflicter of suffering; the reader cannot clearly find a villain or a sentimental hero in this account. This passage draws attention more powerfully than others to Dean Mahomed's conflicting allegiances as a willing collaborator in the East India Company Army, and suggests the shifting positioning which runs through the whole work.

Although Dean Mahomed frequently merges his identity and point of view with the collective identity of the army and its English/Anglo-Irish officers, nevertheless, he is also keen to establish his identity and credentials as a 'Mahometan' and an Indian, and a member of a superior class. In the first two letters, and again in Letter XI, he makes a point of mentioning that his father was related to 'the Nabobs of Moorshadabad [Murshidabad]', a relationship which might be particularly meaningful to his employers and his readers, since it was the Nawab of Bengal and Bihar, whose seat was in Murshidabad, who had most extensively collaborated with the East India Company and given it a mandate to govern and collect revenue in those very substantial and affluent East Indian prov-

---

[3] Kate Teltscher, 'The Shampooing Surgeon and the Persian Prince: Two Indians in Early-Nineteenth Century Britain' (unpublished paper), p. 5.

inces. He also devotes several letters to detailed accounts of Muslim rituals and customs, including circumcision, marriage, and burial, and sets out to correct prejudices and misunderstandings about Muslim attitudes to Mahomet and the significance of Allah. He takes pride in the culture of Muslims, describing them as 'in general, a very healthful people', bearing sickness, when it comes, 'with much composure of mind' and facing death 'with uncommon resignation and fortitude'. Although Dean Mahomed's name creates a continuing identity with the religion, and although his accounts of Muslim practices and beliefs are perhaps better informed and more favourable than for any other group, it is notable that he does not at any point speak of 'Mahometans' as 'we', and his accounts are always given as an objective, slightly distanced, observer's view. There is not much, in terms of tone, to distinguish them from his explanation of Hindu customs, castes (which he terms 'tribes'), and beliefs. In general, these explanations are given far less space and detailed elaboration than those pertaining to the Muslims, but they are nevertheless more sympathetic than accounts given by European travellers. Michael Fisher notes that Dean Mahomed draws substantially on such earlier accounts, in particular those of Jemima Kindersley and John Henry Grose, but mostly to reorient and give a more favourable gloss on particular customs condemned by them.[4]

Dean Mahomed's greatest enthusiasm is reserved for spectacle and for landscape. There are numerous encomiums to the grandeur and scope of Indian scenery, the fertile valleys and great rivers, the tree-lined roads 'shaded with the spreading branches of fruit-bearing trees, bending under their luscious burthens of bannas, mangoes, and tamarinds' and beneath the trees 'many cool springs and wells of the finest water in the universe' (Fisher 1997, 48). More often than not, such landscapes are viewed from the elevation of a grand house, owned by an official in the East India Company. Reading the letters one is struck by the wealth and established nature of these English and Anglo-Irish officials, whose houses and estates overlooking the land they claim to govern are reminiscent of those eighteenth-century houses asserting the ascendancy of the Protestant gentry in Ireland.[5] Perhaps less reminiscent of the Protestant landlord class in Ireland is the apparent respect for the native aristocracy, and

[4]   For a detailed comparison of passages from Grose and Kindersley, see Fisher 1996, 227–33. The citations are from Kindersley 1777 and Grose 1766.
[5]   The description of efforts by these administrators and rulers to give relief to the many dying of starvation during the drought and famine of 1769/70 is also echoed by similar descriptions by members of the Anglo-Irish Ascendancy class

the social interaction between them, and also with and between Hindu and Muslim elite classes. But if the East India army general and the top officials live in considerable splendour, Dean Mahomed takes care to let us know that the palaces and entertainments of Indian princes and rulers are even more magnificent. In his second letter, for example, after his glowing description of the music and dancing laid on for the officers at the Raja's palace, he tells us that the Raja's servants then let off fireworks 'displaying, in the most astonishing variety, the forms of birds, beasts, and other animals, and far surpassing anything of the kind I ever beheld in Europe' (Fisher 1997, 37). The magnificence of the Nawab of Bengal's ceremonial dress and procession is described in minute detail. So too are the Hindu and Mogul buildings of Delhi and Ayodha, and the luxurious palace and lifestyle of the Nawab Shuja-al Daula, who is, however, represented as an example of excess and decadence. One of a half dozen extended anecdotes within the *Travels* is devoted to the fate of this Nawab, who was murdered by a princess he had kidnapped and violated, a fate which Dean Mahomed clearly regards as fitting, and an act by the princess presented, together with her subsequent suicide, as heroically virtuous in true sentimental mode: 'the violated female, with a soul, the shrine of purity, like that of the divine Lucretia . . . disdaining life after the loss of honour, stabbed her brutal ravisher with a lancet, which she afterwards plunged into her own bosom, and expired' (Fisher 1997, 89).

Dean Mahomed's *Travels* alternate between a merging of his identity and point of view with that of the English and Anglo-Irish officers of the East India Company army, and assertion of his identity as a 'native of India', and an informant who can speak with authority not only about those of his own class and religion, but also Hindus and other groups, and correct misconceptions and prejudices perpetrated by European accounts. As an informant, he becomes one of those 'autoethnographers', who, as Mary Louise Pratt defines the term, are 'colonized subjects who undertake to represent themselves in ways that *engage with* the colonizers own terms' (Pratt 1992, 7 [her italics]). Whereas the earlier accounts of the 'pacification' or routing of Maratha and Parahiya warriors represent them as unruly and savage, in his later letters, the separate points of view become less clear, and the accounts of resistance by Indians far more ambivalent. The wavering allegiance and perspective is particularly apparent in his account of the series of encounters which result in the

(for example Somerville and Ross) of attempts to give assistance during the Irish famine of the 1840s.

defeat of Raja Cheyt-singh (Chayt Singh), a ruler who had been 'either unwilling or unable' to pay the revenues demanded by Governor Hastings.[6] Not only does Dean Mahomed devote three long letters to a detailed description of the series of battles which led to the Raja's defeat, he also quotes at length the Raja's eloquent letter in his own defence, in which the Raja asserts that his rule has been an enlightened and constructive one, bringing wealth and harmony to his subjects. Dean Mahomed endorses the Raja's claims, while drawing on vague abstractions to distance himself and the actions of the East India Company from involvement in his defeat in the following words which close his account of the episode: 'Such was the happy situation of the Prince, and the philanthropy of the man, who shortly after became the sport of fortune, amidst the vicissitudes of life, and the trials of adversity' (Fisher 1997, 121).

Fisher speculates that Dean Mahomed's decision to leave the East India Company and travel to Ireland may have been in part a consequence of his growing difficulty in reconciling his allegiance to his country and countrymen with his allegiance to his employer. The final letter (XXXIV) preceding his announcement of that decision perhaps gives support to Fisher's suggestion. Here Dean Mahomed closes his account of further skirmishes, in which the army at times met with 'a degree of courage not to be expected in an undisciplined rabble', with a more explicit acknowledgement of the role and effects of the British occupation: 'The refractory were awed into submission by the terror of our arms; yet humanity must lament the loss of those whom wasting war had suddenly swept away'. His acknowledgement is followed by thirteen lines from a poem detailing the suffering and loss involved in war, suffering brought to innocent and guilty alike, and which can 'sweep, at once, whole Empires to the grave'. Such sentiments might well be considered appropriate by a man who has witnessed the destruction of Raja Chayt Singh's kingdom, and the disempowerment of the Mogul empire and kingdoms.

Dean Mahomed and Ignatius Sancho use the epistolary form in very different ways and for different ends. Sancho addresses his letters to a variety of readers, positioning himself differently with regard to each

---

[6] Michael Fisher points out that Hastings had considerably increased the amount of revenue originally agreed in the treaty between the East India Company and the Raja. Chayt Singh argued 'that these enhanced demands exceeded what the extant treaties required, and that he could not afford to meet them in any case' (Fisher 1997, 24).

reader, and in so doing creating an interaction between the character and status of the recipient and his own persona, an interaction which in turn creates a community of readers. Dean Mahomed adopts a more formulaic mode, addressing each letter to a single unnamed but representative reader who, it is claimed, has been 'very anxious to be made acquainted with the early part of my Life, and the History of my Travels' (Fisher 1997, 34). Although he mentions the entreaties of friends and the 'liberal encouragement' of others as a secondary motive, the 'Dear Sir' to whom each of the 38 letters is addressed stands as the abstract and respected representative of the elite Anglo-Irish community to whom he writes. As a 'native informant' he is, like Equiano and unlike Sancho, always in some sense apart from his readership; as a member of the East India Company army, he becomes an integral part of a community of Anglo-Irish and British men, identified with their role in India, as Equiano identifies with the British crews and merchant traders in his naval voyages. All three writers demonstrate the inadequacy of binary categories which essentialise their identities as either black or Asian or white, African or Indian or English, victims of or participants in empire.

Works Cited

Carretta, V., ed. 1998. *Letters of the Late Ignatius Sancho, An African*, London and New York: Penguin.

Edwards, P., ed. 1968. *Letters of the Late Ignatius Sancho, An African*, London: Dawson.

Edwards, P. and Rewt, P., eds 1994. *The Letters of Ignatius Sancho*, Edinburgh: Edinburgh University Press.

Fisher, M.H. 1996. *The First Indian Author in English: Dean Mahomed (1759–1851) in India, Ireland, and England*, New Delhi: Oxford University Press.

Fisher, M.H., ed. 1997. *The Travels of Dean Mahomet: An eighteenth-Century Journey through India*, Berkeley, Calif.: University of California Press. (Reprints the text first published in Cork in 1794.)

Gregoire, Abbé H.B. 1808. *De la litterature des negres*, Paris.

Grose, J.H. 1766. *A Voyage to the East Indies with Observations*, London: S. Hooper and A. Morley.

Hall, Stuart 1993. 'Cultural Identity and Diaspora', in Patrick Williams and Laura Chrisman (eds) *Colonial and Postcolonial Discourse: A Reader*, London: Harvester Wheatsheaf, 392–403. (Reprint from Rutherford, J., ed. 1990. *Identity, Community, Culture, Difference*, London: Lawrence & Wishart, 222–37.)

Kindersley, J. 1777. *Letters from the Island of Teneriffe, Brazil, the Cape of Good Hope, and the East Indies*, London: Norse.

Myers, N. 1996. *Reconstructing the Black Past: Blacks in Britain 1780–1830*, London: Frank Cass.

Ogude, S.E. 1983. *Genius in Bondage: A Study of the Origins of African Literature in English*, Ife, Nigeria: University of Ife Press.

Pratt, M.L. 1992. *Imperial Eyes: Travel Writing and Transculturation*, London: Routledge.

Sandhu, S.S. 1997. 'Ignatius Sancho, An African Man of Letters', in Reyahn King (ed.) *Ignatius Sancho, an African Man of Letters*, London: National Portrait Gallery, 45–73.

Sandhu, S.S. 1998. 'Ignatius Sancho and Laurence Sterne', *Research in African Literatures*, Vol. 29, no. 4 (Winter), 52–72.

Sandiford, K. 1988. *Measuring the Moment: Strategies of Protest in Eighteenth Century Afro-English Writing*, Selinsgrove: Susquehanna University Press.

Shyllon, F. 1977. *Black People in Britain, 1555–1833*, Oxford: Oxford University Press.

Teltscher, K. n.d. 'The Shampooing Surgeon and the Persian Prince: Two Indians in Early Nineteenth-Century Britain' (unpublished paper).

Uglow, J. 1997. *Hogarth: A Life and a World*, London: Faber & Faber.

Walvin, J. 1973. *Black and White: the Negro and English Society, 1555–1945*, London: Allen Lane.

Notes Towards Reading the 'New' Literatures in Nineteenth-Century Bengal

FIRDOUS AZIM

POSTCOLONIAL THEORETICAL INTERVENTIONS have had far-reaching effects on the study of literature. In its initial phase, postcolonial theory had satisfied itself with a reinterpretation of the established literature canon. In this mode, certain texts such as *Robinson Crusoe* or *The Tempest* were read to bring out the thematic and formal links with colonising processes. This stage can be characterised as an examination of the canon of English literary texts, ranging from rereadings of texts like the above, to looking at specifically colonial writings of writers like Rudyard Kipling, Joseph Conrad or E.M. Forster. An important feature of this kind of post-colonial criticism was the establishment of links between the political and economic processes that marked the colonial venture and the emergence of new literary forms. Thus studies of the novel link the development of the narrative voice with theories of colonial subjectivity.[1] As postcolonial literary criticism reads texts not only for their themes but also for the formal devices and structures of literary representation, the all-pervasive nature of colonial cultural production is revealed. Such readings are not limited to texts that deal directly with colonial stories or are based in 'other' lands, but highlight the politics of cultural production.

A later (though perhaps even a simultaneous phase) is devoted to the recognition of writing in English from once-colonised countries or other anglophone cultures. The concept of 'other' Englishes has effectively challenged conventional English syllabi, and added to the number and widened the scope of texts that have habitually been the concern of English departments. It is now difficult to come across an English department that does not have the writings of V.S. Naipaul, Salman Rushdie or Chinua Achebe on their reading lists. However, the task of reading more and adding other texts to the literature syllabus, though it is a dynamic process, is not a sufficient challenge to conventional English studies. The thrust of postcolonial theory, that is, the highlighting of the links

---

[1] For examples of such works see Edward Said's rereading of *Mansfield Park* (Said 1993), or Azim 1993.

between literary/cultural production and the processes of political and economic domination, needs to be constantly kept in mind while reading new and varied literary texts. In other words, the postcolonial scholar should take special care to ensure that postcolonial literary studies do not translate into a mere reading of more and varied texts, but focus on the power hierarchies involved in cultural production and dissemination. The discovery and recognition of newer materials and different forms of writing tend to create a premature euphoria, distracting from the more difficult and challenging task of theorising and problematising the position of these texts, even as they are given canonical status.

It is this second or later kind of postcolonial intervention that dominates postcolonial English studies today. Courses on 'new' or 'other' literatures in English abound in English departments all over the world, and have indeed added a new dimension and excitement to the study of English literature. However, the theoretical and political thrust of the theory does not seem to come into play in these new readings. Perhaps one of the problems with the 'literatures in English' syllabus is that it has roots in places other than postcolonialism. It also springs out of the older Commonwealth literature movement, where the stress had been on an aesthetic derived from the Western canon, on mutual cultural intelligibility, and at always looking to England as the mother country of the Commonwealth.[2] Thus particular or local interests or aesthetic devices were not taken into account and a concentration on these was seen as diverging from the main project.[3] The political motive behind the Commonwealth literature movement had been to celebrate the widespread area that English writing occupied, and was part and parcel of a celebration of empire. Anti-colonial movements in once-colonised countries had the effect of problematising the position of writers in English. The addition of these writers to the literature syllabus then has to take on board this problematic positioning.

The limitations of the 'new' literatures in English originate in the manner in which they have been added into literary studies. The focus on 'newness' or novelty keeps the field very much English, which is then manifested as an enrichment or broadening of the sphere of English

[2]   This point has been well argued by Moore-Gilbert (1997).
[3]   A manifestation of this can be seen in the teaching of African texts such as Chinua Achebe's texts in South Asian universities. In our own teaching practice at Dhaka University, discussions focus on tragedy and the novel, the status of the tragic hero and so on. Ignorance of Nigerian or Ibo forms of storytelling preclude an analysis of the ways in which those other forms are also working on the text.

literature, in fact, as an accretion to English literature. Postcolonial criticism actually needs to focus on the politics of this accretion and how texts are given literary and canonical status in today's cultural and academic worlds. By focusing on the politics of cultural recognition and establishment, the political significance of postcolonialism, both as theory and pedagogical practice, can be reiterated. These 'new' literatures must be made to come out of the strict confines of English literature, and into dialogue with other literatures. Most 'Third World countries' have more than one literature department – English or any other colonial language, the native literatures, be they Bengali, Urdu or Hindi in South Asia or Swahili or Arabic in Africa. To these, more recently, have been added departments of cultural and media studies. Postcolonial theory and studies seem to have been most effectively integrated into the study of English literature, but the kind of traversing that it needs to do between these various fields of cultural studies has not been so effectively realised. One of the reasons for this is perhaps the very special and esoteric language that this theoretical field has devised for itself. The criticism often levelled against it – that it is a product of Western universities and hence not of relevance to the study of 'our' literatures – cannot be so easily dismissed.[4] Another and perhaps more serious limitation is that postcolonial theory has so far failed to make direct inroads into any other sphere, such as, let us say feminism has done. Feminist theory and activism actively engage with each other, enriching both. The failure to do so on the part of postcolonialism can be traced back to the exclusively 'literary' nature of its intervention, or at least of the manner in which this intervention manifests itself in once-colonised countries. Its Commonwealth literature roots need also to be brought out and critiqued, so that the notion of collaboration or opposition to the colonial power can be made more obvious. The parameters of postcolonial theory need to be pushed further to make it relevant to literary and cultural studies as a whole, instead of being limited, as it seems to be so far, to the task of widening the English literary canon.

Colonial History and the Politics of Reading

Thus the postcolonial modification of the English syllabus or the addition of the 'new' literatures in English seems to dwell on the 'newness' and fails to theorise or even historicise it adequately. Moreover, English writings

---

4 The most well-known such critique is made by Ahmad (1993).

are read in isolation, and hence the way that these texts are received within their own cultures is often overlooked. 'Other' Englishes have their being in more than one cultural site, and their status within these other sites needs to be considered simultaneously. A dramatic instance of such difference in reception is provided by *The Satanic Verses* controversy. When texts belong in two or more cultures, they have a different status and when we talk of the plurality of meaning, we must try and look at the different contexts in which texts are brought into being and circulation. Looking only at the metropolitan reception and concentrating on the status that recognition from such centres imparts to literary texts makes for very limited and sometimes dangerously erroneous perceptions and readings.

Colonial history shows us the ways in which postcolonial societies have struggled with the forces of colonialism in order to define for themselves a space from where cultural and national struggles can take place. Historical readings can help to contextualise the texts that form the 'new' literatures in English. The example that I will take to illustrate such a struggle is the literary/linguistic and pedagogical sphere of nineteenth-century Bengal, as it, even in its elite circles, constructs a cultural field for self-representation. Gauri Viswanathan in *Masks of Conquest* (1990) has shown how English literary studies came into being within a colonial field and helped to deflect attention away from the rapacious nature of British colonialism, and established a notion of British cultural superiority. The basis of this educational enterprise had been laid in Macaulay's (in)famous *Minutes on Education* in 1835, where he had spoken of the 'intrinsic value of our literature' and deemed it to be 'the most useful to our native subjects' as impressing on them the cultural superiority of their colonial masters. However, and this is a point that Gauri Viswanathan fails to make, the establishment of an educational system with English literary studies as its centre, was not thrust forcibly on to 'native subjects', but was an enterprise in which the native elite participated directly. Guided by the practical or market value of a knowledge of English, the Bengali elite established private educational institutions, where English and English literature were taught in a very central manner. The Hindu College in Calcutta, established in 1817, is the most well-known example of Bengali collaboration with the colonial educational project.

The educational establishments that sprung up in nineteenth-century Calcutta were by no means uniform, and were divided by the use of the language of instruction. The division into English or Bengali 'medium' in schools and colleges also reflected the various social tiers of the time. The vernacular tier of this educational spectrum was part of a process of 'filtration', and the higher rungs were occupied by English 'medium' education. But even within this filtration process, the place of literature was central, and the creation of a notion of Bengali literature echoed many of the motives that the creation of a field such as English literature served in the colonial sphere. Thus cultural superiority was a notion that could be applied to both Bengali and English, as both devised a literary history for itself. But whereas the English were concerned with colonial governance and domination, the Bengali used the literary sphere to propagate a notion of national and cultural development. I find this best illustrated in a little-known document entitled 'Notes on the Sanskrit College' (1852), written by Iswarchandra Vidyasagar, who is one of the key figures in both the literary and reformist movements of the mid-nineteenth-century Bengal renaissance.[5] Vidyasagar is one of the founding fathers of modern Bengali education, as well as being known for the leadership that he gave to reformist movements such as those involving widow remarriage and female education. These notes were written while he was the principal of the Sanskrit College in Calcutta. This was a state college established by the colonial British power and where the medium of education was Bengali. The main purpose of this institution was to produce teachers for the 'normal' schools that were being set up all through the Bengal presidency. The medium of instruction in these schools was Bengali.[6] These notes were written as a part of a debate with the British educational authorities or his employers, regarding the course of studies that this college was meant to follow. Disagreement regarding the syllabus resulted in his resignation from the college.

Let us look at the 'Notes on the Sanskrit College'. They are perhaps the most succinct expression of the relation between English and the development of Bengali. They begin:

1. The creation of an enlightened Bengali literature should be the first object of those who are entrusted with the superintendence of Education in Bengal.
2. Such a Literature cannot be formed by the exertions of those who are not competent to collect the materials from European sources and to dress them in elegant expressive idiomatic Bengali.

(Vidyasagar 1991, 682)

[5] The 'Notes on the Sanskrit College' are anthologised in ed. Prafulla Kumar Patra, *Vidyasagar Rachanabali*, 682–6.
[6] See Ghosh 1984, for a detailed picture of the kinds of education available to a student in mid-nineteenth-century Bengal.

In both the Anglicist school of thought, represented by Macaulay and colleagues and in the concerns expressed by the Bengali writer and peda-gogue, literature remains central. Education in Bengal is to be geared towards the creation of a new literature. Vidyasagar's notes go on to identify who these new literateurs could be. He dismisses the anglicised students of institutions such as the Hindu college and thinks that if the students of the Sanskrit college, with their training in the Indian classics, 'be made familiar with English literature, they will prove the best and ablest contributors to an enlightened Bengali Literature' (Vidyasagar 1991, 683).

What we see here is a desire to create a new Bengali, both as literature and nation. 'Enlightened' is the key word that describes this new Bengali, and this enlightenment is to come from European sources or European literatures. At one level, this new Bengali seems to be constructed merely as translation – from the colonial source to the native ground. Limiting ourselves to this level, that is, of looking at the new Bengali merely as a process or even as a product of translation, we can still see processes of hybridisation that Bhabha has theorised as a crucial part of the formation of colonial subjectivity and identity. Crucially, this new Bengali is not concerned with a return or recovery, even through the medium of language, to a precolonial or pre-English stage. Indeed the new Bengali literature that did come into being during the Bengal renaissance does not read unproblematically as a narrative of anti-colonial cultural struggle. Mainstream Bengali criticism has tended to valorise this literary production as part of anti-colonial struggle, but a more nuanced reading shows us a fraught and fissured terrain in which the colonised subject, elite or otherwise, finds new spaces for cultural expression.

The Bengali being created in this colonial terrain is new in the sense of being enlightened and Europeanised. Looking at this process as the tran-sition to modernity, we are faced with the phenomenon of a colonised modernity. The literature that is produced in the period reflects this mixed nature of the modernising process. Perhaps the most celebrated poem from this period in Bengal is Michael Madhusudan Dutt's 'Bangab-hasha' or 'Bengali Language' (1866). This poem envisages the poet as a traveller on foreign shores wandering through foreign lands, while the immense wealth that lies in the motherland remains neglected. It cele-brates the return of a prodigal son, and is read as the poet's definite rejec-tion of poetic efforts in English to concentrate on writing in Bengali. This celebrated return, however, is rendered in a 14-line sonnet, written in Bengali blank verse. Indeed, the literary venture of the Bengal renais-sance was marked by this adoption or translation of English literary forms into Bengali, beginning with the creation of blank verse in Bengali, the writing of sonnets, the development of prose narratives like the novel or the inauguration of the proscenium theatre. Hence this reformulation of Bengali, which was even then recognised as a part of a process of reform and nation making, was based on European forms and models. So the 'enlightenment' or modernity that was being desired expressed itself not merely in theme, but also effected the form.

This amalgamation between Bengali and English represents the colonised desire to traverse and stitch together the cultural split that colonialism had brought in its wake. This desire often finds expression as a rejection of the coloniser's culture, but nevertheless takes on board many of the forms and themes that a colonial cultural sphere is composed of. A similar and perhaps more well known and certainly more recent 'return' has been made by Ngugi wa Thiong'o, who has given up writing in English for Gikuyu and has called this renunciation 'part and parcel of the anti-imperialist struggles of Kenyan and African peoples' (Ngugi wa Thiong'o 1988). The colonial pedagogic process is seen as creating a rift in the idyllic, because unified, life of the child. This rift is perceived as a 'homelessness' (cf. Dutt's image of the poet 'wandering on foreign shores'). The child has to negotiate between the world of his home and of his native language and the world of the school where the colonial language dominates. A sense of exile and homelessness characterises these split linguistic terrains. To return to Vidyasagar's notes: the split becomes the site of creation, a site from where a new voice – a new literature – can emerge.

On both sides of the colonial divide the struggle seems to be over the language of literature. In colonised worlds, the public–private split has its linguistic dimensions, and language is put across this binary so that we have a public language of commerce, business and industry, of law and public life opposed to a private and affective language of the home. The language of literature remains such a bone of contention because it straddles both spheres. At one level, it appears as a site of 'authenticity' – Wordsworth had described it as a 'spontaneous' and 'real'.[7] Modern psychoanalytic theory would also read it as an 'authentic' site, as an irrup-

---

7 William Wordsworth's 'Preface to the *Lyrical Ballads*', 1802 is often thought to be the 'manifesto' of the Romantic Movement in English literature and definitely is a wonderful example of the way poetry and politics merge. Whilst the 'Preface' was first written in 1800, it was subsequently revised. References here are to the 1802 version.

tion of the unconscious, as the language of dreams and desires.[8] But it is also one of the most public uses of language, the most political in the sense that literature is the site through which a nation or culture spins its dreams and desires, and also represents itself to others. It is used as a national emblem, as a representation of the nation/culture. It is this twofold status of literature that makes the linguistic medium in which it is expressed so crucial. Hence, political writings – be they by Gandhi or Nehru or Mandela – are easily accepted in the coloniser's language; it is only when poems and stories appear in the coloniser's tongue that the issue of language becomes so central.[9] To use the example of Bengal again: the writer Rabindranath Tagore had protested against the use of English in anti-colonial political struggle as belying its own purpose. He had recommended the use of Bengali because of its wider outreach. In his exordiums and critique of the anti-colonial Congress movement, we do find a notion of the language of the people and its separation from the coloniser's language.[10] But were we to put Tagore's pronouncements through the same process of critique to which Coleridge had subjected Wordsworth's ideas, the same questions would emerge. What defines the 'real' language – where is this site of authenticity to be found?

The historical and political forces that determine and guide the use of English and other European languages in once-colonised nations have always been fraught. The tendency to renounce English or other colonial languages has been one of the ways that writers have tried to establish their anti-colonial credentials as well as find a relevance for their works in their own countries. But even while they were doing that, colonial influences had seeped into national culture, modifying and transforming literary writings in their own languages. Another manifestation of this kind of self-reflexivity in postcolonial writings is the use of 'other' modes of liter-

---

[8]   Perhaps the most direct adumbration of this theory is to be found in Freud's essay, 'Creative Writers and Day-Dreaming' (Freud 1990). See also Rose 1996, to see how nation making and the deepest and most inner recesses of our mental life interconnect with each other and find mutual expression in social and political reality.

[9]   Even the memoirs of these political leaders are written in English. What could be more intimate or authentic than a recounting of one's childhood? All these writers have recounted their lives in English, but nowhere have I found the kind of soul-searching that Madhusudan Dutt made himself undergo in the nineteenth century in Bengal, or that Ngugi has done in more recent times.

[10]   Tagore, in a series of essays which have been collected under the titles of 'Atyashakti' (1901–1905) and anthologised in *Rabindra Rachanabali*, Vol. 3, 246–83, has examined the notions of nation making, of language and religion, and the notion of internationalism (Tagore 1985).

ary writing in English. Again this is completely overlooked in analyses of 'new' literatures in English. For example, Salman Rushdie has been rightly praised for his use of magical realism as well as the self-consciousness of his narration. But somehow this has led to the impression that this is an 'Indian' way of writing. This does bring about a misunderstanding – as Indian writing itself is varied and variegated, and a tight-knit realism can equally be regarded as Indian. Salman Rushdie is perhaps most 'Indian' in his use of the English language, marked as it is by the direct translation of words and even phrases from Urdu. This is illustrated in his use of endearments such as 'little piece of the moon' in *Midnight's Children* or names such as Gup and Chup in *Haroun and the Sea of Stories*. The 'accretions' to English that we have noticed earlier can be made to wield a richer reading if read with knowledge of the vast and diverse fields from which these writings emerge, rather than lumping them together as 'literatures in English'.

While English is being moulded and reformed into new shapes and functions, the writer in English is perhaps faced by another worry. The role of 'native informant' as defined by Gayatri Spivak has a historical background in the nineteenth-century colonial educational venture. Macaulay in the 1835 *Minutes on Education* had seen the role of the English-speaking native as a 'conduit', the passage through which Western civilisation and culture would seep into Indian soil and the Indian soul. The writer in English, by bringing to view Indian ways of life and writing, may at best be reversing the process, but, more crucially, is in danger of playing the role of tourist guide to Western travellers to the east. Keeping these doubts in mind may result in a more critical analysis of the recent appreciation of 'other' writings in English in Western countries, and more importantly, it may help to evaluate the nature and purpose of the writing itself. There are many reasons for a writer choosing to write in the language of the former colonisers. English has been largely accepted as the language of the present globalised world, and hence writing in English has a larger purview. But this fact in itself has a great political significance, which can be highlighted in order to analyse the place of local, regional and national cultures in the future. As audio-visual culture takes over, or at least exists side by side with so-called literary culture, the use of images and the aesthetics of literary production may also be undergoing a change. In India, for example, English writing can be read all over the country and in fact in the region as a whole, and is the only cultural form that may hope to have the same purview as the audio-visual film and television industry. What does this bode for writing in Urdu or Bengali? This bi- or multi-lingual literary sphere needs to be seen in its entirety. The

Caribbean writer in English, on the other hand, uses the language in a very different way. Here English is claimed as the mother tongue, and hence not seen as the property of the former colonisers, but of today's users. So in one once-colonised region, English is the means of communication, and always in conflict with other languages, and in another, it is a means of self-definition, and is used in defiance of the cultures that consider it its 'natural' property. The many places that English sits in need to be brought into fuller view so that these different rhythms can be heard more clearly.

Woman as Home and Other

While feminist and postcolonial literary criticism have been contrasted on the basis that feminist critics are more in touch with their political counterparts, it will be useful to look at postcolonial treatments of the figure of the woman in literature. This will serve as an example of the ways in which reading literary texts merges with other social and political concerns.

The figure of the woman has functioned as a metaphor in postcolonial theoretical considerations. Fanon's examination of the veiled Algerian revolutionary and the demonstration of the use of colonial stereotypes to puzzle and deceive the colonial power has provided postcolonial literary theory with an example of the ambiguity of the figure of the woman in colonial discourse. Further, *Orientalism* (Said, 1978) has seen the difference in power positioning between the coloniser and the colonised as similar to that between the active male and the passive female. Keeping the focus on representation and the speaking voice in literature, we can see how the figure of the woman becomes emblematic of the ambiguity and the shifting positioning of postcolonial readings.

Feminist literary criticism has to a large extent been involved with discovering a 'woman's' voice in literature. While the status and nature of this voice has been much debated, the discovery and bringing-into-view of women's writing remains one of the main concerns of feminist criticism. An analysis of the woman's voice in literary texts from a postcolonial perspective is provided by Gayatri Spivak in 'Three Women's Texts and a Critique of Imperialism' (Spivak 1985). Through a reading of three novels by women – *Frankenstein*, *Jane Eyre* and *Wide Sargasso Sea* – the question of a specifically female voice in literary writing is brought to view. These readings reveal the colonial nature of these women's texts. Even Jean Rhys's novel, which is often read as a rewriting of *Jane Eyre* from the point of view of the colonised, is shown to be complicit with the processes of colonial cultural production. This essay, in a way, lays the foundation for her later and more detailed examination of the subaltern voice in 'Can the Subaltern Speak?' (Spivak 1988). Postcolonial theory has used the figure of the woman as the emblem of colonial domination. *Orientalism* (Said, 1978) had highlighted the erotic dimensions of colonial conquest, where conquered lands were depicted as passive women waiting to be ravished. Spivak has taken the metaphor further, to show that colonial domination renders the woman/subaltern mute, making it impossible to decipher her voice except in a tangential and masked manner.

Postcolonial theory has pointed out how woman as metaphor has been used extensively by colonial literary discourse. On the other hand, the figure of the woman has also been wielded and used by the anti-colonial and emerging national discourses. In the public–private divide that accompanied colonialism, woman was seen as aligned with the private sphere. Such a division renders the domestic into a domain that is sheltered from the forays of the colonial overlord, and where women are kept as the upholders of tradition and language.[11] This woman, in turn, is caught within the various poles of the public–private divide, between the traditional sphere of the home and the forces of colonial modernity. She is at the same time figured in colonial discourse as a sign through which non-European colonised cultures are classified as 'backward' or even 'barbaric'. Women in colonial contexts are placed in contradictory spheres, both as emblematic of society's modernity – a sign of the 'enlightenment' of a culture – and as the upholder of traditional values. In the previous section we had looked at Vidyasagar's envisioning of a new Bengali literature. This emerging Bengali literature uses woman as a metaphor for home, the traditional, the precolonial and as that sphere which has somehow evaded the colonial onslaught. At the same time, women are also the objects of the modernising reform movement, and it is in the genre of the novel that images of the 'new' woman are drawn.

The creation of a new literature in Bengal entailed a wholesale rewriting of ancient Sanskrit myths. In this process of rewriting, the figure of the woman is remoulded and made to emblematise the nation. The nation in turn is equated with a mother figure. Notions of mother/nation/goddess/earth are conflated in this literary-cultural redrawing of woman. It will be interesting at this point to look at how a woman writer wields this image for herself. I will turn to the poetry of Toru

---

[11] This formulation is spelt out by Chatterjee (1989).

Dutt, who, writing in English in the 1870s in Calcutta, can definitely be seen as placed within this public–private divide, and within this project of reformulating the figure of the woman as a literary/cultural symbol. 'Savitri' (1882) is a long poem that portrays this well-known figure from Indian mythology, but a woman who has become the symbol of wifely devotion.[12] Ironically enough, in Toru Dutt's rendition, 'Savitri' becomes a symbol of freedom, of freedoms that were once enjoyed by women in India, but which were now lost to us. Thus

> In those far-off primeval days
> Fair India's daughters were not pent
> In closed zenanas . . .   (Dutt 1882, Part 1, lines 72–75)

The contrast or the dichotomy between the inside and the outside is drawn as between the present and the past. It is in the present that Indian women are confined within their homes. So while there may be a notion of a 'better' because more liberated past, Toru Dutt seeks freedom not in ancient India, but in modern Europe. Were we to read her poetry along with her letters, we would notice in both forms of writing an intense desire for freedom. 'Freedom' is not seen as political freedom here, but as freedom of movement, as freedom to wander and roam.[13] Whether nationalistic discourse could accommodate these differing notions of freedom is open to question. Savitri is shown as wandering 'in boyish freedom', and one of her main freedoms was the choice of life partner. This contrast between an imagined and ancient India and the present sense of confinement finds expression in her letters as the contrast between her confined life in her family home in Baugmaree near Calcutta and the freedoms and friendships she had enjoyed during her sojourn in England. Ancient India is thus compared with contemporary England or Europe. The movement is both backwards in time – to the glories of the classical past – but also outwards – outside – for 'other' images of freedom. The notion of the comforts of the mother-nation is offset by the drawing of other sites and arenas where Indian daughters are more comfortable and crucially enjoy a sense of freedom.

The other literary form where the position of women was intensely debated is that of the novel. If the English novel with its domestic themes was the cultural delineation of the private sphere, and used women as its

---

12 'Savitri' is anthologised in Dutt 1882, a posthumous collection of the poems of Toru Dutt.
13 A very good reading of the desire for freedom expressed in Toru Dutt's letters is to be found in Grewal 1996.

central motif, the emerging novelistic form in nineteenth-century colonial Bengal, was similarly deployed to such a purpose. Again, in the pages
of the novel, nation making and the positioning of women are juxtaposed. But unlike the reformulated heroines of ancient myths, these
novel heroines struggle with 'new' middle-class bourgeois values. The
novel is part of the modernising discourse through which the emerging
national elite learns to negotiate the transformations to domestic and
affective life.[14] The new educated Bengali middle class needed to
resituate itself within new class and social formations. The novel, by
focusing on domestic life, uses women as the central emblematic figure
through which the process of social transformation is shown. Moreover,
growing literacy amongst middle-class women also draws in women as the
main readers of the genre, so that the novel becomes a vehicle of social
change as well as a reflection of this change. The novelist Bankimchandra Chatterjee (1838–1894) becomes the first best selling writer in
Bengal. His readers were mainly from the emerging middle class, but
women formed a large part of this readership. The new woman has often
been criticised as being too involved in novel reading, even neglecting
her duties in the kitchen.[15]

Literary history can thus be seen to provide us with examples of the
ways that women were being brought into discourse within a colonial
context. An abstracted female figure worked as the most potent symbol
for the nation, and women themselves were drawn in as producers and
consumers of literature. From within this plethora of experiments and
innovations, where are we to find a woman's voice? Again an involved
reading of literature would bring to us perhaps not that voice, but the
spaces that need to be negotiated for women's issues and concerns to find
expression.

One of the questions that faces postcolonial critics is the predomi-
nance of men in the 'new' literatures canon. In fact, even going through
the names I have mentioned, men seem to be the progenitors of this field.
Do we really need women's voices? Perhaps we do, and what the presence
of the woman may do is to unsettle some of the notions that seem to easily
accrue to postcolonial texts. On the question of homelessness and exile,

---

[14] The best reading of the ways that the novel reflects the changes in Bengali
domestic life is to be found in Chaudhuri 1968.
[15] The popularity of Bankimchandra Chatterjee's novels with middle-class
Bengali women is illustrated in Satyajit Ray's film, *Charulata*, where the heroine is
shown as taking out one of his novels as she whiles away the idle hours in her
house.

for example, the binaries drawn by a writer like Ngugi would undergo a different rendition. We have seen how Toru Dutt has destabilised the meaning of 'freedom'. In today's world, the easy schematic division between private and public does not hold any longer, and it is the presence of women in various discursive fields that has effectively challenged and undone this division. Literature also perhaps needs to blur the boundaries between so-called literary writings and other forms of expression. In today's variegated cultural sphere, women's voices can perhaps be heard through many other sites, and a juxtaposition of these will help to not merely undo, but reformulate the literary. So instead of merely adding Anita Desai or Bharati Mukherjee to the list of male 'greats', we need to be more innovative. We could look at many other places – interviews, films, songs – or the documents through which the international movements for women's rights put forward their demands – for the ways in which women are making their entry into the field of culture and politics. As feminism's earlier agonising over the status and universality of women's voices has shown us, differences in women's positioning – even when they pertain to the writings of so-called Third World women – need to be kept at the fore. Otherwise we are in danger of repeating the earlier mistake of valorising a dominant voice as representative. In short, the process of analysis becomes even more intense when we bring feminist concerns into postcolonial readings and into the emerging canon of 'new' literatures. The highlighting of gender difference brings into play other forms of difference, which undergo yet another analysis in this light.

Postcolonial interventions have changed the face of literary and cultural studies in the past three decades. They have brought to the fore the links between political economic power and the production and dissemination of culture. They have examined the question of literary and cultural representation, and shown how cultural stereotyping influences 'real' processes such as economic and social policies. Finally and most importantly, a constant re-examination of the cultural field may also open up ways in which social hierarchies can be understood and hopefully transformed.

Postcolonial approaches to literature have acquired a new relevance and significance. Bengal is the first site of a colonial literary pedagogical practice, and the history of teaching literature needs to be explored further. With the renewed and enhanced status of English in the globalised situation, the power that was associated with this language during colonial times has taken on a different aspect. The plethora of literary efforts in English from all over the world is one of the manifestations of this new 'rise' of English. The meeting between cultures is part of other social, political and economic relations that govern the world, whether such a meeting had taken place in the past, as in the colonial world, or in the influences and cross-fertilisations of the emerging global order. The pleasure(s) of reading are indeed enhanced once texts are made to speak from all the sites they occupy and with all the voices that resonate through them.

Works Cited

Ahmad, A. 1993. *In Theory: Classes, States, Nations*, London: Verso.

Azim, F. 1993. *The Colonial Rise of the Novel*, London: Routledge.

Bhabha, H. 1986. Foreword to F. Fanon, *Black Skin, White Masks*, London: Pluto Press.

Bhabha, H. 1993. *The Location of Culture*, London: Routledge.

Chatterjee, P. 1989. 'The Nationalist Resolution of the Women's Question', in K. Sangari and S. Vaid (eds) *Recasting Women: Essays in Colonial History*, New Delhi: Kali for Women, 233–53.

Chaudhuri, N.C. 1968. *Bangali Jibane Ramani*, Calcutta: Mitra and Company.

Dutt, M.M. 1987. 'Bangabhasha', in Khetra Gupta (ed.) *Madhusudan Rachanabali*, Calcutta: Sahitya, Sangsad, 159.

Dutt, T. 1882. 'Savitri', in *Ancient Ballads and Legends of Hindustan*, London: Kegan, Paul Trench and Co., 3–45.

Freud, S. 1990. 'Creative Writers and Day-Dreaming', *The Standard Edition of the Complete Psychological Works*, London: The Hogarth Press, Vol. IX, 141–54.

Ghosh, B. 1984. *Vidyasagar O Bangali Samaj*, Calcutta: Orient Longmans Ltd.

Grewal, I. 1996. *Home and Harem: Nation, Gender, Empire and the Cultures of Travel*, London: Leicester University Press.

Macaulay, T.B. 1935. *Speeches, with the Minute on Indian Education*, London: Oxford University Press.

Moore-Gilbert, B. 1997. *Postcolonial Theory: Contexts, Practice, Politics*, London: Verso.

Ngugi wa Thiong'o 1988. *Decolonising the Mind: The Politics of Language in African Literature*, Nairobi: Heinemann.

Rose, J. 1996. *States of Fantasy*, Oxford: Oxford University Press.

Rushdie, S. 1981. *Midnight's Children*, New York: Knopf.

—— 1990. *Haroun and the Sea of Stories*, London: Viking and Granta.

Said, E. 1978. *Orientalism*, London: Routledge and Kegan Paul.

—— 1993. *Culture and Imperialism*, New York: Alfred Knopf.

Spivak, G.C. 1985. 'Three Women's Texts and a Critique of Imperialism', *Critical Inquiry*, Vol. 12, No. 1, 243–61.

—— 1987. *In Other Worlds: Essays in Cultural Politics*, London: Methuen.

—— 1988. 'Can the Subaltern Speak?', in C. Nelson and L. Grossberg (eds) *Marxism and the Interpretation of Culture*, Basingstoke: Macmillan, 271–313.

Tagore, R. 1985. 'Atyashakti', in *Rabindra Rachanabali*, Calcutta: Viswabharati Press, Vol. 3, 246–83.

Vidyasagar, I. 1991. 'Notes on the Sanskrit College', in Prafulla Kumar Patra (ed.) *Vidyasagar Rachanabali*, Calcutta: Patra's Publication, 682–6.

Viswanathan, G. 1990. *Masks of Conquest, Literary Study and British Rule in India*, London: Faber & Faber.

Wordsworth W. 1966. 'Preface to Lyrical Ballads with Pastoral and Other Poems, 1802', in P.M. Zall (ed.) *Literary Criticism of William Wordsworth*, Lincoln: University of Nebraska Press.

Venetian Spaces: Old–New Literatures and the Ambivalent Uses of Jewish History

BRYAN CHEYETTE

THIS ESSAY WILL FOCUS on the imagined geography of Venice which has long since been represented as the decaying heart of European civilisation. In modern times (from the late nineteenth century onwards), Venice was specifically racialised as a liminal space where Europe and Africa or the Occident and Orient, meet. At the turn of the century, the poetry of T.S. Eliot and Ezra Pound pointed to the Semitic racial hybridity of Venice as a key instance of the radical lack of connection between a European tradition and the individual artist. In recent times, the fiction of Caryl Phillips and Anita Desai have redrawn the literary map of Venice so as to embrace its unbounded territory and to locate the Jewish diaspora within a postcolonial narrative. The essay will begin by looking at the resistance of one strand of postcolonial theory to the incorporation of Jewish history or the history of anti-Semitism into an understanding of a colonising Western modernity. It will then move on to show that much colonial and postcolonial fiction has a wider construction of the diaspora than current contemporary theoretical orthodoxies allow. To this end, I will bring together the fiction of Caryl Phillips with the poetry of T.S. Eliot and the fiction of Anita Desai and E.M. Forster. But I will begin with the theoretical impediments which seem to discourage such a comparative project.

Resisting Jewish History

In a recent essay on English ethnicity, Robert Young notes that most nineteenth-century theories of race were devoted to analyses of European ethnicity. He goes on to state that: 'Of this only anti-Semitism is widely known, but it was part of a much wider project of analysing European races' (Young 1997, 127). Later on in the essay he refers to the racial theories of M.F. Edwards which situated Jews in relation to Egyptian history and the Jewish diaspora as a whole (which included much of Asia and Africa). Young's comment, however, once again confines 'the Jews' to the history of Europe: 'the example of the Jews provided both the evidence and the model of a racial theory that was eventually to end with the attempt to exterminate them' (Young 1997, 132). The 'evidence', according to Edwards (which Young seems to endorse), particularly concerns the 'permanence of racial types' (Young 1997, 132). In this reading, Jews are either archetypal victims or exemplary Europeans to the extent that, according to Young, the 'British Israelite movement in this period was . . . claiming that the Anglo-Saxons were actually the true descendants of the Jews' (Young 1997, 140).

Young's confusion about whether Jews are part of European majoritarian history, or a victimised minority – whether they are white or black in other words – also extends to much of his longer work. His *White Mythologies: Writing History and the West* (1990) speaks of the history of anti-Semitism as a form of internal orientalism in the West, thereby simultaneously including and excluding it from the realm of his inquiry. This equivocal gesture is done without linking the history of anti-Semitism to German orientalism, which was the main variant of internalised Western orientalism. This history of German orientalism is, as we shall see, evoked tellingly in Anita Desai's *Baumgartner's Bombay* (1988). In his more recent book, *Colonial Desire: Hybridity in Theory, Culture and Race* (1994) Young argues that every Victorian racial theorist, however doctrinaire, was in reality 'ambivalent', 'uncertain' and 'anxious'. The only racial category in *Colonial Desire* which is unambivalent concerns the 'positive' representations of Jews in Victorian Britain which is surprising given the ubiquity of these rather exhausted equivocations throughout the book. It is as if Benjamin Disraeli can be taken at his own word on the matter of Jewish racial superiority.

As Robert Young's work indicates, there is a strand of postcolonial theory which is unable to perceive Jews as anything other than as part of the majoritarian tradition. Henry Louis Gates's rightly influential anthology, *'Race', Writing and Difference* (1986), for instance, includes little or no discussion of Western anti-Semitism among its essays which Tzvetan Todorov, in particular, objected too in the epilogue to the collection. Gates in the volume, subsequently reprinted in his *Loose Canons: Notes on the Culture Wars* (1992), speaks routinely of a homogenous and dominant white 'Western Judeo-Christian' culture. Edward Said in his *Culture and Imperialism* (1993) follows Gates in this regard and, because of this, does not address the non-Christian minorities within Europe.[1] The inevitable contradictions in this one-eyed perspective can be found in

[1]   For a detailed discussion of this issue see Marshall Grossman, 'The Violence of the Hyphen in Judeo-Christian', *Social Text* 22 (Spring 1989), 115–22.

Said's *The Question of Palestine* (1979) where, at one and the same time, he reads 'the Jews' in George Eliot's *Daniel Deronda* (1876) as both 'European prototypes' and as 'curiously . . . "Eastern" ' (Said 1979, 65).

Once one speaks of a supposedly common white Judeo-Christian tradition then 'the Jews' can only belong to this culture as an aspect of European oppression. Such essentialising, by definition, flattens out the ambivalent position of Jews who were historically at the heart of European metropolitan culture and, at the same time, banished from its privileged sphere so that ascendant racial and sexual identities could be formed and maintained. But, while acknowledging this uncertain history, one also needs to recognise the reasons for the diffident (to put it kindly) stance of many postcolonial theorists towards a minority Jewish history. This resistance, I believe, takes three main forms and concerns, in particular, the history of individual Jews as part of the colonial project; the more general history of Zionism; and the contemporary cultural politics of many American Jews and African Americans. I want to briefly engage with these issues so as to acknowledge both the theoretical limitations inherent in this strand of postcolonial theory as well as the genuine difficulties in incorporating Jewish history into a postcolonial perspective.

Present-Day Hostilities

As an example of a Jewish internalisation of colonial discourse it is hard to ignore the towering figure of Benjamin Disraeli. Although baptised, Disraeli was avowedly Judeocentric and can be said to have successfully promoted English Jingoism along with the Victorian cult of Empire. The fact that Disraeli as a Jewish-born individual suffered from virulently racialist attacks about his 'Semitic' origins clearly pales into insignificance when placed next to his imperial policies.[2] What is more, Disraeli inspired a generation of colonial novelists, such as John Buchan, Rider Haggard and Rudyard Kipling, in arguing that Imperialism enacted the superiority of Judeo-Christian values throughout the world. While many individual Jews colluded with the apparatus of colonialism, it is clear that during times of crisis they were regarded with the utmost suspicion as

---

[2]   See *Jewish History* 10:2 (Fall 1996) for a recent collection of essays devoted to Disraeli's racialised Jewishness and David Feldman 1994, *Englishmen and Jews: Social Relations and Political Culture, 1840–1914* (New Haven: Yale University Press), chapter 4.

racial others.[3] In these terms, the whitening of European Jewry needs to be understood historically as a failed quest for invisibility and not merely naturalised as the signifier of Jewish empowerment.

What is most curious about the postcolonial response to the Disraelian narrative tradition is that it simply reinforces Disraeli's essentialising beliefs that Judeo-Christianity was transcendent and all-encompassing. As I have shown elsewhere, colonial writing found it impossible to unproblematically subsume 'the Jew' as a facile aspect of a dominant imperial discourse. Such figures as Buchan, Haggard and Kipling reveal the transparent difficulties which the dominant culture had in making Jews unambivalent – fixed in their 'whiteness' or 'Judeo-Christian' superiority.[4] There is clearly a profound blindness about the complex nature of Jewish history in the West when such crude colonial literature is able to expose the short-comings of postcolonial theorists in this regard. By dismissing Jews merely as European subjects, it is as if the current privileged position of post-Holocaust, post-Zionist Western Jewry can be read back in time and space.

At the same time, the history of Zionism does point to the historic collusion of a large number of European Jews with colonial discourse and practices which continues to this day. One can not understand Edward Said's underdetermined representation of Jews in his *Orientalism* (1978) without recourse to this history and the consequent victimisation of Palestinians since the turn of the century. For Said, the 'Jew of pre-Nazi Europe' (Said 1978, 286) becomes 'bifurcated': 'one Semite went the way of Orientalism, the other, the Arab, was forced to go the way of the Oriental' (Said 1978, 307). Instead of incorporating the history of anti-Semitism into his study he, therefore, regards orientalist discourse as the 'strange secret sharer of Western anti-Semitism' (Said 1978, 27). To reinforce the manichaean divide between post-War Arab and Jewish 'Semites', Said's *Culture and Imperialism* simply does not mention the shadowy history of anti-Semitism within Imperial culture.

As his *The Politics of Dispossession: The Struggle for Palestinian Self-Determination 1969–1994* (1994) makes clear, however, there is an understandable anti-Zionist dimension to Said's bifurcation of post-war

3   Bryan Cheyette 1993, *Constructions of 'the Jew' in English Literature and Society: Racial Representations, 1875–1945* (Cambridge: Cambridge University Press), chapter 3.
4   For this argument in full see Bryan Cheyette, 'Neither black nor white: The figure of "the Jew" in Imperial English Literature', in Tamar Garb and Linda Nochlin (eds) *The Jew in the Text* (London and New York: Thames and Hudson, 1995), 31–41.

'Semites'. What this book shows is the extent to which present-day representations of the Holocaust have been used as a tool of Palestinian oppression (Said 1994, 167–69). But it is precisely because Jewish suffering has been so crudely essentialised, in the name of Israeli nationalism, that it needs to be engaged with outside of a national narrative. Ella Shohat, for instance, has long since written against all nationalist discourses which dominate most discussion of Zionist history. In this context, Shohat calls for the disentangling of the orientalist distinction of East versus West, Arab versus Jew by inserting a range of diverse histories, communities and identities into the Middle East which fall outside of these crude binarisms. She concentrates especially on Sephardi (or Mizrahi) Jews from North Africa, Asia and the Middle East. These groups, most obviously, point to an interconnectedness with other postcolonial histories and with the interplay of communities within and across borders. It is these kinds of comparative histories – impure, unbounded and diasporic – which have been taken up by Anita Desai and Caryl Philips in their fiction. These non-national histories need to be placed against what Shohat rightly calls the 'professionalised study of compartmentalised historical periods and geographical regions' (Shohat 1997, 88).

Part of the problem in trying to institutionalise disruptive histories which cross received racial and national boundaries is that they often can not be contained within current academic orthodoxies. Paul Gilroy, in this spirit, has recently asked 'why does it remain so difficult for so many people to accept the knotted intersection of histories' which, in his example, brings together black American soldiers as witnesses to the horrors of the Nazi death camps (Gilroy 1998, 287). However it is clear that a history of common oppression, which Gilroy has begun to outline, is also distorted by the contemporary deformation of black-Jewish relations (both within and outside the academy) in the United States. In his *The European Tribe* (1987), Caryl Phillips notes with some disbelief the 'virulent anti-Semitism that seems to permeate much black thought' (Phillips 1987, 53) in America. While anti-Semitism in general is on the decline in the United States, most agree that it is on the increase in the black community which is largely due to the influence of the Nation of Islam on poorer African Americans. Cornell West, Henry Louis Gates and bell hooks have all intervened against the Nation of Islam to rightly temper its worst anti-Semitic excesses and its extreme cultural nationalism and politics of separation.[5]

5   Paul Berman ed., 1994, *Blacks and Jews: Alliances and Arguments* (New York: Delacorte Press) contains key essays by Cornell West, Henry Louis Gates and bell

The attempt to build bridges across supposedly different histories of the diaspora in the United States has, from one perspective, resulted in the appropriation of black experience by the Jewish community. As David Biale has noted, the Holocaust in the United States has been over-determined as the dominant model of racism with all forms of historical oppression expected to fit into this framework. Phillips understands, in this context, that 'an American black might respond with contempt to an American Jew who told him, "I know what it is to be persecuted; I am a Jew" ' (Phillips 1987, 53). Biale rightly notes that the institutionalised presence of the Holocaust in the United States makes it a convenient filter through which other more immediate American histories of oppression – such as the history of slavery and the genocide of Native Americans – can be under-played. What is more, the double-edged nature of Jewish victimhood in the United States produces a community which both insists on its minority status and, at the same time, has the power to place a Holocaust museum in the political heart of Washington DC. As Biale notes, it serves American state interests to award the 'genocide of Europeans by Europeans . . . canonical status' while the 'home grown mass sufferings of African and Native Americans' still remain largely outside of the national canon (Biale 1998, 28).

By associating racism and genocide with a Europe that has long since been transcended by the myth of the New World, the Holocaust is thus able to fit comfortably within dominant constructions of American identity. The Americanisation of the Holocaust, in other words, allows the United States to forget or play down its policies of genocide and racial oppression on its own back door. This tension has corrupted present-day black-Jewish relations which have gradually deteriorated since the late 1960s. James Baldwin's much anthologised 1967 essay entitled, 'Negroes Are Anti-Semitic Because they Are Anti-White', indicates the faultlines between blacks and Jews which have continued to this day. Phillips in *The European Tribe* cites a key passage from Baldwin's essay: 'The Jew must see that he is part of the history of Europe, and will always be so considered by the descendants of the slave. Always, that is, unless he is willing to prove that this judgement is inadequate and unjust' (Phillips 1987, 52). The fact that Baldwin insists on the agency of Jews, with regard to an alternative set of values to the majoritarian white tradition, indicates the possi-

hooks. See also Paul Gilroy 2000, *Between Camps: Race, Identity and Nationalism at the end of the Colour Line* (Harmondsworth: The Penguin Press), for an exemplary account of these issues.

bility of re-imagining the present on completely different racial lines. It is precisely this possibility that informs Phillips's *The Nature of Blood* (1997).

Reimaging Europe

It is clear that the present-day histories of Zionism and black-Jewish relations in the United States – as well as the past complicity of Jews with colonial discourse – has reinforced the racialised separate spheres between Jews and other ethnicities within the academy. It is at this point, as Phillips (1987) notes in *The European Tribe*, that an avowedly European perspective paradoxically helps to break down these rigid divisions. Unlike the Americanisation of the Holocaust, the Jewish dead on the continent of Europe are still able to challenge the received order of European states and their national boundaries. What is more, the long history of a lethal European modernity, as Homi Bhabha has argued, is most obviously shared by the 'histories of slavery and colonialism, where the racist desire for supremacy and domination turns the ideas of progress and sovereignty into demonic partners in a *danse macabre*' (Bhabha 1998, xv). Because the deformed myth of progress is more readily exposed in a contemporary European context, both Phillips and Anita Desai are able to engage productively with Jewish history in relation to their own Indian and Black-British histories. Phillips, for instance, is quite explicit in *The European Tribe* about his 'fascination' with 'the Jews' (Phillips 1987, 66) and, to this end, 'Shylock has always been [his] hero' (Phillips 1987, 55).

As Jonathan Boyarin has argued, Gayatri Spivak's resonant postcolonial question, 'Can the Subaltern Speak?' (1988), also informs its European post-Holocaust equivalent, 'Can the Dead Speak?' (Boyarin 1992, 82). The ineffability of representation raised by Spivak, most famously in her essay 'The Rani of Sirmur' (1985), applies equally to the post-Holocaust critical orthodoxy that the victims of the death camps are beyond representation. What is more, her sense of the inevitability of Western critical appropriation of colonial histories can be placed next to the equivalent Jewish fears that the voice of the camp victims is too easily adopted by non-survivor narratives. In contrast to much postcolonial theory, Boyarin suggests that we construct Otherness not merely spatially – where the other is perceived exclusively in relation to colonialism – but also temporally. This temporal perspective enables an engagement with the Jewish dead who, in Europe at least, continue to unsettle received narratives of Western modernity.

Instead of thinking of time and space as contrasting axes, Boyarin wishes to complicate the postcolonial stress on spatiality as it tends to discount minority history *within* Europe. That is, spatial organisation – the emphasis on 'other worlds' – denies the existence of more than one time frame or more than one kind of Europe. Boyarin contends suggestively, in these terms, that one should begin to think of 'different times [existing] in the same place' (Boyarin 1992, 82) to account for the Jewish dead who are not merely spatially but also temporally displaced. What is interesting about this argument, from the point of view of this essay, is that Caryl Phillips's fiction can be precisely characterised as a form of writing where 'different times . . . exist in the same place'. Phillips, above all, is the kind of novelist who reconstructs history – especially European history – from the viewpoint of those who have been marginalised or written out of this story. He writes impressionistic histories, in other words, from the perspective of those who have been displaced and excluded. His novels such as *Cambridge* (1991) and *Crossing the River* (1993) all defamiliarise dominant modes of address in relation to minority histories.

Phillips's project in *The Nature of Blood* is explicitly announced in *The European Tribe* where he notes that the sixteenth-century Venetian ghetto was the model for all other ghettos in the world. He rightly notes that 'Jews were forced to wear a special hat, they were not allowed to move in and out of the ghetto after dark, and its iron gates were guarded by Christians' (Phillips 1987, 52). That the ghetto was created to protect Jews from lethal assaults from the surrounding population also relates to the later history of European genocide. In a characteristic move, he places an early history of the ghetto, legally created in 1516, next to the 'two groups of Venetian Jews taken in 1943 and 1944 to die in the concentration camps of the Holocaust' (Phillips 1987, 52). This timeless view of history feeds directly into *The Nature of Blood* and points to his construction of an endless victimisation of both the Jewish and black minorities of Venice. It is this teleological sense of continuous history, running from the past to the present and back again, that has always concerned Phillips. His choice of Venice in this novel was, in this regard, dictated by his decision to address the silenced voices in both Shakespeare's *Othello* and *The Merchant of Venice*.

Racialised Venice

Before looking at *The Nature of Blood* in more depth, I want to briefly explore the extensive literary appropriation of Venice which prefigured

Phillips's novel. There is little doubt that Phillips is drawing on a long tradition of Venice as a hybrid space which most clearly contests Europe's supposedly self-evident superiority. In his book on Venice, Tony Tanner asks, in parenthesis, 'why *did* Shakespeare set his two plays with figures from marginalised groups . . . as protagonists in Venice?' (Tanner 1992, 5). Although this appears to be a rather minor question for Tanner, the history of Venice has long since challenged Europe's contested borders. Richard Sennett has, for instance, recently mapped out the colonial history, since medieval times, which made Venice the 'gatepost between Europe and the East and between Europe and Africa' (Sennett 1994, 214). As early as the year 1000, Venetians began trading in Indian spices, pepper from the east coast of Africa, and cinnamon from Ceylon (Sennett 1994, 217–18). In the words of William McNeill, the city acted as the 'hinge of Europe' (McNeill, 1974) by bringing this produce to Northern and Western Europe which attracted a good many marginal peoples who were barred from official citizenship.

By the end of the Victorian period, the long history of imperial dominance and uncontained racialised difference made Venice a significant mirror for colonial anxiety. Throughout the nineteenth century it was adopted by a range of romantic discourses as an enchanted place in the throws of decay and decline. Venice, in these terms, became a 'central site for the European imagination' (Tanner 1992, 4) as it signified a Western ascendancy which could no longer contain its racial other. The most extreme representation of the racialisation of Venice, as a space which signified the irrevocable decline of Europe, can be found in the poetry of T.S. Eliot and Ezra Pound. This move reached its low point in Eliot's 'Burbank with a Baedeker: Bleistein with a Cigar' (1919) which explicitly compares the former grandeur of Venice with the utter confusion generated by the contemporary bestial Jew in the guise of Bleistein, Sir Ferdinand Klein and, ultimately, Shylock. The 'watery impermanence' of Venice, together with the timeless solidity of its colonial history, has always made it a peculiarly 'bewitching mixture' (Tanner 1992, 8) for the modern Western literary imagination. Eliot, in his deliberately incoherent and overwrought epigraph to 'Burbank with a Baedeker', draws on six disparate accounts of Venice through the ages (in as many lines) which indicates both the ageless continuities of its millennial history and its dream-like instabilities:

Tra-la-la-la-la-la-laire – *nil nisi divinum stabile est; caetera fumus* – the gondola stopped, the old palace was there, how charming its grey and pink – goats and monkeys, with such hair too! – so the countess passed on until she came through the little park, where Niobe presented her with a cabinet, and so departed.

Here we have western culture as an inchoate jumble in the guise of 'St Sebastian' by Mantegna (1431–1506), Shakespeare's *Othello*, the *Entertainement of Alice, Dowager Countess of Derby* by John Marsdon (1575–1634), 'A Toccata of Galuppi's by Robert Browning (1812–1889), *Variations sur le carnivale de Venise* by Théophile Gautier (1811–1872), and *The Aspern Papers* (1888) by Henry James. The kaleidoscopic account of Europe's crumbling centre captures, in miniature, the method of the poem as a whole, especially in its 'multiplicity of partial dramatisations' (Ricks 1988, 38). It is the refined irrelevance of these historical allusions which makes them symptomatic of the very incoherence which is meant to be the poem's subject. Bleistein, like all of Eliot's 'jews', is a hybrid creature – 'Chicago, Semite, Viennese' – who combines an originary primitivism with a cosmopolitan modernity. The grotesque doubleness of Bleistein – part animal, part materialist – is condensed in the all too literal phrase, 'money in furs'. His ever-present cigar smoke is, in other words, an ideal figurative expression of a racialised confusion which obscures the cultural significance of the past:

> The smoky candle end of time
> Declines. On the Rialto once.
> The rats are underneath the piles.
> The jew is underneath the lot.
> Money in furs.

The location of 'the jew . . . underneath the lot', ravaging the foundations of Venice, is meant to explain the decline of the 'mind of Europe' (Eliot 1975, 51) as Eliot put it in his 'Tradition and the Individual Talent' (1919). But if Bleistein's diseased, smoke-ridden eye makes it impossible to assess the centrality of Venetian culture, then the poem itself can also be said to have been infected by such Semitic confusion. Even the all-explaining 'jew' cannot be disparaged with any certainty as Eliot's 'jew' appears at the beginning, the middle, and at the end of time in a myriad of contradictory guises. Just a few of his poetic guises include: a diseased eye, an eternal parasite, a cosmopolitan, a plutocrat, a usurer – Bleistein, Sir Ferdinand Klein, Shylock – as well as the whole of Venetian Jewry. The poem's allusions, as Christopher Ricks felicitously puts it, 'conceal by exposure' (Ricks 1988, 35–6) and are no less mired in equivocations than Bleistein himself. Venice, with its labyrinthine streets and watery fluidity, refuses to be reduced to a single meaning.

Shylock and Othello

What is paradoxical about Phillips's *The Nature of Blood* is that it has, to a large extent, adopted the teleological and impressionistic method of Eliot's poetry but to very different ends. Phillips has signalled his use of Eliot's classical modernist techniques in *The Final Passage* (1985) where he not only cites part of Eliot's 'Little Gidding' (1942) as his epigraph but, as Lyn Innes has shown, has detailed allusions to Eliot's poetry throughout the book (Innes 1995, 24–6). Phillips's quote from Eliot at the beginning of the book speaks especially to his narrative design:

> A people without history
> Is not redeemed from time, for history is a pattern
> Of timeless moments. So, while the light fails
> On a winter's afternoon, in a secluded chapel
> History is now and England.

Innes is right to note the 'double-edged' (Innes 1995, 24) quality of this quotation which simultaneously allows a 'people without history' to enter the temporal sphere while recognising the historicism of those with power: 'History is now and England.' Phillips's historical narratives are self-consciously thought of as a 'pattern of timeless moments' and, to this end, Anthony Ilona has usefully characterised his novels as 'chronicles' of the Black diaspora. Utilising the distinction which Hayden White makes between the 'historian proper' and the 'chronicler', Ilona notes that Phillips's chronicles are open-ended and are, usually, an 'unconnected record of events' (Ilona 1995, 6). His novels, written as chronicles, thus bring together a series of separate stories which only obliquely cohere. Phillips's chronicles culminate with *Crossing the River* although all of his fictions encompass a range of disparate traditions which make up his cultural influences. This can be seen most clearly in his collection, *Extravagant Strangers: A Literature of Belonging* (1997), which juxtaposes entries by Eliot, Rudyard Kipling and Joseph Conrad with Jean Rhys, C.L.R. James, and Samuel Selvon. *The Nature of Blood*, along with *Higher Ground* (1989) – which it partially rewrites – is Phillips's most explicit attempt to mix different cultures and traditions into a diverse whole.

It is the project of challenging separatisms and nationalisms on all sides which enables Phillips to reclaim the hybridity and modernity of Venice for minority discourse. In a stark reversal of Eliot's 'Burbank with a Baedeker', *The Nature of Blood* represents a timeless Venice not in terms of Jewish corruption of Europe history but, instead, as a site of Jewish victimisation. Phillips therefore represents the brutal persecution of fifteenth-century Venetian Jewry as a lethal prefiguration of European anti-Semitism. *The Nature of Blood* is quite explicit about this teleology where Jews are burnt at the stake in an unmistakable reference to the Nazi crematoria or where Venetian mass suicide is once again re-enacted during the Holocaust. Different times exist in an ageless Venice in a determinedly aestheticised view of history. The motifs of *Othello* shape the novel in slightly different ways – crossing boundaries between black and white, feminine and masculine, home and exile – and are an essential strategy in interweaving Jews and blacks or Shylock and Othello as archetypal victims of a European modernity.

Phillips, throughout his career, has always veered between the specificities of black British culture and history and a more amorphous diasporic history. *The Nature of Blood*, in particular, is part of a diasporic project which is concerned with, equally, uncovering the hidden stories of the lives of peoples of African descent while, at the same time, making connections with these peoples and other oppressed groups now located in Europe. I read Phillips as a diasporic writer who transcends a too easy afrocentricism and strives for a higher ground. Irene, in Phillips's story 'Higher Ground', is an early version of Eva Stern in *The Nature of Blood* as both are victims of Nazism who have a suicidal response to their sufferings. As Jewish women, they repeat the Othello-story of racial intermarriage: Irene with a black-British immigrant who returns to the Caribbean and Eva with a British soldier who liberates her from Belsen. Left alone at the close of 'Higher Ground', Irene sees 'the snow falling against the black sky' (Phillips 1989, 218) and recites the seminal prayer of the Hebrew bible, 'Hear, O Israel: the Lord our God, the Lord is one'. In this way, Phillips manages to evoke the final words of James Joyce's 'The Dead' as an epiphanous image of racial assimilation – black and white merging – as well as a more conventional illustration of religious transfiguration.

In *Higher Ground*, the traditional gospel cry acts as the book's epigraph – 'Lord plant my feet on higher ground' (Phillips 1989, 5) – which Phillips reinterprets in aesthetic terms. His novelistic 'higher ground' turns out to be the artistic transcendence of the particularities of exile and dispossession so as to create a more general 'literature of belonging'. Phillips both wants to chronicle an alternative version of received history, one which adds another dimension to what we already know of the past, while ignoring the pitfalls of an ever-present identity politics. In other words, he does not just want to confine his alternative history to peoples of African descent as it would then become a form of cultural nationalism. A key to this diasporic project can be found in *The Nature of Blood* when his

Othello-figure contemplates the fears and desires inherent in his wooing of a white woman. Phillips's Othello says the following:

> Once more, I looked upon myself in the mirror. It was true. The wooing of this lady [Desdemona] did indeed threaten the very foundations upon which my life was constructed, but surely it was the coward's way to remain in secure military bachelorhood and learn nothing more of the world beyond my own life. I abandoned the mirror and made my way towards the door.   (Phillips 1997, 144)

The Nature of Blood, in general, is concerned with mixing different cultures whether they be black and white, or Jew and gentile, and finally, of course, black and white Jews (in the Zionist counter-narrative). The telling question at the end of *The Nature of Blood* from the Ethiopian Jewish immigrant to Israel – '*would our babies be born white?*' (Phillips 1997, 203, italics in original) – points to the danger of Israel's assimilating completely into a dominant Western mode. Phillips focuses on the Ethiopian immigrants to Israel, and their opposition to '*this land of clocks*' (Phillips 1997, 209, italics in original) rightly points to a non-colonial model of Jewish identity and statehood. Othello's abandonment of the mirror – in other words the culture of narcissism – is crucial in this regard. Phillips's Othello refuses simply to gaze upon his own reflection in the mirror and, like Phillips himself, makes for 'the door' which opens upon other histories and cultures. In this way, Phillips is a black British writer who has transformed himself into a diasporic writer who both encompasses Afro-Caribbean history but can also be extended to include other diasporic histories such as that of the Jews. For this reason, Phillips does not just depict a single individual or national history in his novels but, instead, he focuses more broadly on the plural history of the diaspora which encompasses Europe, Africa, America and the Caribbean. It is in these expansive terms that he is able not only to rewrite the history of Venice from the margins but also to abandon a too easy self-regard.

Liminal Venice

A racialised Venice was to signify both the fears and desires of a hybrid history as well as, in the Victorian period, an idealised form of European colonial order. This can be seen, for example, in Margaret Oliphant's *The Makers of Venice* (1888) where she describes Venice as a place where the 'harsh, artificial sounds which vex the air in other towns' were 'replaced by harmonies of human voices and by the liquid tinkle of the waves' (Oliphant 1888, 1). She goes on to speak of Venice, at the height of its imperial power, as 'supreme in the seas the arbiter of peace and war through all the difficult and dangerous East, the first defender of Christendom against the Turk, the first merchant, banker, carrier whose emissaries were busy in all the councils of the world' (Oliphant 1888, 3–4). Oliphant evokes the long history of Venetian legalism and commercialism – to combat the unruly East – but also hints at the uncontrollable nature of wealth which crosses all boundaries and encourages unchecked desires. Thus, as well as signifying a civilising progress, Venice has been associated with a luscious sensuality which, popularised most notably by the poetry of Byron, the paintings of Turner and the histories of Ruskin, have also been at the heart of Victorian versions of the city. In these terms, Venice was 'all wonder, enchantment . . . brightness and the glory of a dream' (Oliphant 1888, 2).[6]

The extent to which fin de siècle Venice was contrasted with its colonial other can be seen when Fielding visits Venice in E.M. Forster's *A Passage to India* (1924). With an anachronistic imperial certainty, reminiscent of Oliphant's *The Makers of Venice*, Fielding regards the city as the epitome of 'the harmony between the works of man and the earth that upholds them, the civilisation that has escaped muddle, the spirit in a reasonable form with flesh and blood subsisting' (Forster 1985, 278). This view of Venice as an idealised Christian locale – precisely because of its sacramental balance of the body and the spirit – is pointedly contrasted with the muddle and confusion of India:

> Writing picture-postcards to his Indian friends, he felt that all of them would miss the joys he experienced now, the joys of form, and that this constituted a serious barrier. They would see the sumptuousness of Venice, not its shape, and though Venice was not Europe it was part of the Mediterranean harmony.   (Forster 1985, 278)

While Fielding's perspective is not the same as Forster's, his stress on the European virtues of form and harmony clearly speak to the impossibility of turning India into an ordered imperial narrative. At times, Forster is well aware of the severe limitations of Fielding's colonising vision and the ambiguities inherent in the word 'form'. As Aziz states, 'this pose of "seeing India" . . . was only a form of ruling India' (Forster 1985, 301). By

6   For a recent account of Oliphant's book see Linda Rozmovits 1998, *Shakespeare and the Politics of Culture in Late Victorian England* (Baltimore: The Johns Hopkins University Press), chapter 4. See also Manfred Pfister and Barbara Schaff eds, 1999, *Venetian Views, Venetian Blinds: English Fantasies of Venice* (Amsterdam: Rodopi).

the end of A *Passage to India*, Aziz reads an unopened letter from Heaslop to Fielding to indicate the extreme danger of searching for a harmonising and all-explaining narrative of India: 'You are lucky to be out of British India at the moment. Incident after incident, all due to propaganda, but we can't lay our hands on the connecting thread. The longer one lives here, the more certain one gets that everything hangs together. My personal opinion is, it's the Jews' (Forster 1985, 303). In this way, 'the Jews' act as a serio-comic 'connecting thread' – as Forster describes the clown-like Heaslop as 'the red-nosed boy' (Forster 1985, 303) – to account for the uncertain future of British India. But, implicitly at least, Forster is associating the aesthetically pleasing equanimity of Venice with the false, because materialistic, concord of Jewish power.

As we have seen in relation to T.S. Eliot, one should not underestimate the role of Venice in relation to the history of modernism which Tony Tanner has outlined with regard to Henry James, Marcel Proust and Ezra Pound. Pound, significantly, even wanted to be buried in Venice. The importance of John Ruskin – who described Venice as 'too big' a subject for him in a letter to Charles Eliot Norton (cited in Tanner 1992, 368) – is considerable in stimulating twentieth-century preoccupations with the city. Given the importance of Venice to the history of literary modernism, it is not a coincidence that the German-Jewish social theorist, Georg Simmel, was to construct Venice as a site of 'absolute ambiguity' (cited in Tanner 1992, 366) and as the exemplar of modernity. Unlike Eliot and Pound, who associate Venice with a racialised Jewishness, Simmel, in his essay 'Venedig' (1922), embraces the otherness of Venice as symptomatic of the strangeness of all cities:

> The character of the squares is ambiguous, devoid of vehicles their narrow symmetrical enclosed nature gives them the appearance of rooms . . . Ambiguous, too, is the double-life of the city, at once a maze of alleyways and a maze of canals, so that the city belongs to neither land nor water – rather each appears like the protean garment, with the other concealed behind it, tempting as the true body. Ambiguous too are the dark little canals whose waters move and flow so unquietly without revealing the direction in which they flow, constantly moving, without going anywhere.   (Cited in Tanner 1992, 367)

Simmel, who famously constructed 'the stranger' as someone who defies both temporal and spatial separation, thinks of Venice as, quite literally, estranged – 'constantly moving . . . going nowhere' – from the 'true body' of an ordered landscape. No longer the bastion of imperial progress, Venice is now a city of strangers, full of ghetto-like spaces – 'narrow symmetrical enclosed' – which threaten the mastery of the West from the inside. The city of Venice signifies the stranger within the heart of Europe and a history that is literally going nowhere. It has, in other words, once again been appropriated as prefiguring the post-modern city of the future.

Distorting Mirrors

Writing sixty years after Simmel, Anita Desai's *Baumgartner's Bombay* also constructs Venice, in a stark rewriting of Forster, as a city of strangers. Her displaced German-Jewish anti-hero, Hugo Baumgartner, has to spend a week in Venice after leaving Berlin for Bombay shortly before the start of the Second World War. After drifting around Venice in search of the Jewish quarter Baumgartner encounters an 'eastern market' and at last feels at home:

> [H]e stood there, as entranced as he was alarmed. Venice *was* the East, and yet it was Europe too; it was that magic boundary where the two met and blended, and for those seven days Hugo had been a part of their union. He realised it only now: that during his constant wandering, his ceaseless walking, he had been drawing closer and closer to this discovery of that bewitched point where they became one land of which he felt himself the natural citizen.   (Desai 1988, 63)

By thinking of Venice as a blend of Europe and Asia, Baumgartner is, in Zygmunt Bauman's terms, 'ambivalence incarnate' (Bauman 1998, 146). As a 'natural citizen' of this imaginary landscape, he disrupts the spatial and temporal boundaries of both 'black' and 'white', 'east' and 'west' and begins to feel at ease with his strangeness. In these terms, Baumgartner is Simmel's classical stranger who 'contaminated' (Desai 1988, 20) with uncertainty all whom he comes into contact with. Early in the novel, in fact, Desai describes him as: 'Accepting – but not accepted; that was the story of his life, the one thread that ran through it all. In Germany he had been dark – his darkness had marked him the Jew, *der Jude*. In India he was fair – and that marked him the *firanghi* [foreigner]. In both lands the unacceptable' (Desai 1988, 20). Baumgartner is doubly exiled – a Jew in Nazi Germany and a European in India – and so reflects Desai's own double heritage as she has an Indian father and a German mother. But it is precisely this double consciousness which enables Desai to view Indian history through European eyes and European history through Indian eyes.

Desai is careful not to simply make Baumgartner's homelessness a facile 'imaginary homeland' (Rushdie 1992) which is constructed primarily through the literary imagination. Because Baumgartner finds himself in such radically different historical circumstances there is no attempt simply to elide the fantastically divergent contexts in which he finds himself. For this reason, she characterises his Jewishness as 'both in [the East] and travelling to it, at a distance and yet one with it' (Desai 1988, 64). In a telling lack of closure, Baumgartner never quite manages to enter the Jewish ghetto in Venice as this would have been a too easy resolution of his incommensurable identity. Unlike Forster's A *Passage to India*, which echoes slyly throughout the novel, Desai does not want the strangeness of Venice to resolve her unrealisable attempt to bring together India and Europe, Bombay and Berlin, in the figure of Baumgartner.

In endeavouring to contain Europe and its others within Baumgartner's fluid identity, Desai is able to view East and West not as fixed opposites but as mutual deformations of each other. At the beginning of the novel, Baumgartner remembers his father's wonderfully ornate furniture shop made up of 'Empire suites', 'gilded rococo frames' and 'lamp shaded with mosaics of glass' (Desai 1988, 26). Even at this early stage, Desai is playing with the idea of Baumgartner's German orientalism –in the guise of his father's imperial kitsch – which acts as a means of distorting his supposedly recognisable Western identity: 'Mystifying and alarming were the three-piece mirrors that sat on the dressing tables and showed you unfamiliar aspects of your head, turning you into a stranger before your own eyes as you slowly rotated to find the recognisable' (Desai 1988, 26). This, in miniature, is the imaginative method of Desai's novel which constructs warped mirror-images of India in Germany and Germany in India. Unlike Phillips, where the mirror is a form of narcissism, Desai introduces a series of grotesque counterparts to stress the orientalist German depictions of India inherent in his mother's cult of Tagore and the exoticisation of the East (Aronson 1943).[7]

As the book is filtered through Baumgartner's consciousness, Desai constructs *Baumgartner's Bombay* around parodic versions of European and Indian history as reflected through each other's distorting lenses. Thus, the ethnic cleansing which accompanied Indian independence – with Habibullah forced to flee to Dacca from Calcutta – echoes the forms of racial purification in Europe which drove Baumgartner out of Germany. His imprisonment in an anti-alien internment camp is turned into a domestic version of the concentration camp where Baumgartner's

---

[7] For an extended discussion of *Baumgartner's Bombay* in these terms see Newman 1995, chapter 4.

mother died. The extreme poverty which he encounters in Bombay especially reminds him of the ghettoisation and impoverishment of
German Jewry in the late 1930s. In fact, the plot revolves around his final
murder by a German back-packer which is a tragi-comic recapitulation of
European fascism. As with Phillips's *The Final Passage*, Desai begins her
novel with an epigraph from T.S. Eliot's *Four Quartets* (this time 'East
Coker' (1940)) which helps convey her characteristically understated
sense of messianic time:

> In my beginning is my end. In succession
> Houses rise and fall, crumble, are extended,
> Are removed, destroyed, restored . . .

Although Desai incorporates a cyclical history into her novel it is not a
form of religious redemption, as it was for Eliot, but is instead a means of
restoring a sense of reality beneath a myriad of false images. Only when
Baumgartner first arrives in the Taj Hotel in Bombay does he begin to
understand that the vastness of India can not be reduced to his mother's
orientalist fantasies. Baumgartner both suffers these child-like racial
oppositions and realises their laughable inadequacy:

> India flashed the mirror in your face, with a brightness and laughter as
> raucous as a street band. You could be blinded by it. But if you refused
> to look into it, if you insisted in walking around to the back, then India
> stood aside, admitting you where you had not thought you could go.
> India was two worlds, or ten. She stood before him, hands on her hips,
> laughing that blood-stained laugh: Choose! Choose!   (86)

Here Baumgartner's adopted mother – Mother India with her hands on
hips – can no longer be contained as a racialised mirror-image which
helps define the Western self. India, in these terms, is associated with
endless imaginative choice and, in its plenitude, is able to reduce even the
Holocaust to 'little family quarrels' in the words of Frantz Fanon (Fanon
1986, 115). By re-enacting the Holocaust in India, in the guise of the
murderous Kurt, Desai shows just how marginal this European history is
in a postcolonial context. In the end, unlike Forster, Desai refuses to
name this incommensurable India and, instead, constantly holds in play a
range of partial versions of this history. As Shirley Chew has noted,
'Baumgartner's increasing concern is to negotiate a space for himself as
best he can and, by the stratagems of silence and evasion, to avoid being
plunged once more into chaos' (Chew 1988, 787).

Desai, in this regard, has learnt from the life-long silences of her friend

Ruth Prawer Jhabvala. The daughter of a German-Jew who committed suicide in 1948, after hearing of the loss of his family and friends, Prawer Jhabvala has refused to speak about her family's traumatic history (Newman 1995, 29–30). To this extent, Baumgartner's story is inspired by Prawer Jhabvala's post-Holocaust sense of being surrounded by millions of people needlessly dying in India which, eventually, became a way for her to articulate the Holocaust. Hers and Baumgartner's inability to speak of their suffering, contrasts starkly with Phillips's untroubled and detailed representations of the horrors of racial oppression in *The Nature of Blood*. Whereas Desai upholds the limits of representation – in endlessly distorted mirror-images – Phillips wishes to create a transcendent aesthetic realm which can represent absolutely everything. There is a sense in which Phillips's intertwining histories – even in a city as multifaceted and hybrid as Venice – can still reduce ethnicity to a purist form of identity politics. The articulation of identity as sameness in his work implies, paradoxically, a sense of historical uniqueness which needs to be bridged. Perhaps Desai's eloquent silence is the only means of enacting the refusal of identity. But, without a rudimentary comparative diasporic history, an increasingly combustible identity politics will surely follow.

Works Cited

Aronson, Alex 1943. *Rabindranath Through Western Eyes*, Calcutta: RDDHI.

Bauman, Zygmunt 1998. 'Allosemitism: Premodern, Modern, Postmodern', in Bryan Cheyette and Laura Marcus (eds) *Modernity, Culture and 'the Jew'*, Cambridge: Polity Press, 143–56.

Bhabha, Homi 1998. 'Joking Aside: The Idea of a Self-Critical Community', in Bryan Cheyette and Laura Marcus (eds) *Modernity, Culture and 'the Jew'*, Cambridge: Polity Press, ix–xi.

Biale, David 1998. 'The Melting Pot and Beyond: Jews and the Politics of American Identity', in David Biale, Michael Galchinsky and Susannah Heschel (eds) *Insider/Outsider: American-Jews and Multiculturalism*, Berkeley, Calif.: University of California Press, 17–33.

Boyarin, Jonathan 1992. *Storm from Paradise: The Politics of Jewish Memory*, Minneapolis: University of Minnesota Press.

Chew, Shirley 1988. 'Life on the Periphery', *Times Literary Supplement*, July 15–21, 787.

Desai, Anita 1988. *Baumgartner's Bombay*, London: Heinemann.

Eliot, T.S. 1975. 'Tradition and the Individual Talent', in Frank Kermode (ed.) *Selected Prose of T.S. Eliot*, London: Faber, 37–44.

Fanon, Frantz 1986. *Black Skin, White Masks*, London: Pluto Press.

Forster, E.M. 1985. *A Passage to India*, Harmondsworth: Penguin Books.

Gates, H.L. ed., 1986. *'Race', Writing and Difference*, Chicago: University of Chicago Press.

———— 1992. *Loose Canons: Notes on the Culture Wars*, Oxford: Oxford University Press.

Gilroy, Paul 1998. 'Not Being Inhuman', in Bryan Cheyette and Laura Marcus (eds) *Modernity, Culture and 'the Jew'*, Cambridge: Polity Press, 282–97.

Ilona, Anthony 1995. 'Crossing the River: A Chronicle of the Black Diaspora', *Wasifiri*, no. 22 (Autumn), 3–9.

Innes, C.L. 1995. 'Wintering: Making a Home in Britain', in A. Robert Lee (ed.) *Other Britain, Other British: Contemporary Multicultural Fiction*, London: Pluto Press, 21–34.

McNeill, William 1974. *Venice the Hinge of Europe, 1081–1797*, Chicago: University of Chicago Press.

Newman, Judie 1995. *The Ballistic Bard: Postcolonial Fictions*, London: Arnold.

Oliphant, Margaret 1888. *The Makers of Venice*, London: Macmillan.

Phillips, Caryl 1985. *The Final Passage*, London: Faber.

———— 1987. *The European Tribe*, London: Faber.

———— 1989. *Higher Ground*, London: Faber.

———— 1991. *Cambridge*, London: Faber.

———— 1993. *Crossing the River*, London: Faber.

———— 1997. *Extravagant Strangers: A Literature of Belonging*, London: Faber.

Phillips, Caryl 1997. *The Nature of Blood*, London: Faber.

Ricks, Christopher 1988. *T.S. Eliot and Prejudice*, London: Faber.

Rushdie, Salman 1992. *Imaginary Homelands: Essays in Criticism 1981–1991*, London: Granta.

Said, Edward 1978. *Orientalism*, London: Routledge.

———— 1979. *The Question of Palestine*, New York: Times Books.

———— 1993. *Culture and Imperialism*, London: Chatto & Windus.

———— 1994. *The Politics of Dispossession: The Struggle for Palestinian Self-Determination 1969–1994*, London: Chatto & Windus.

Sennett, Richard 1994. *Flesh and Stone: The Body and the City in Western Civilisation*, New York: W. W. Norton.

Shohat, Ella 1997. 'Columbus, Palestine and Arab Jews', in Keith Ansell Pearson, Benita Parry and Judith Squires (eds) *Cultural Readings of Imperialism: Edward Said and the Gravity of History*, London: Lawrence & Wishart, 88–105.

Spivak, G.C. 1985. 'Three Women's Texts and a Critique of Imperialism', *Critical Inquiry*, Vol. 12, No. 1, 243–61.

———— 1985b. 'The Rani of Sirmur', in Francis Barker *et al.* (ed.) *Europe and its Others*, Colchester: University of Essex, 128–51.

———— 1988. 'Can the Subaltern Speak?', in C. Nelson and L. Grossberg (eds) *Marxism and the Interpretation of Culture*, Basingstoke: Macmillan, 271–313.

Tanner, Tony 1992. *Venice Desired*, Oxford: Basil Blackwell.

Young, Robert 1990. *White Mythologies: Writing History and the West*, London: Routledge.

———— 1994. *Colonial Desire: Hybridity in Theory, Culture and Race*, London: Routledge.

———— 1997. 'Hybridism and the Ethnicity of the English', in Keith Ansell Pearson, Benita Parry and Judith Squires (eds) *Cultural Readings of Imperialism: Edward Said and the Gravity of History*, London: Lawrence & Wishart, 127–50.

Imagining the Postcolonial Writer[1]

ABDULRAZAK GURNAH

WHO IMAGINED THE POSTCOLONIAL WRITER? How did he or she come to be? I do not ask this because I expect an answer, though it is none the less a real question. Indeed my question is not entirely hostile. I phrase the matter in this way as a means of framing the issue of this category's invention. A subsequent and easier question is: how have we come to be so content as we appear to be with the category *postcolonial* at all? The question requires a qualification. It is noticeable that enthusiasm for the language of postcolonial theory and its assumptions is markedly cooler in African and Caribbean discourses and in their publications, both in institutions located in Africa and the Caribbean, and in those that wish to emphasise the specific locational context and dimension of their approaches. There are reasons to do with precedent and practice to explain the resistance of some disciplines to the comparative tendencies of postcolonial analysis (linguistics or ethnology, for example) for these discourses privilege specificity and *hard* content, more so, in any case than literary discourse. And historians of European colonialism, itself a most literate phenomenon, still seem to prefer reading through the inexhaustible colonial archives than studying Jacques Lacan. It is inevitable that academic structures will impose limits on themselves, identifying priorities and possibilities as a principle of organisation. If a perception is that the possibilities apparently suggested by postcolonial methods, which are multi-disciplinary and culturally located, is unprofitable for answering certain kinds of questions, then this might constitute a structural limit beyond which some practitioners are not interested in going. We can distinguish this from a perception that this trajectory of enquiry leads misleadingly nowhere, or more mercifully, that it leads to a conversation which the West is conducting with itself and with a handful of intellectuals of the colonial diaspora employed in institutions in the West, who, in Aijaz Ahmad's phrase, are 'coerced by the centre' (Ahmad 1992, 210).

---

[1] This essay is an extended version of a short paper originally delivered at a seminar held at the University of Alcala in Spain in March 1997 on 'Writing (and) Race'.

It is the discussion of the 'literary', of writing, which has turned out to be the most amenable form for the exercise of postcolonial methods in institutions in the West and elsewhere, and this is no doubt due to its links to 'literary theory'. It would not be contentious to say that 'theory' is characterised by its challenge to constitutive narratives of origin and cultural hierarchies. And in its institutional dimension, 'theory' has generated its sternest challenge to the arts and the humanities, even though its beginning was in linguistics. For despite privileging the humane in the name of a universal moral instinct, it is *the humanities* that have clung tenaciously to cultural hierarchies when other institutional practices have abandoned them for interdisciplinarity in the interests of use and legitimacy. It is in this locale that the post-structuralist challenge to the universal, to narratives of truth and knowledge, proved so devastating. And it is out of this that postmodernity emerges, if we agree with Lyotard that postmodernity is the recognition that reason cannot validate itself but only appears to acquire legitimacy through a fragmented set of discursive practices. So the narrative of postmodernity is characteristically de-centred, denying the universal its privileged space and de-legitimising the narrative of mythic origins. This is the fragmented space that is claimed by postcolonial theory and which energises arguments for postcolonial identity. The crux of Bhabha's argument lies (at times) around here: the liberating plurality of the postmodernist position allows the ambivalent moment to emerge from behind, or beside, the grand narrative of modernity (Bhabha 1994, 171).

But if the liberating potential of ascendant postmodernism allows the emergence of postcolonial conceptions of identity in difference, these conceptions find only a muted echo, or worse, in African and Caribbean critical discourses. Kwame Anthony Appiah scrutinises the connection between postcolonial and postmodern in his eloquent article 'Is the Post-in Postmodernism the Post- in Postcolonial?',[2] and in the process arrives at a distinction of the possibilities of the category:

Postcoloniality is the condition of what we might ungenerously call a *comprador* intelligentsia . . . In the West they are known through the Africa they offer; their compatriots know them both through the West they present to Africa and through an Africa they have invented for the world.   (Appiah, 1991, 348)

---

[2]   Appiah 1991, 336–57.

Whether ungenerous or not, this description certainly gives the postcolonial intellectual undeserved powers of agency, seeming to set aside briefly the preceding narratives of difference that prompt the contesting position of postcolonial discourse. Appiah establishes the different senses of the *post* in postcolonial, between that sense understood by the postcolonial theorist as a rejection and transcending of the coloniser's discourse of otherness, what Aijaz Ahmad had called 'a monstrous machinery of descriptions',[3] and that other sense which does not acknowledge or seek to refuse, which seems insensitive to, the 'claim to exclusivity of vision' (Appiah 1991, 348) seen as characteristic of cultural imperialism. Appiah makes the particular point that the latter sense is true of contemporary *popular* African cultural life, and that it is a characteristic of popular culture to be insensitive to the politics of its borrowings, and this is precisely the argument of postmodern theory as it concerns the international commodification of culture. While this might seem to suggest that theories of postmodernism are relevant here, this would only be misleadingly so, argues Appiah, for despite appearances, 'these artworks are not understood by their producers or their consumers in terms of a postmodernism', in terms of a rejection of or a challenge to a dominant antecedent narrative or practice. He develops this argument in an analysis of Yambo Ouologuem's *Le Devoir de violence* (1968). Ouologuem's novel can be read as both a response to African writing of the independence and post-independence period, whose impulse Appiah suggests was 'the imaginative recreation of a common cultural past' (Appiah 1991, 349), and a challenge to more wide-ranging nation-building pieties which were unavoidable at the time. In the first reading, Ouologuem refuses the nationalist sub-text of this reconstruction, because by 1968 events had already demonstrated that the idea of nation in the African context would have to be rethought in both its historical as well its progressivist senses. Unlike Achebe's precolonial community in *Things Fall Apart*, where despite the ugliness of specific injustices social

---

[3] 'It was by assembling a monstrous machinery of description – of our bodies, our speech acts, our habitats, our conflicts and desires, our politics, our socialities and sexualities, in fields as various as ethnology, fiction, photography, linguistics, political science – that those discourses were able to classify and ideologically master colonial subjects, enabling the transformation of descriptively verifiable multiplicity and difference into the ideologically felt hierarchy of value' (Ahmad 1992, 182). Ahmad is on his way to offering yet another ferocious critique of the postcolonial intellectual at this point, but as the quotation indicates, he is just as aware of the totalising nature of the discourse of imperialism and is just as keen to reject it.

order prevailed, Ouologuem's Kanem goes through century after century of cruelties, of violence, of civil disorder and irresponsibility. Greedy Native rulers, barbaric Muslim invasions, rapacious European colonialisms contribute to and sustain this oppression. In other words, Ouologuem's text repudiates the narrative of national historical retrieval just as much as the imperial one. It does so by repudiating the content of such narratives and also its characteristic realist form. In this respect, *Le Devoir de violence* has an appearance of agreeing with postmodern delegitimation of mythic origins, but misleadingly so, because, argues Appiah:

> it is grounded in an appeal to an ethical universal; indeed it is based, as intellectual responses to oppression in Africa largely are based, in an appeal to a certain simple respect for human suffering, a fundamental revolt against the endless misery of the last thirty years.
>
> (Appiah 1991, 353)

Its privileging of the humane is figured in the 'niggertrash', the nationless oppressed of Africa who have endured the suffering visited on them through the centuries. Ouologuem's challenge to narratives of both historical nation and imperialism is in terms of this privileging of suffering humanity, and for this reason can only misleadingly be seen to be an ally of Western postmodernism. The implication of Appiah's argument is that postmodernism disavows the ethical, and postcolonial theory's expedient alliance with postmodernism disarms the text that is the subject of its analysis, and empties it of its political and ethical meaning.

Appiah worries, then, that the imprecision of the connection between postcolonial and postmodern, and the sense in which they reflect different historical and cultural experiences, is an expression of expedient but misplaced parasitism. And if in his own account Appiah is, to a large degree, imprecise about *Africa*, and its history of suffering, and how its ethical universal is any different from anyone else's, including for that matter the postmodern theorist's and the postcolonial critic's, who apparently deny its legitimacy, his analysis serves to disentangle important issues and clarify the theoretical debate. Other responses have been less tolerant than this. From some critics and writers, postcolonial conceptions have impelled outright and outraged resistance: because they are held to distort and homogenise, and are held to be dependent on a formulaic jargon that allows the critic to pronounce without having any detailed knowledge of the context. Postcolonial critical discourse, in this account, intellectually appropriates the object of its analysis, colonising that object into a homogenised Other, and perpetuating an institutional hegemony of the West. In an editorial to a special issue of *Research in*

African Literatures focused on 'the place of theory in the apprehension of meaning' in African writing, Abiola Irele expresses sympathy with these concerns and invites a debate on the issue:

> The dissatisfaction that attended the introduction of the term ['post-colonial'], which seeks to designate a whole category of non-Western literary texts and to inaugurate a new mode of interpreting them, has not hindered its widespread adoption as one of the key terms of contemporary critical discourse. At the same time, its very success seems to have inspired a debate as to its appropriate terms of reference. At issue is the fact that, in its use . . . the term's very generality tends to obscure the fundamental problem it is concerned with, that of the deliberate marginalization of an ongoing discourse on history in the literatures of the so-called Third World.   (Irele 1995, 1)

His editorial makes clear his own doubts about postcolonial conceptions and methods, especially, as the above quotation demonstrates, with the marginalisation of *history* and the specific, detailed experience of post-colonial reality which is adjacent and contiguous with it. He quotes the Nigerian poet and academic, Niyi Osundare, who is quite stern on the 'inadequacy' of postcolonial theory, and who sees it as voguish and confused, an expression of the thrall 'the world of African scholarship' feels for 'the Western academy' (Irele 1995, 2), though which African scholars Osundare has in mind is less obvious and less easy to guess from this account. For Osundare, it is only possible 'to deal adequately with the complexities and varied cultural provenance of postcolonial writing' (Osundare 1993, 8) by reference to concrete experience. Osundare's objections, then, refer to what he sees as the generalising tendencies of postcolonial methods.

But it is Karin Barber's powerful article, 'African-Language Literature and Post-Colonial Criticism' (1995), that Irele nominates as a 'valuable' and 'extremely thoughtful' contribution to 'the role of theory' in African writing, and in part this is because Barber lucidly develops the objections Osundare refers to above. This is how she opens her discussion:

> The 'postcolonial' criticism of the 1980s and 90s . . . has promoted a binarized, generalized model of the world which has had the effect of eliminating African-language expression from view. This model has produced an impoverished and distorted picture of 'the colonial experience' and the place of language in that experience. It has maintained a centre-periphery polarity which both exaggerates and simplifies the effects of the colonial imposition of European languages. It turns the

colonizing countries into unchanging monoliths, and the colonised subject into a homogenized token . . . an Other whose experience is determined so overwhelmingly by his or her relation to the metro-politan centre that class, gender, and other local and historical and social pressures are elided.   (Barber 1995, 3)

Barber distinguishes two forms of 'postcolonial'. The first one, exempli-fied by Said, Spivak and Bhabha, is concerned with the production of a counter-narrative to colonial discourse. This 'style of postcolonial criti-cism' only obliquely invokes what Barber calls 'indigenous discourses', and largely as a point of vantage from which to demonstrate both the invention of the colonial Other and the limits of the authority of that invention. The emphasis of this form of 'postcolonial', in other words, is on the deconstruction of the imperial narrative rather than on recuper-ating its Other. The latter procedure, in fact, is to be carefully avoided for its implication of 'nativism'.

The second form of 'postcolonial', which Barber refers to less respect-fully as 'buoyant-type postcolonial criticism', is exemplified by Ashcroft et al. It is to this second form that Barber devotes her attention. She presents this second 'postcolonial' as a position which turns on the argu-ment that postcolonial writing is the expression of suppressed voices of those cultures silenced by colonial experience. The most potent form of this silencing is the privileging of colonial language, to the point that indigenous languages became unusable for 'expressive purposes'. So the discovery of an articulacy in an appropriated form of the colonial language, in a new and refashioned English, for example, is also a refusal of otherness and a reconstitution of the self. It is this breaking of the silence which links 'all postcolonial texts'[4] and which defines the moment of subjectivity and identity. In her article, Barber demonstrates unanswerably how the 'finding a voice' argument assumes that until that moment of recognition that colonial languages could be fashioned to contest the imperial ethos, native cultures had been mute about their ex-perience of colonialism. She shows how this argument, therefore, 're-enacts the very erasure of indigenous languages and cultures that it takes as its initial problematic' (Barber 1995, 7). In the 'finding a voice' argument, 'indigenous' languages are a medium for articulating the precolonial world, an authenticating register for evoking the integrity of what preceded rupture. Paradoxically, writing in native languages is also the ambition of the future, when the postcolonial subject would, presum-

4   Ashcroft et al. 1989, 187 (quoted in Barber 1995, 6).

ably, have gone beyond the indeterminacies of the present and learnt to speak without angst. Barber then demonstrates how partial and ill-informed such a position is by a discussion of writing in Yoruba, its historical sources and its promotion by colonial policy, its contemporary viability as a popular cultural form, and its intertextual complexity. She demonstrates, in other words, how in this example and in others she refers to (Kiswahili and Hausa, among others), the silence imagined by the postcolonial argument was nowhere widespread and complete, and that, just as importantly:

> Contemporary African-language written literature, gaining additional resonance and extension from its location in huge, heterogeneous, popular cultures, is fully as capable of confronting contemporary 'postcolonial' experience as European-language literature. (Barber, 1995, 12)

Focusing so exclusively on writing in English, Barber argues, to the point of making the use of colonial language the qualifying criterion of postcolonial writing, is to offer a misguided and even false representation of postcolonial cultures and their cultural productions.

I am mindful in this presentation of the problematic dimensions of postcolonial theory that so often a discussion of the uses of *postcolonial* ends up as a summary of its inadequacies and wrong-headedness. In a witty and characteristically sharp-eyed review of Spivak's new book, Terry Eagleton makes fun of what he represents as the ritual disavowal of postcolonial theory by postcolonial theorists themselves:

> There must exist somewhere a secret handbook for post-colonial critics, the first rule of which reads: 'Begin by rejecting the whole notion of post-colonialism.' . . . The idea of the post-colonial has taken such a battering from post-colonial theorists that to use the word unreservedly of oneself would be rather like calling oneself Fatso or confessing to a furtive interest in coprophilia. Gayatri Spivak remarks with some justification in this book that a good deal of US post-colonial theory is 'bogus', but this gesture is de rigueur when it comes to one post-colonial critic writing about the rest. (Eagleton 1999, 3)

Eagleton has a point, even if its patronising formulation here disguises another habitual whine of the Left intellectual, that every position except the one she or he occupies is politically directionless. Later on in the review, Eagleton makes precisely this criticism of Spivak, ascribing her obscurantism and her 'endless self-interruptions' to her nonadherence to 'a major political project' (Eagleton 1999, 3). It may be that Eagleton has a specific idea of 'political' here as referring to the theoretical debates of the Left, but to speak of Spivak's 'project' as non-political is to allow the theatricality of her avant-gardist language to obscure the sustained challenge to humanist and feminist assumptions about the West and its representations of the non-West. Her challenge, and that of Edward Said and Homi Bhabha among others, has been to the cultural and academic institutions of the West, and in that respect their interventions have transformed the cultural debate in the West and its relation to the non-West. Critics of the terms of this challenge, as we saw in Appiah's discussion of 'postcoloniality' earlier, may wish for a more concretely political position, but this is not to say that postcolonial theory is void of a political project.

I would now like to turn briefly to why postcolonial methods appeared such an attractive, or even indispensable, way forward for the literary discourse of non-Western writing. As a way of speaking about a category of writing, this term was preceded (though not necessarily in that order) by the post-imperial Commonwealth literature, the truly clumsy emergent literatures, the apparently innocent new literatures, and the socio-political thematisations of Third World literature – which all had their heyday and still have a currency. This is not the place to enter into a discussion of the history of these terms and why it was they seemed right or bearable at the time they were in institutional vogue, but their currency and supersession demonstrate, at the very least, their provisional usefulness. It also expresses the tentativeness with which liberal institutional discourse has groped towards describing and naming cultural difference in the aftermath of an empire which was constructed by wide-ranging and aggressive narratives of hierarchy and power. This institutional tentativeness derived from uncertainty about how to revise a way of speaking of cultures bluntly constructed as lesser by inflated narratives of self-description. The promoters of this institutional revision were often people who had worked in the colonial services as administrators and teachers, and for many of them the progressive optimism about the viability of the cultures of the colonised was a vindication of the profound changes the independence period seemed to promise. The uncertainty about how to speak of non-European cultures afflicted not so much these progressive optimists but the institutions themselves. For how to speak of non-European culture was also part of the self-description within which unequal difference was so critical. To imagine this, we might consider the institutional discomfort of offering a course on Charles Dickens alongside one on Chinua Achebe or R.K. Narayan. To offer such courses alongside each other was to give up their hierarchical relationship, whereas to contain them in a distancing term that was unambiguously othering was to sustain difference. In addition, the process of finding a way of speaking about the cultural products of the colonised, was also (progressively) to allow space in the developing discourse for the Othered who was aspiring to become a Self.

Within the institution, this uncertainty about terms derives partly from a desire to avoid the more blatant cultural supremacist accents which are an aspect of dominance. The failure to fulfil this desire, which I believe is evident in the hectic substitution of categories to contain non-European cultures, and in particular their writing, reveals the difficulty of disentangling the affiliated signifiers that make up the transcendental narrative of the world in the Western era. That is to give more credit than is perhaps deserved, because this failure may also be to do with bad faith, a refusal to let go of the sustaining myths of narratives of knowledge, their genealogies and transmissions, and the hierarchies which inform their ordering. Hence implied in such terms as new literatures, Third World literature and Commonwealth literature – to say nothing of emergent literatures – is a trope of such smug magnitude, on the one hand, and such an ardent liberal reaching for something lukewarm and inoffensive, on the other, that the result is contradiction and logical discomfort. In one way or another, these terms and their contexts, signify difference and an arriviste transparency, and a congenitally knowable lack of complexity which makes the writing accessible from within a reading practice informed by complex and sophisticated textual provenance. That certainly would be true of 'new' and 'emergent', and in a more sinister way, it would also be true of 'Third World'. There is something of the clang of the compound gates in that phrase, distancing the pathologically different. 'Third World' is where there is famine and casual and grotesque violence, and whose writing can be taken uncritically to be the wails of the oppressed to be applauded without putting too fine a point on the flourishes of the text. As for 'Commonwealth', it makes perfect sense that the term should exclude British writing, otherwise it would make for a grotesquely over-balanced object – but it does make the category historically appealing and something of an indulgent euphemism for boogie writing, for *their* writing.

If that describes the uncertainties of Western liberal institutions in speaking of non-European cultures, in producing knowledge of those cultures, how might we describe the uncertainties in this context of the historically Othered. I am still thinking of writing and the categories to contain it and its subject, and I am still thinking of institutions that are part of this discourse. I suspect the discomforts for those I call 'historically othered' are even more acute in this context. Not only are these categories clumsy and partial in the way I have described, but they contain within them implicit seductions. In whatever limited form, such descriptions are inclusive, they appear to endorse the cultures of the Other, and they give unprecedented authority to the non-Western intellectual.

In this sense, postcolonial seems to be an advance as a way of speaking of non-European cultures, though non-European in the use of this term appears to include, quite problematically, European settler cultures. I say quite problematically, because the settler was, and probably still largely is, the visible beneficiary and token of European colonialism. In any case, 'postcolonial' enables a discussion of culture that is not based on insider authority, whether this authority is that of the orientalist scholar or of the native claiming an essentialist proprietorship on visceral grounds. Both appear to be superseded by the larger analytic structure derived from the common experience of colonisation. Such an analytic structure, which I have argued is post-structuralist in conception, inevitably involves a challenge to ideas of truth, authenticity or even a cultural identity that is located in *place*. But because postcolonial sites its readings of non-European texts at the encounter of Europe and the native, it fails to avoid the seductions implicit in such a generalised synthesis, precisely the argument put forward so effectively by Karin Barber. The emphasis then falls on incommensurable difference between the European and the native, and in the process the fragmentations of the colonised culture recede into unimportance, into a kind of necessary detail to the larger issue. The critical literary discourse of non-European cultures as it is institutionalised in Western institutions by such terms as postcolonial, is also a way of avoiding having detailed knowledge of those cultures, and ultimately to seem to be suggesting that those cultures do not have a particularity.

The objection to such a conception of culture is that it is a colonised one, one derived from colonial mapping of the world as the West and the Rest. Let me give an example. One of the myths of colonial construction is the homogeneity of the colonised territory and its natives, simultaneously with their complex unknowability except by the initiated coloniser, who can only seek to know their difference disparagingly and instrumentally. By accepting this myth of homogeneity (as Appiah seems to in his image of the *suffering African* as a political constituency), the colonised writer implicitly, where it suits other agendas, observes the same homogeneity. So Nigerian writing in English says little or nothing of the North of Nigeria, except to endorse colonial tropes of semi-oriental vapidity and despotism. For example, in Soyinka's *Season of Anomy*, the North is there only to figure as the Underworld of violence and bizarre sexual indulgence into which his Orpheus-like hero will descend to rescue his Eurydice. Also, Ngugi's account of Kenyan history is the dispossession of the Gikuyu, and their eternal contest with the land-grabbing European settler. Present in both these accounts are structures which originate in the historical accounts which were constructed by an imperial discourse. On the one hand, in the case of Nigeria, it was imperial construction that saw the Muslim North as an oriental despotism, although not without a kind of back-handed admiration of one stern administrator for another though less efficient one. On the other hand, in the case of Kenya, imperial concerns could only focus on the consequences of European settlement in Kenya. These accounts, then, as they are taken up and elaborated on by Soyinka and Ngugi to their contrasting agendas, do not contradict the regional integrity given to them by colonising discourse.

I come from Zanzibar, and the history of the colonisation of East Africa in the 1890s sees European intervention as a benign deliverance of Africans from Arab slavers. As a result, the decline of the coast is seen as a 'national' response of the now liberated nation – the expulsion of alien invaders. This is now the authoritative account, despite the impossible construction of nation in retrospect, an impossibility tolerated in other colonial-constructed territories and their nominal histories and cultures. In the case of Zanzibar, this account has now been internalised or naturalised into history, but it was not one which ever even felt complete.

Let me develop this notion with an example. In Kiswahili, the word for culture or cultural accomplishment used to be *ustaarabu*, the way of the Arabs. It is a dramatic expression of a consciousness of culture as something that can be represented by a principal authority. It reflects the hegemony of Arab Islam over the hierarchy of values which had been internalised into and then represented in language. Its agents were not, of course, Arabs themselves. If they were, *ustaarabu* would be a term to express crude cultural domination and self-valorisation, and no doubt it had utility in this sense in a parochial and rigid understanding of the historical relations between Arabia and the east coast of Africa. For first-language speakers of Kiswahili, especially in the period before independence, the slippages in what the term signifies would not have been problematic, on the whole, but would have been a dimension of its plenitude, in the sense of its capacity to evade precise definition. Even such a permissive sense of plenitude still implies an originary and coherent and infinite myth of reference, but it is precisely because of this diffusion that a term like *ustaarabu* refuses a concrete reading, and as with similar words, is liable to capture in order to endorse cultural hierarchies. It had certainly exceeded its literal sense by the time I refer to here, though this is not to say that 'the way of the Arabs' did not signify the highest forms of refinement and accomplishment in someone's cultural vocabulary. For example, *mstaarabu*, which is the personal form of the abstract term, might have referred to someone who spoke with a certain flourish and command of language, to someone who observed social etiquette with punctiliousness, just as much as it might have referred to someone who demonstrated a concern for the welfare of others or who had a reputation for honesty and reliability. It is clear then that *ustaarabu* was a privileged term comparable to *civilised* in English, and equally as flexible in its capacity for extension.

This is not to suggest that either of these two terms are innocent and open-ended, as the examples above no doubt demonstrate. The very use of these terms to refer to cultural practice implies the opposite, that there exists a consensus, at times rational at others visceral, about what constitutes them in application. My interest in these terms here is not in their capacity to describe representations of such practices accurately, but in the sense that they are expressions of self-perception, or what in a loose and popular sense is sometimes described as identity. I shall stay with 'identity' for the time being, despite the obvious problems with the implication of essence and uniqueness which the abstraction implies, a limitation which is a familiar hazard when we talk about culture.

I have spoken of *ustaarabu* as the Kiswahili word for culture in the past tense, as if it is no longer used to mean that. So what has changed? In varying degrees, the campaign for independence in East Africa polarised on arguments of ancestral ownership and alien usurpation of rights to the land. By *rights*, I mean the right *to*: to make the laws, police the citizens, plan strategies of change, admit and expel and so on. I distinguish here between anti-colonial resistance movements, which in retrospect seem desperate and vain attempts to prevent the inevitable, and the campaign for *rights* which largely characterised independence movements in Africa. Clearly, in a context where culture is already valorised as suppressed identity, as the denial of the expression of the full self, to cite it as 'the way' of the oppressing alien is inconceivable, despite the ambivalences I mentioned earlier. When it came to the campaign for independence in the 1950s, the politics of Zanzibar polarised along 'racial' lines. One of the parties, the Afro-Shirazi Party, saw itself as representing the oppressed and dispossessed natives against aliens and Arabs. Since this party triumphed with its *coup-d'etat* in 1964, the expulsion of *ustaarabu* was both a linguistic as well a general priority. In this context, the ambivalent dimensions of the term were secondary to the larger symbolism of expelling emblems of alien domination. To some extent, then, by independence or soon after, *ustaarabu* had become implicated in a reinterpretation of history and identity, and its deliberate obsolescence was a refusal of the principal authority it apparently proposes.

What has all this to do with postcolonial theory? Apparently nothing. The inattentiveness of postcolonial analysis to particularities of the fragmentations within colonised cultures is to do with its emphasis on their encounter with European colonialism above all. The inattention to the fragmentations within these cultures, which are of profound consequence in any understanding of their cultural products, and most of them far more spectacular than the example I gave of little Zanzibar, are most clearly evidenced in the complete lack of interest in writing in native languages. The very detail with which such writing would speak of the competing relations within the cultural hotch-potch of colonised territories, would complicate the otherwise coherent and homogenous narrative of postcolonialism. In this respect, postcolonial theory is a triumph of the imagination over a more problematic reality, and the postcolonial writer, shed of her or his complicating difference, comes into being.

If the encounter with European colonialism is the defining category for speaking about culture, as it would be if we were to take postcolonial to derive from a common historical experience of colonisation, then the particularities of this encounter are critical in order to evade the homogenising and ahistorical narratives of difference which brought the colonised into being. That the critical category postcolonial falls far short of this, and is inclined in the opposite direction, is inclined towards the production of homogenised ahistorical narratives, means that as method it falls far short of *theory*, however determinate its mode of pronouncement. It still seems to me a method worth having, for the reasons I discussed earlier and because of the way postcolonial analysis has opened up texts in a way that the more culturally contextualised accounts are not interested in doing, especially since so much contemporary writing thematises dislocation and estrangement. But it is a method we can make best use of if we remain clear about its provisionality and the limitations of its scope as a mode of enquiry.

Works Cited

Achebe, Chinua 1958. *Things Fall Apart*, London: Heinemann.

Ahmad, Aijaz 1992. *In Theory*, London: Verso.

Appiah, Kwame 1991. 'Is the Post- in Postmodernism the Post- in Postcolonial?', *Critical Inquiry*, Vol. 17, No. 2 (Winter), 336–57.

Ashcroft, B., Griffiths, Gareth and Tiffin, Helen eds 1989. *The Empire Writes Back: Theory and Practice in Post-colonial Literatures*, London: Routledge.

—— eds 1995. *The Post-Colonial Studies Reader*, London: Routledge.

Barber, Karin 1995. 'African Language Literature and Postcolonial Criticism', *Research in African Literatures*, Vol. 26, No. 4 (Winter), 3–30.

Bhabha, Homi 1994. *The Location of Culture*, London: Routledge.

Eagleton, Terry 1999. 'In the Gaudy Supermarket', *London Review of Books*, Vol. 21, No. 10 (13 May) (a review of *A Critique of Post-Colonial Reason: Toward a History of the Vanishing Present* by Gayatri Chakravorty Spivak [Harvard, 1999]), pp. 3–6.

Irele, Abiola 1995. 'Editor's Comments', *Research in African Literatures*, Vol. 26, No. 4 (Winter), 1–2.

Ngugi wa Thiong'o, 1987, *Matagari*, Oxford: Heinemann International.

Osundare, Niyi 1993. *African Literature and the Crisis of Post-Structuralist Theorizing*, Monograph Series; Dialogue in African Philosophy, No. 2, Ibadan: Options Book and Information Service.

Ouologuem, Yambo 1968. *Le Devoir de violence*, Paris: Seuil. Translated as *Bound to Violence*, trans. Ralph Manheim, London: Heinemann Educational, 1968.

Soyinka, Wole 1973. *Season of Anomy*, London: Rex Collings.

Reading the Referent: Postcolonialism and the Writing of Modernity

SIMON GIKANDI

I

LIKE ITS COUSINS in postmodernism – feminism, cultural studies, and ethnic studies – postcolonial theory functions under the anxiety of modernity and its universal theories of reason, history, and the human subject. This anxiety has unexpected implications for reading literary texts produced in formerly colonized, or Third World, countries, for the most powerful moments of postcolonial theory are the ones in which it tries to rewrite and reread the experience and discourse of modernity while seeking to affirm an alternative regimen of interpretation, one that is both indebted to, but also located above, the history of colonialism. Postcolonial writers and intellectuals have to claim modernity because it is the force that brought into being their objects of analysis, namely colonialism and decolonization. But beneath the postmodern language favored by many proponents of postcolonial theory, modernity lurks as the source of the critical language of postcoloniality, the force animating a cultural grammar that revolves around powerful categories such as race, time, nation, and identity even as it claims to reject all categories. At the same time, however, postcolonial theory needs to disavow modernity because, to the extent that its objects of analysis and their attendant terms are in association with the establishment of European hegemony over the rest of the world, they need to be purged of their Eurocentrism. The language of postmodernism appears attractive to postcolonial intellectuals because it provides both the alibi and the means for exorcizing Eurocentrism from the narrative of modernity. This is how postcolonial theory comes to function as what Homi Bhabha aptly calls the 'translation of modernity': it is both inside and outside the categories of modernization and modernism (Bhabha 1994, 241).

After years of pretending to play postmodern games, then, the best postcolonial work has come to acknowledge that the central problems it confronts emerge from within the problematic of modernity because colonialism – the primary subject of postcolonial theory – was, in the end, the highest stage of European modernity and its dominant ideologies of secularization and rationalization. This shift in postcolonial discourse from the epistemology of postmodernism to the politics of modernity marks, as Bhabha recognizes at the end of *The Location of Culture*, a significant shift within the tradition of postcolonial writing and criticism: 'There is an attempt to interrupt the Western discourses of modernity through these displacing interrogative subaltern or postslavery narratives and the theoretical-critical perspectives they engender' (Bhabha 1994, 241). Indeed, once postcolonial intellectuals have accepted the fact that their discipline is not about postcolonial countries *per se* but the logic of colonial rule and conquest – that is, the modernizing drive of Eurocentricism – then they cannot but recuperate all the debates and disputes about periodization and postcolonial time as what Stuart Hall has called 'the retrospective re-phrasing of Modernity within the framework of "globalisation" in all its various ruptural forms and moments' (Hall 1996, 250). Instead of being presented as abstract products of a postmodern theory that is defined by its 'incredulity toward metanarratives' (see Lyotard 1984, xxiv), postcolonial theory has been forced to pause and reconsider the extent to which colonial and postcolonial subjects are now produced in 'the discursive historical discontinuity' of modernity (Spivak 1999, 33). In short, the time for historicizing the postcolonial moment has arrived.

This historicization of postcoloniality, nevertheless, calls attention to several questions that have been the source of considerable puzzlement to both proponents and opponents of postcolonial theory: what was the postcolonial condition and how is it to be read in its fictional texts? What are its signs, narrative languages, and terms of reference? And why do the canonical texts of postcoloniality, the narratives produced by African, Indian, and Caribbean writers in the great period of nationalism and decolonization, falling roughly between 1895 and 1960, seem to be absent from discussions of the postcolonial condition and its literature? Why does postcolonial theory, as Aijaz Ahmad and others have complained, seem to be concerned with narratives and conditions of migrant subjects and writers and not the politics of everyday life in the postcolony itself? (see Ahmad 1992, 1–5). If there is a postcolonial condition, as there was a colonial condition, why has it not, its theorizing notwithstanding, produced protocols of reading that are not exclusively postmodern or post-structuralist?

The truth is that not even the most powerful commentaries on a postcoloniality condition (the most controversial example is Achille Mbembe's 'Postcoloniality and the Banality of Evil', 1992) have been able to escape the prisonhouse of a postmodern/post-structural institution of exegesis. Even when such works seem to draw on the examples of specific historic and cartographic postcolonial moments, to name post-colonial countries and to recite their unfortunate experiences after decolonization, the weight of evidence always seems to confirm presuppositions that have already been predetermined by metropolitan theories. While works such as Mbembe's seem to appeal to metropolitan readers because of their majestic representation of the postcolony, their popularity – and indeed authority – is derived from the images, tropes, and practices of the postcolony that seem to confirm what the West imagines these places to be; in this sense, these commentaries can be categorized as affirmation of tropes as old as the European discourse on the other. The difference, though, is that alterity is articulated by the others who have learnt to speak for themselves. In North American academies, to cite the example I am most familiar with, postcolonial theory has currency only to the extent that it provides a conduit for universalizing 'our' theories and applying them to 'their' experiences and practices; representations of the postcolony that speak 'our' language have greater legitimacy than the ones that try and understand these 'other' worlds in their own terms; the postcolonial world has value as raw material for analysis and reflection, but any suggestion that it can be the source of theoretical reflection is often met with hostility.

Even more troublesome is the resistance, among metropolitan critics and native informants alike, for literary texts that seem to operate outside the circuit established by postcolonial theory. It is not by accident that the literary texts that dominate the discourse of postcolonialism, quite often the works of British colonial writers like Forster, Kipling, and Conrad read in conjunction with migrant writers such as Salman Rushdie, or self-consciously postmodern writers like J.M. Coetzee, are the ones which seem to confirm *a priori* theories of colonialism or postcolonialism, or to fit into 'the reading formation' current in the Western university (see Bennett 1983, 214). The great texts that defined postcoloniality – works by Chinua Achebe, Flora Nwapa, Mulk Raj Anand, R.K. Narayan, N. Saghal, George Lamming, V.S. Naipaul, and Kamau Brathwaite – rarely seem to enter the celebrated canon of postcoloniality. By the same token, it is not by accident that in the postcolonial countries themselves, the texts that have been at the center of the discussion about postcoloniality are works which only a few specialists in the European and American academies have read or written on. Ahmadou Kourouma's *Les Soleils des indépendences* (*Suns of Independence*) is a case in point: the novel was considered to be a major narrative intervention in the debate on the postcolonial condition in Francophone West Africa, but in the

European and American institutions, it has been overshadowed by minor writers who have won major international awards (see Miller 1990, 201–45). Metropolitan scholars who place Coetzee at the center of their postcolonial projects would be surprised to discover that in his native South Africa he comes at the end of one of the most remarkable periods in the production of literary culture in Africa, preceded by black icons such as H.I.E. Dhlomo and Sol Plaatje. It is rare to see these founders of the African literary tradition in any notable discussion of postcolonial literature.

How do we account for this unevenness in the cultural capital of postcolonial theory and discourse? And why do the native informants who mediate the exchange between the postcolonial space and its metropolitan interlocutors acquiesce so easily in this uneven configuration of knowledge? It is not enough to account for this absence either in terms of the preferences of individual critics, or the ideological failure or blindness ostensibly inherent in postcolonial theory, nor is it enough to lament this situation as the logical outcome of a Eurocentrism that has been further legitimized by the theoretical instruments that were supposed to deconstruct it (see Ahmad 1992, 1–9). A more productive approach to this problem is to think about it with the difficulty, conceptual and historical in nature, that is implicit in any attempt to read postcolonial texts without a proper understanding of its context or its implied and real readers, its conditions of production and reception. For once we look beyond the postcolonial literature produced for metropolitan consumption, the vast majority of postcolonial readers write for readers located specifically in their own countries; indeed, over ninety per cent of postcolonial literature in the Indian sub-continent is produced in non-European languages. Clearly, the conditions in which, as Bennett would say, postcolonial texts are activated for certain readers are important determinants of how we read this literature (Bennett 1983, 214). If a reading formation is the product of a specific historical and material condition, and if 'the social relations of reading' expose the 'contradictory cross-currents' of a period (Bennett 1983, 216), then the problem that concerns me here – the absence of the postcolonial text, its reader, and its referent from postcolonial theory – is the result of a radical disjunction between postcolonial theory and postcolonial narratives.

The following attempt to think through what a postcolonial reading formation might look like is based on the premise that in order for postcolonial theory to perform the task it set itself – that of displacing the central concepts of modernity – it had to negate the means of accounting for its modern conditions of production and reception; it had to repress its means in order to valorize its ends. Three of these means are particularly crucial: the first one is the category of the referent. Coming of age at a time when theories of referentiality had been displaced by indeterminacy, postcolonial theory could not provide its readers with the tools for reading specific local histories as they made their way into literary texts. The second problem concerned the status of literary history as a mode of accounting for what John Frow aptly describes as 'a knowledge of conditions and functions' (Frow 1986, 121). Now, this does not mean that postcolonial theory did not have a sense of the historicity of literary texts; indeed, one of its most important literary categories – intertextuality – was the mark of an acute awareness of how its protocols of reading were being driven by debates on the relation between literature and history, narrativity and historiography. The problem – and this is the third point – was that postcolonial theory was not always attuned to the simple fact that within its disclaimer of referentiality and universalized modes of kr.owledge was also the repression of 'a historical given with determinate historical effects' (Frow 1986, 121).

II

While it is true that postcolonial literature and theory operated under the premise, powerfully articulated by Julia Kristeva that it was through intertextuality that 'the poetic utterance' was subordinated to 'a system of a larger whole' (Kristeva 1980, 65), its understanding of what history was, not to mention its articulation of the forms and effects of the historiographic, was often limited and asymmetrical. The problem here was that the intertextual system had a fundamental relation to the condition of production of a text or its history only to the extent that readers were able to make this connection. In other words, readers had to be able to recognize intertextuality not merely as the relation between a set of texts but between these texts and their contexts. The force of intertextuality, then, would have to be determined by the specific circumstances in which texts were produced, the histories they invoked, and, most importantly, their conditions of reception.

This point can be made more clearly by way of two examples from Dambudzo Marechera's 'The House of Hunger':

> Do you remember Lobengula's letter to the Queen? 'Some time ago a party of men came into my country, the principal being a man named Rudd. They asked me for a place to dig gold and said that they would

give me certain things for the right to do so. I told them to bring what they would give, and I would show them what I would give. A document was written and presented to me for signature. I asked what it contained and was told that in it were my words and the words of those men. I put my hand to it. About three months afterwards I heard from other sources that I had given, by that document, the right to all the minerals in my country. I called a meeting of my indunas, and also of the white men, and demanded a copy of that document. It was proved to me that I had signed away the mineral rights of my whole country to Rudd and his friends'.   (Marechera 1978, 42)

Philip came in. His hands looked like Macbeth after the murder of Duncan. But when he came closer I saw that those hands were really spotless, clean. He held out his hand to Nestar.

(Marechera 1978, 55)

Readers easily recognize the second example. It makes an intertextual reference to a text that is familiar to readers of English literature almost everywhere: Philip's unruffled condition is elaborated, powerfully and precisely, through the invocation of Shakespeare's text, a text which is so common that it is not even mentioned by title. In contrast, the first example is more complicated, not so much within the context of Marechera's novella, but in regard to the assumption it makes about the readers of this text. 'Do you remember Lobengula's letter to the Queen?' The intertextual referent is paradoxical because, while it might appear enigmatic to audiences unfamiliar with the history of Zimbabwe, it takes it for granted that the implied reader knows the citation and its complicated history. Any product of the school system in most of postcolonial Africa, and especially Zimbabwe, knows about Lobengula's letter to Queen Victoria: it is both a famous episode in the history of colonialism in the region and a prominent feature of any standard historical text. Within the economy of Marechera's text, the narrator and the reader share a common (perhaps conspiratorial) universe of meanings and evaluation.

But this regime of meaning also excludes the reader who has not had access to the primers of colonial history and historiography in Southern Africa. What often happens when texts like these enter the metropolitan scene of reading is that the first example is not recognized as intertextual both because its referent and primary text is unfamiliar to readers while the second referent, the one from Shakespeare, tends to be privileged and to be transformed into the vantage point of interpretation. Can we develop protocols of reading that take both of these intertextual referents and their historical effects as important elements of the postcolonial text?

I want to suggest that we can only do so by dealing with a set of interpretative problems that were at the center of a set of fictional texts produced on the eve of, and after, decolonization. These texts, rather than the familiar narratives of postcolonial migrancy and hybridity, were the first to represent, or will into being, the postcolonial condition. The problem, of course, is that such texts as Chinua Achebe's or Wole Soyinka's early works speak a postcolonial grammar that often appears to be at odds with the central claims of postcolonial theory. Our task, however, is to make the *postcolonial* concerns of these works central to the discourse on postcoloniality and we can only do so if we take their referential claims seriously.

The first step in this process is to distinguish between a historical and figural intertextuality. In the example from Marechera above, the first intertextual reference is historical to the extent that it refers both to a real event and its representation in the historical record. Postmodernism may have forced us into the habit of putting the 'real' in quotation marks, but such signs of indeterminacy miss the simple fact that events such as imperial duplicity – and poor Lobengula's letter to Queen Victoria – were the pivot around which the history of colonialism (and postcolonialism) in Zimbabwe revolved. In contrast, the second reference is figural: it is an event that exists solely in a text as a text; it may have been based on a real event, but this has become lost in the sense that its veracity makes no difference to its regime of evaluation. In other words, the existence or non-existence of Duncan or Macbeth has no effect on our understanding of Scotland or its destiny, while the whole history and politics of Zimbabwe are a consequence of the encounter between Lobengula and Rudd.

A second step is to extend the range of intertextual reference beyond the familiar 'contrapuntal' reading of colonial and postcolonial texts. Now, there is no doubt that one of the most powerful theories of reading postcolonial literature involves what Edward Said has called the comparative reading of the literature of imperialism, the recognition that the histories of metropolitan texts and colonial spaces are intertwined and overlap (Said 1993, 18). The primary limitation of this kind of reading, however, is that it unwittingly makes the metropolitan text the primary referent, or host, while the postcolonial text (and thus experience) serves as its guest. So long as we read Tayib Salih's *Season of Migration to the North* (*Mawsim al-hijra ila al-Shamal*) in relation to Conrad's *Heart of Darkness*, the latter will always seem to be the foundational text; the central motif of the protagonist's journey in the novel will continue to be read as a reversal of the Conradian voyage into the heart of darkness

even when the book's Arabic title calls attention to other equally important movements such as the classical movement of seasons (*Mawsim*) and
pilgrimage (*al-hijra*). One way out of this problem is to expand the contrapuntal reading and its terms of reference – to move beyond the Western
canonical text.

In addition, even when we continue to insist that postcolonial literature is intertextual by nature, it is important to show how this intertextuality cuts across genres and traditions. This point can be illustrated
through a brief exploration of what I will call internal intertextuality in
African fiction. Consider the repression and recuperation of gender in
the postcolonial African text. The canonical texts of African nationalism, which emerged initially to counter colonial images of Africa and to
call into question the politics of imperialism, were notorious for
repressing the experiences of women, or for turning women into icons of
male desire and power struggles. In classic African texts such as Chinua
Achebe's *Things Fall Apart* and Cyprian Ekwensi's *Jagua Nana*, the figure
of woman was either the embodiment of the morality of tradition or its
radical transgression. In the circumstances, the production of literature
by African women in the first decade of independence was, as Susan
Andrade has shown in an outstanding essay, driven by the desire to represent women outside the tradition/modernity dichotomy established by
nationalist male writers; and they could only do so by interrogating both
the claims and methods of the canonical male texts (Andrade 1990,
91–110). This is how African women writers came to establish their own
community of writing through self-conscious intertextual opposition not
simply to colonial or even nationalist texts, but to one another's works.

If Flora Nwapa's *Efuru* is one of the most misunderstood and under-
rated texts in African literature it is because, as Andrade has argued
convincingly, its 'silent' interrogation of the works by Achebe and
Ekwensi was lost to most commentators not familiar with its precursors or
even basic African literary history. Nwapa's text did not appear to have
political value because, in contrast to the canonical texts of nationalism,
it was concerned with the private life of a woman trying to cope with the
conflicting claims of modernity and tradition. But it was precisely in its
silences – about nationalism, about the polis, and about power – that
Efuru transformed the tropes that had come to define modern African
literature in its foundational moments. It interrogated Achebe and
Ekwensi's texts by refusing to follow their narrative tactics or to valorize
their ideologies. And as soon as this act of intertextual interrogation was
recognized by readers, it was no longer possible to dismiss *Efuru* as an
apolitical representation of Igbo womanhood; its politics were apparent

in the interpretative challenge the novel presented readers of African literature who, forced to reread their canonical texts from the vantage point established by Nwapa's novel, could not but notice the repression of gender in the nationalist texts that preceded it. By the same token, to the extent that the second generation of African women writers often produced narratives intended to question the premises of Nwapa's novel, they could not be evaluated outside this intertextual relationship. The most famous example of this kind of text was, of course, Buchi Emecheta's *The Joys of Motherhood* which 'literally (and literarily) begins where *Efuru* ends', renaming and revisioning its central themes and claims about motherhood (Andrade 1990, 100).

III

I have already intimated that what we call the postcolonial condition was not simply the product of the political and social practices that followed decolonization but also a condition willed into being by a certain body of texts seeking to find a grammar for representing what Fanon called 'the pitfalls of national consciousness' (Fanon 1968, 148–205). The point here is not that a network of literary texts came to supplement the politics of decolonization; rather, these texts, to the extent that they seemed to speak to a uniformed condition of disenchantment across countries, regions, and cultures, established the historical specificity of postcoloniality. In its series of 'interdiscursive repetitions or transformations', the postcolonial literary system established the historical dynamic of the postcolonial condition (Frow 1986, 124).

Consider how the image of shit became the metaphor for postcolonial failure in Africa. It first appeared in Soyinka's first novel, *The Interpreters* (1965), where one of the characters, confronted daily by night-soil men, was forced to conclude that next to death shit was 'the most vernacular atmosphere of our beloved country' (108). By the time the imagery of shit was taken up by Ayi Kwei Armah in *The Beautyful Ones Are Not Yet Born*, it had become the embodiment – and mediator – of social relations in the postcolony. This point is illustrated by two vivid examples from Armah's novel. The first one comes at a turning point in the narrative where Koomson, a former trade unionist who has risen to become a minister in the Ghanaian government, visits his old school mate (the man who embodies postcolonial failure) and needs to use the latrine:

The man got off his chair. 'Fine,' he said. 'Let's go.' The two men left their women and went off toward the bathroom and the latrine. The cement of the yard was slippery underfoot with a wetness that increased as they got closer to their goal. When they came to the latrine, they found its door locked, and had to wait outside. The agony and the struggle of the man inside were therefore plainly audible to them, long intestinal wrangles leading to protracted anal blasts, punctuated by an all-too-brief interval of pregnant silence. It was a long battle, and the man within took his time. Koomson stood peering into the darkness around the bathroom hole, and though he could see nothing, the atmosphere itself of the place seemed to subdue him. Once the man could hear him swallow very audibly. A man who had escaped, now being brought close to all the things he had leaped beyond.   (Armah 1969, 134)

For the minister of state, decolonization has become the means of escape from the world represented by the latrine but in the process, as almost every chapter in the novel makes clear, his success could only be achieved through the reduction of the whole country into a shit hole.

The second example represents the reversal of Koomson's fortune: the regime has been overthrown and the fallen minister has gone to the man, whose family he had earlier swindled out of a boat, seeking help to escape from the soldiers who have come to power. In his hour of need, Koomson not only realizes that he can only be saved by the man he treated with contempt, but that he can only escape from the country by creeping through the latrine that had subdued him only a few months earlier:

It took Koomson some time to make up his mind, but in the end like a man at his own funeral, he stuck his hand in the other side of the hole and touched the can. Together they shifted it to one side. The touch of the can had something altogether unexpected about it. It was cold, but not at all wet or slippery. It felt instead as if a multitude of little individual drops had been drying on the can for ages, but had never quite arrived at a totally dry crispness. When the can itself was shifted, a new smell evaporated upward into the faces above the hole. It was rather mild, the smell of something like dead mud. A very large cockroach, its color a shiny, deep brown, flew out from under the can, bit Koomson's white shirt front and fell heavily on top of the box seat before crawling away into a crack down the side.   (Armah 1969, 167)

From this example, we can see how Armah thematizes power relations in the postcolony and the apotheosis of decolonization, but the significance of the set of repetitions and transformations here also establish 'a structure of discursive authority' (Frow 1986, 129) for subsequent writers such as Marechera trying to narrate postcolonial failure (see 'House of Hunger', 1978).

The larger question here is how to read literary history, not simply history, in the postcolonial text? We can begin, for a start, by admitting that sometimes texts foreground elements at odds with our cultural experiences and training as readers, that the difference or familiarity of a text determines what we consider to be its historicity and its place in the literary tradition. Take the thematization of modernity which opened my discussion: the literature of postcolonialism in Africa, which was produced almost two decades before postcolonial theory emerged as an important discursive formation, was primarily concerned with the promise and limit of modernity. As Appiah has noted, critics who assume that the postcolonial and the postmodern are synonymous are bound to miss this point (Appiah 1992, 137–57). More importantly, postcolonial texts thematized modernity in a very specific sense: they were concerned not only with the consequences of modernization on traditional society, but the disenchantment that followed when the promise of progress and social upliftment was betrayed either by the colonizer or their successors. It is hard to find a text produced in Africa between 1945 and 1975 that does not taken up this question. From Ferdinard Oyono's *Unie vie boy* (*Houseboy*) to Tsitsi Dangarembga's *Nervous Conditions*, postcolonial African fiction was the story of African subjects in crisis, a crisis generated by the promise of colonial modernity and the prize that had to be paid in the quest for the impossible dream.

How do we recover these important elements of the postcolonial text for the institutions of knowledge and exegesis? We can achieve this goal, I believe, by insisting on the distinction between what I called the real and imaginary postcolonial condition. On one level, this distinction might appear false for two reasons: first, the most important lesson we have learnt from post-structural theory is the way in which the real is the effect of its figuration; secondly, the works of fiction in question were produced as imaginary representations of the condition of postcoloniality. My complaint against many variations of postcolonial theory, however, is that they tend to treat the imaginary as both the source and end of the act of narrativity without paying attention to the referent that was the subject of figuration in the first place. And yet the most powerful postcolonial texts in Africa foregrounded their referent blatantly because that was the only way they could have political effect. The truth is, the regime of meaning in texts such as Wole Soyinka's *A Dance of the Forest* and Ayi Kwei Armah's *The Beautyful Ones Are Not Yet Born* is bound up with both their referent and condition of production. Indeed, the allegorical power of a text such as A *Dance of the Forest* depended on the thematization of its moment of production – the commemoration of Nigeria's independence in 1960 – and its ironic representation of the fantasy of an African past, the fantasy that was driving the passions of the new ruling class on the continent.

The architects of the new African nation, believing that the sanction of the nationalist project depended on a discourse of commemoration, or at least the performance of an imagined history, sought to have the phantasm of the past legitimized in the works of the nation's leading writers. But Soyinka, already aware of the gap between the dream of independence and compromised decolonization, produced a play in which the main topic was the repressed that had returned to call into question all versions of African history. The postcoloniality of this play, then, was apparent in its agonistic sense of a narrative of decolonization wrapped up in its imaginary and haunted by its reality. The intellectual project of decolonization was presented clearly by the court historian Adenebi:

ADENEBI: Oh. Well, in addition I said; . . . no, you said, and I took it up, that we must bring home the descendants of our great forebears. Find them. Find the scattered sons of our proud ancestors. The builders of empires. The descendants of our great nobility. Find them. Bring them here. If they are half-way across the world, trace them. If they are in hell, ransom them. Let them symbolize all that is noble in our nation. Let them be our historical link for the season of rejoicing. Warriors. Sages. Conquerors. Builders. Philosophers. Mystics. Let us assemble them round the totem of the nation and we will drink from their resurrected glory.   (Soyinka 1973, 31).

One of the most remarkable things about Soyinka's play was implicit in the role the work of art was asked to play in the plotting out of the phantasm of postcoloniality – the ghosts of an imagined heroic past would be transformed into the icons of a nationalist future in the form of the totem of the nation referred to in the above quote. The choice of the word 'totem' here is significant for two reasons: first of all, the totem or fetish was the sign of an imaginary representation or symbolism that was unreal but, at the same time loaded with religious, mystical, or magical authority. Commissioned by the Nigerian ruling class to write a play that would celebrate its ascendancy to power, Soyinka chose to open his text by mocking this demand, by confronting the dream of newness with the 'phantasmagoria of protagonists from the dead' (Soyinka 1973, 45). The dramatic moment in A *Dance of the Forest*, the ironic reversal, as it were, was generated by the realization that instead of sending illustrious ancestors to witness the moment of decolonization, the gods had let loose a group of restless losers; the decolonized future would not be judged by its invocation of a dubious past, but 'by reversal of its path' (Soyinka 1973, 59). In the circumstances, as Tom Conley has noted in a different context, 'the repressed resurges as something seen as other, and recognizably different from what conveys it' and historiography comes to be 'rewritten in the abyss between the idea of the repressed and the fear of its continuous return' (Conley 1988, xix).

Secondly, and more specifically within the context of the play, one of the defining vectors of postcoloniality was the call on artists, by the political elite, to produce works that would embody the national imaginary. In Soyinka's play, as readers will recall, the 'tragic' conflict arises when the artist, represented by the carver, Demoke, discovers that he cannot fulfil his or her mandate except through an act of radical transgression. Demoke was commissioned to carve a totem to commemorate decolonization; but in order to produce a work of art that would commemorate the great reunion that was nationalism, Demoke, possessed by the spirit of Ogun, the patron saint of artists in the Yoruba pantheon, chose to carve his totem out of the sacred tree of Oro, the spirit of death. Herein lay the dilemma of the postcolonial artist at the moment of decolonization: in order to produce an aesthetic of identity, he or she had to simultaneously assert the necessity of nationalism (it is hard to think of a single African writer who opposed decolonization) and to transgress against a set of interests seeking to claim postcoloniality as their domain: the political elite who felt that the work of art had not done justice to the romance of independence; the ghosts of the historical past who saw the aesthetic as several times removed from the violence of colonialism and slavery; and from the immanence of the work itself, which was, like Demoke's carving, only visible as a mutilation of its raw materials (the sacred tree of Oro).

The point here is that the writing of postcolonialism was not a retrospective scriptural gesture, masterminded by émigré intellectuals and their metropolitan patrons; rather, it was concomitant with the moment of decolonization itself, a period defined by the authors' awareness of the dangers of the repressed past, the stillborn nature of independence, and its compromised terms. Indeed, by 1968, when Ayi Kwei Armah published *The Beautyful Ones Are Not Yet Born*, the writing of modernity in Africa was no longer about the promise of secularization and modernization, but about the desirability – and impossibility – of this project on the postcolonial sector, of their historical belatedness and absolute necessity. In its use of scatological language and images of decay, Armah's novel was, as I have already shown, a dramatic intervention into the debate on postcoloniality in Africa. This intervention was achieved not so much through the thematization of political failure – other novels from those memorable years from 1965 to 1968 had done the same – but for the form in which it cast the failure of national consciousness. Three aspects of this form were particularly crucial in the demarcation of what we would now call postcoloniality. The first one was its blatant display of the African – the subject of postcoloniality – not merely as a subject in crisis (this always denotes a condition to be overcome), but as deprived of all desire and agency. From its memorable opening to its ironic ending, Armah's novel was concerned with the disembodiment of the African body and the absolute terror of modern life. Indeed, what made the novel a new phenomenon on the African literary scene when it was first published in 1968 was its ability to turn the most quotidian aspects of everyday life into allegories of national failure.

The question that still remains is a simple one: how are we to read these scenes of national failure in the postcolonial text? Are we to consider them as part of the abstract rhetoric of failure that postcolonial writers had inherited from high modernism or is there a certain historical particularity that has to take precedence over the universal grammar of the modern condition? In reading texts such as *The Beautyful Ones Are Not Yet Born*, it is tempting to focus either on its allegorical language as signs of modern failure or, conversely, to reject such a universalistic reading for the particularities of Ghanaian history. Significantly, the text itself provides many visible signals on how it should be read. The image of shit and dirt is consistently built up as a reference to what the nation has become; one does not need to place the text in its referential situation to understand its allegorical meaning. But reading the text within its own internal semiotic economy is not enough, for the motif of betrayal in the novel demands that the reader establish an extratextual relationship with the text – that is, the novel insists that its semiotic signs be extended to the world beyond its confines. In this regard, the text has established a normativity, which, nevertheless, remains incomplete unless the reader has some knowledge of its referent.

This point can be made more clearly by referring to the scene of betrayal in the middle of the novel. The period is just after the second world war and a new politician has appeared at historic Cape Coast, a landscape dominated by melancholy and disappointment, promising freedom and redemption. As one of the characters, Sister Maanan, remembers it, the young nationalist mesmerizes his audience because he has the power to articulate the deepest desires of the colonized (Armah

1969, 86); but it is important that this ability to generate the eros of nationalism is recalled from the moment of failure and atrophy that defines postcoloniality. Indeed, the erotics of nationalism is invoked in order to foreground the question that dominates Armah's novel and post-colonial literature in general: 'How could this [the dream of decoloniza-tion] have grown rotten with such obscene haste?' (Armah 1969, 87). Since the novel is dominated by images of youth seduced by power, of the stillborn babies of independence, the perverted dreams of decolonization and 'the powerful ghost of its promise' (Armah 1969, 87), it is easy to privilege an allegorical reading. We could read these scenes as autono-mous units of meaning (and focus on their figuration), or read them in an intertextual relation to other extra-literary discourses of decolonization, most notably Fanon's *The Wretched of the Earth*. But the text takes it for granted that its ideal reader will know, without much prompting, that the messiah who betrayed his ideals was none other than Kwame Nkrumah, the first prime minister of Ghana and one of Africa's leading nationalists. What the text takes for granted, then, is what often gets lost in postcolo-nial readings.

One issue is central to the two forms of reading – the allegorical and the contextual – discussed above: it concerns the role of the reader in the postcolonial text, 'the rim of social and institutional conditions' (Frow 1986, 187) that determine the range of interpretations available to readers. If postcolonial texts seem to have a different regime of meaning in different contexts – the divide that interests me here is between metro-politan and postcolonial readers – it is because of crucial variations in the interpretative frame. Consider Bhabha's assertion that the postcolonial perspective forces us 'to rethink the profound limitations of a consensual and collusive "liberal" sense of cultural community. It insists that cultural and political identity are constructed through a process of alterity' (Bhabha 1994, 175). Such a claim will almost immediately make sense in those postcolonial texts that have been produced by cultural and ethnic minorities on the margins of metropolitan cultures in Europe and North America. Major writers in this tradition often posit the consensual community as one of the greatest threats to the difference on which they hope to construct their identity; they narrate alterity as a productive means of rethinking their identity and their relationship to the national culture.

But there is another postcolonial tradition in which the key terms in Bhabha's lexicon are turned upside down as it were: here the primary failure of decolonization is seen as its inability to create a consensual and democratic sense of community and the exploitation of alterity for selfish political ends. In some of the most powerful texts of decolonization in Africa, for example, the claim of alterity is often represented as a mode of social death, a radical retreat from the temporality of modernity and its consensual community. But, then, there are many kinds of postcolonial African texts.

IV

The final point I want to make, then, concerns the identity of the post-colonial text itself: what is at issue here is not merely the association of postcolonial theory with a language of difference and social marginality, but the assumption that the postcolonial intellectual project preempts 'the problematics of signification and judgement that have become current in contemporary theory – aporia, ambivalence, indeterminacy, the question of discursive closure, the threat to agency, the status of intentionality, the challenge of "totalizing" concepts' (Bhabha 1994, 173). But what are we to do with postcolonial texts – and intellectual pro-jects – that seem to question this economy of discourse? Take, for example, Tsitsi Dangarembga's *Nervous Conditions*. The first thing readers will notice about this novel is that it relies on the most traditional forms of narrative style (realism) to map out the colonial and postcolonial experience in Zimbabwe, that its language is not that of aporia, ambiva-lence and indeterminacy, but a sustained attempt to recall the colonial experience as real and palpable, objectified, unified and totalized, for it is only by doing so that the author can narrate the painful alienation of the colonized. In Dangarembga's novel, the role of time is not to differentiate social categories but to homogenize and periodize them; modernity and modernization are foregrounded, not undermined, because they are the categories that express colonial and postcolonial failure. It is within what are clearly delineated as the objective conditions of modernity that the twin themes of the novel – 'the poverty of blackness on one side and the weight of womanhood on the other' (Dangarembga 1988, 16) – are articulated.

But the most remarkable aspect of this novel is how it complicates the existing discourse on the culture of colonialism, not merely in relation to the question of gender but the modern/tradition divide that was one of the most powerful tropes in colonial discourse and nationalist African fiction. Two points are pertinent in this regard. First, there is the para-doxical fact that the burden of womanhood in the novel, contrary to the discourse of colonialism and nationalism, arises because of the conjuncture of tradition and modernity. Tambu and Nyasha, the main characters in the novel, are driven by the difficult awareness that they are perceptual prisoners of a patriarchy that is rooted both in the traditional Shona cosmos and the world of colonial modernity. Tambu's embracement of her education arises from the belief that 'the more I saw of worlds beyond the homestead the more I was convinced that the further we left the old ways behind the closer we came to progress'; Nyasha's education has convinced her that the ideology of progress only imprisons the African further into the colonial world (Dangarembga 1988, 147).

The second point, however, is that the distinction between tradition and modernity is not as clear as these positions might suggest. Indeed, what makes patriarchy so powerful in the novel is the fact that it is both traditional and modern. This is apparent in the figure of Babamukuru (the older father), a man whose authority over the whole of his extended family is derived from the fact that he is a modern bourgeois subject, the key link to colonial culture, but, as his name suggests, Shona culture has bestowed him with the instrumental and spiritual force to dominate and reorganize other people's lives. Patriarchy in this novel is shown to be a product of both shifting class relationships and the modernization of traditional beliefs. In these circumstances, novels such as *Nervous Conditions* are important not because they exist as materials for theoretical reflections, but because they deconstruct theories that have come to take their authority for granted.

Works Cited

Ahmad, Aijaz 1992. *In Theory: Classes, Nations, Literatures*, London: Verso.

Andrade, Susan Z. 1990. 'Rewriting History, Motherhood, and Rebellion: Naming an African Women's Literary Tradition', *Research in African Literatures*, Vol. 21, No. 1, 91–110.

Appiah, Kwame Anthony 1992. *In My Father's House: Africa in the Philosophy of Culture*, New York: Oxford University Press.

Armah, Ayi Kwei 1969. *The Beautyful Ones Are Not Yet Born*, London: Heinemann Educational Books.

Bennett, Tony 1983. 'Texts, Readers, Reading Formations', *Literature and History*, Vol. 9, 2.

Bhabha, Homi 1994. *The Location of Culture*, New York and London: Routledge.

Conley, Tom 1988. 'Translator's Introduction: For a Literary Historiography', in Michel de Certeau, *The Writing of History*, New York: Columbia University Press.

Dangarembga, Tsitsi 1988. *Nervous Conditions*, Seattle: Seal Press.

Fanon, Frantz 1968. *The Wretched of the Earth*, trans. Constance Farrington, New York: Grove Press.

Frow, John 1986. *Marxism and Literary History*, Cambridge, Mass.: Harvard University Press.

Hall, Stuart 1996. 'When was "the post-colonial?" Thinking at the Limit', in Iain Chambers and Lidia Curti (eds) *The Post-Colonial Question: Common Skies, Divided Horizons*, London and New York: Routledge, 242–60.

Kourouma, Ahmadou 1981. *The Suns of Independence*, trans. Adrian Adams, London: Heinemann Educational Books.

Kristeva, Julia 1980. *Desire in Language*, ed. Leon S. Roudiez, trans. Thomas Gora, New York: Columbia University Press.

Lyotard, Jean-François 1984. *The Postmodern Condition: A Report on Knowledge*, Minneapolis: University of Minnesota Press.

Marechera, Dambudzo 1978. 'House of Hunger', *House of Hunger: Short Stories*, London: Heinemann Educational Books, 1–82.

Mbembe, Achille 1992. 'The Banality of Power and the Aesthetics of Vulgarity in the Postcolony', *Public Culture*, Vol. 4, No. 2, 1–30.

Miller, Christopher 1990. *Theories of Africans: Francophone Literature and Anthropology*, Chicago: University of Chicago Press.

Oyono, Ferdinand 1966. *Houseboy*, trans. John Reed, London: Heinemann Educational Books.

Said, Edward 1993. *Culture and Imperialism*, New York: Vintage.

Soyinka, Wole 1965.*The Interpreters*, London: Heinemann Educational Books.

Soyinka, Wole 1973. *A Dance of the Forest* (1963) in *Collected Plays 1*, Oxford: Oxford University Press.

Spivak, Gayatri Chakravorty 1999. *A Critique of Postcolonial Reason: Toward a History of the Vanishing Present*, Cambridge, Mass.: Harvard University Press.

Caribbean Creole: The Real Thing?
Writing and Reading the Creole in a
Selection of Caribbean Women's Texts

DENISE DE CAIRES NARAIN

We hear about the natives but we still don't hear them.
(Brathwaite 1995, 70)

I want to say this in decent quiet voice. But I hear myself
talking too loud and I see my hands wave in the air.
(Rhys 1966, 61)

It is the voice I hear.   (Brodber 1994, 161)

he loved the sound of my voice, so for days I would not utter a
word;   (Kincaid 1996, 217–18)

Both during independence struggles and in postcolonial societies, certain cultural productions – songs, rhythm, testimony –
continue to invoke the ancestors' strength and to confront
new struggles in the decolonization process.
(Katrak 1989, 178)

THIS PAPER ADDRESSES some of the issues raised in a recent discussion
between Kamau Brathwaite and Peter Hulme, conducted in *Wasafiri*,[1] in
which Jean Rhys's literary designation was the site of considerable contestation. It is Rhys's white Creole 'derivation', and the credibility of her
representations of the black Creole, which is one of the focal points of the
disagreements which I am interested in pursuing. The meanings associated with the word 'Creole' are of interest in this discussion and I will
note at the outset the shift in usage of the word – so that it is now predominantly used to refer to the demotic speech of West Indians (in all its
island/mainland variants), rather than to refer to those Europeans born in
the West Indies (such as Jean Rhys). The disagreement between Hulme
and Brathwaite can partly be explained by the respective emphases they
place upon this word and I will locate this within the broader critical

---

1   *Wasafiri*, 20, Autumn 1994, 5–11; *Wasafiri*, 21, Spring 1995, 69–78; *Wasafiri*,
23, Spring, 1996; *Wasafiri*, 28, Autumn 1998, 33–8.

contexts of Caribbeanist/nationalist and postcolonial discourses. In varying degrees, Creole speech has been invested with considerable critical clout as a medium for cultural transgression in many nationalist and postcolonial discussions and I will discuss a selection of these. The bulk of the discussion will then focus on the very diverse representations of the Creole-speaker and of Creole speech to be found in a selection of texts by Jean Rhys, Merle Hodge, Phyllis Shand Allfrey, Jamaica Kincaid and Erna Brodber. The selective use of literary texts to facilitate a focus on Creole speech, combined with the decision to locate Rhys alongside other Caribbean women writers, is motivated by a desire to interrogate some of the claims made in the name of 'orality' and the demotic along-side its use in literary texts and to suggest other possibilities for contextu-alizing Rhys' work beyond the wary/weary battles over her designation as 'West Indian', 'modernist', 'feminist' or 'postcolonial'.

The shift in meaning of the word 'Creole', from its early use in the seventeenth century to refer to those Europeans 'born and bred' in the New World, to its widespread contemporary usage to refer to the language of West Indians,[2] is indicative both of its volatile etymology and its centrality to perceptions and constructions of Caribbean identity. Most accounts of Caribbean writing argue that the writing of the region came into its own and *found its voice* when writers of the region started to make use of the speech of 'the folk', Creole. Space does not permit a detailed account of this literary history but there is general agreement that the shift away from the derivative mimicry of European forms which charac-terized the 'early' period began with attempts to name the local – its land-scape and social contours – before coming more fully into its own when an increasing number of writers in the 1950s (Selvon, Salkey, Lamming, Naipaul, to name a few) began to make use of the rhythm and syntax of the demotic speech of the West Indies. Brathwaite, in addition to his powerful poetic contribution in the form of *The Arrivants* (Brathwaite 1973), has offered several seminal essays which account for the creoliza-tion of the literary in the West Indies. 'A History of the Voice' places the Creole-speaking voice at the centre of any strategy for resisting imposed cultural forms and for constructing a more appropriately indigenous writing. Brathwaite's focus here is on poetry and he argues that the domi-nance of the pentameter can be resisted by the *noise* he associates with the Creole word:

[2]   See Allsopp 1996, 176, for a succinct definition.

Now I'd like to describe for you some of the characteristics of our nation language. First of all it is from as I've said, an oral tradition. The poetry, the culture itself, exists not in a dictionary but in the tradition of the spoken word. . . . When it is written, you lose the sound or the noise, and therefore you lose part of the meaning.

(Brathwaite 1993, 271)

The emphasis Brathwaite places on the voice is perhaps most dramatically demonstrated in his comments after playing a recording of the Jamaican Claude McKay reading his sonnet, 'St Isaac's Church, Petrograd'. Brathwaite suggests that McKay's 'Clarendon syllables' and his pronunciation of 'the' as 'de', 'subtly erode, somewhat, the classical pentametric of his sonnet' (Brathwaite 1993, 277). The *literal* voicing of the poem here is seen to undermine the *literary* voice which the poet employs. Brathwaite seems here to be using *voice* as the authentic marker of native presence in the literary text and to be questioning the use of literary disguises which the device of 'the speaker' makes possible. Interestingly, it is only when this poem is *performed* that this supposed cultural 'gap' is exposed.

Carolyn Cooper, a Jamaican critic, sets up a similarly binary opposition between the world of the spoken/performed Creole word and that of the Standard English printed word in her book, *Noises in the Blood*. She argues that the transgressive irreverence of Creole culture, its noisy 'slackness', challenges the hegemony of the book:

The revised sub-title of *Noises in the Blood – Orality, Gender and the 'Vulgar' Body of Jamaican Popular Culture* – denotes an ideological shift of emphasis to foreground both text (Orality) and fully emergent subtext (gender). The sub-title also amplifies the figure of the body, intimating the openness of the dilatory text to promiscuous turns of meaning. Sexual punning on orality – a vulgar trope – is at the root of this transgressive discourse on marginality, identity and voice. . . . These vulgar products of illicit procreation may be conceived – in poor taste – as perverse inversions of the tightly-closed orifices of the Great Tradition.   (Cooper 1993, 7–9)

This binary is repeated in Christian Habekost's *Dub Poetry*, in which, in the process of celebrating 'dub poetry', the black man's body and Creole-speaking voice are seen to epitomize radical alterity. The emphasis on the unruliness of Creole in Habekost's account is driven by a desire to place dub poetry in confrontation with the politeness, and elitism, of 'conventional' poetry.

Dub Poetry has nothing to do with the 'lyricists' poetry that fills traditional (classic) poetry anthologies. . . . 'Dub', on the contrary, can't
even be roughly clarified by looking into a dictionary. For 'dub' is not a
word but a phenomenon, a movement, a musical hypnosis, bass &
drum, the heartbeat of a people.   (Habekost 1986, 13–37)

What Habekost's account also does is to foreground the pervasiveness of
male-dominated definitions in constructions of cultural resistance:

the poet on stage with flying dreadlocks, an angry expression on his
black face, murderously kicking into the air with his motor-bike boots
just as the police boots kicked him . . . then it gets under the whitest of
skins and is enough to 'blacken' the whitest soul.

(Habekost 1986, 36)

The emphasis on the physical presence of the poet, and on the (literal)
voice of the poet in these accounts, suggests that body/voice are being
invoked *as* authenticity. In a context where, as Brathwaite suggests
above, the native is spoken *about*, then the appeal to the speaking voice
may appear to provide possibilities for short-circuiting the mediating
voice of the metropolitan/postcolonial critic. A poem by Jimi Rand,
'Nigger Talk', offers an example of one of the more direct versions of this
appeal to speech as the marker of authenticity:

Cause me no talk no London talk
Me no talk no Europe talk
Me talking black, nigger talk;
Funky talk
Nitty gritty grass-roots talk.   (Rand 1984, 114)

Debates about the use of Creole in Caribbean literary and cultural forms
did not really engage with the gendered implications of its use until the
late 1980s. Clearly women writers were making use of Creole in their
work before that and male writers had made frequent use of women
speakers when using Creole in their texts but, on the whole, as indicated
above, women's use of Creole has been associated with rather more
'domestic' articulations than that of their male counterparts. An extract
from Louise Bennett's poem, 'Nayga Yard',[3] may help foreground this
difference:

[3]   Louise Bennett is a Jamaican poet, performer and folk archivist who works
exclusively in Creole.

> So, nayga people, carry awn;
> Leggo yuh talents broad.
> Member de place fi-yuh –
> Jamaica is nayga yard.   (Bennett 1982, 104)

In their different ways, both Rand and Bennett attempt to retrieve the 'n' word and make it resonate beyond the narrowly racist parameters of its widespread use. In both poems, *voice* is deployed to indicate the socio-political location of the speaker which makes such locutions necessary. Such voicings, with their insistence on both inscribing and *performing* 'racial derivation', have been of strategic use but their very locatedness also suggests the limitations of such a strategy.

Postcolonial discourse has tended to be less interested in the Creole-speaker than in the hybridity and oppositionality which Creole symbolizes. Postcolonial critics have regularly invoked Caribbean Creole as a symbol of the subversive possibilities of an indigenous language. So, in *The Empire Writes Back*, the plurality of linguistic practices which Ashcroft et al. associate with Caribbean Creole 'offers a paradigmatic demonstration of the abrogating impetus in postcolonial literary theory' (Ashcroft et al. 1989, 47). Conversely, Ketu Katrak, in the concluding sections of her essay, 'Decolonizing culture: toward a theory for postcolonial women's texts', argues that the lack of a written tradition in Africa and the Caribbean and the presence of one in India resulted in major differences with regard to language:

> Although the British assumed a stance of racial superiority in their attempt to educate natives in all the colonies, the levels of linguistic and cultural denials in African and Caribbean communities were certainly more devastating than in India. . . . This linguistic scenario is one among other reasons for the most radical revisions/'violences' to the English language coming not from Indian but from African and Caribbean writers.   (Katrak 1989, 170)

Katrak concludes her essay by pointing to the work of Sistren, a Jamaican working-class women's theatre group, as emblematic of the possibility for harnessing 'the oral' to a transformative politics:

> In Sistren's use of 'patwah', of African rituals in their dramas, of figures like Ni from the oral tradition, we find the many empowering elements of culture.   (Katrak 1989, 178)

Gayatri Spivak, in 'Three women's texts and a critique of imperialism', tells the reader that *she* registers the impact of Rhys's use of Creole in *Wide Sargasso Sea*:

> Christophine is the first interpreter and named speaking subject in the text. 'The Jamaican ladies had never approved of my mother, "because she pretty like pretty self" Christophine said,' we read in the book's opening paragraph (*WSS*, p. 15). I have taught this book three times, once in France, once with students who had worked on the book with the well-known Caribbean novelist Wilson Harris, and once at a prestigious institute where the majority of the students were faculty from other universities. It is part of the political argument I am making that all these students blithely stepped over this paragraph without asking or knowing what Christophine's patois, so-called incorrect English might mean.   (Spivak 1985, 271)

Spivak herself, of course, does not offer an interpretation of what these specific patois words mean; she only points to *the fact that it is patois*. The implication here is that, in their non-recognition of the innate subversiveness of Christophine's patois, Spivak's students reveal their inability to *world* Christophine's *word*. Nonetheless, despite the importance which Spivak recognizes Rhys as ascribing to Christophine's Creole word power, she concludes that:

> She cannot be contained by a novel which rewrites a canonical English text within the European novelistic tradition in the interest of the white Creole rather than the native.   (Spivak 1985, 272)

To be fair, Spivak's reading of *Wide Sargasso Sea* is only a part of her larger argument but the quotes above suggest a contradictory approach to Rhys as a white Creole writer. Christophine's use of Creole *speech* is registered as having subversive impact (even if Spivak's students don't get it) but, while it is obviously Rhys who 'gives' Christophine these words, Spivak is categorical in the second quote about Rhys's inability to *contain* Christophine's native presence, given the text's emphasis on the white Creole, Antoinette. Spivak, to use one of her own formulations, argues that Rhys *cannot make the subaltern speak*. This denial of voice is too categorical, and it denies the possibility of strategic constructions – and deconstructions – of subjectivities and voices. I would argue, instead, that Rhys privileges Christophine's speech but also recognizes the parameters within which Christophine can exercise that vocal power – when 'the man' invokes the word of the Law, Christophine understands its, and his, power precisely. Spivak points to the moment in the novel when Christophine makes her exit and argues:

Well before the conclusion, she is simply driven out of the story, with neither narrative nor characterological explanation or justice. ' "Read and write I don't know. Other things I know." She walked away without looking back.' (*WSS*, p. 133) (Spivak 1985, 272)

It is part of Rhys's argument, in this text, to suggest that the world of the book which *this* book is inextricably bound up in, *can* be challenged by the subaltern's words but the political realities of the historical moment, and Rhys's own ambivalent and complex racially-inflected symbolism, mean this challenge can only go so far. Veronica Gregg puts it succinctly:

> It seems to me that Parry [reference to Benita Parry, 'Problems in Current Theories of Colonial Discourse', 1987] is right that the subaltern can speak. But it is also true that Christophine is constructed according to the stereotypes of black promiscuity and the black mammy who privileges the white child over her own. In short, there are several points in the novel at which Christophine is put back in her 'place'. (Gregg 1995, 42)

I think Gregg's more mobile interpretation recognizes that Rhys both affirms a belief in indigenous sources of power and, simultaneously, undermines that 'native power' because of her insistence on it, in this narrative, as separate from the world of the book. This is confirmed in one of her letters to Diana Athill in which Rhys initially expresses concern about Christophine's perhaps unbelievable articulacy, before concluding, 'Besides there is no reason why one particular negro woman shouldn't be articulate enough, especially as she's spent most of her life in a white household' (Wyndham and Melly 1984, 297). It appears that, in Rhys's construction, for Christophine's presence in the text to resonate with subversive possibilities she must be fully grounded in a Creole world unaffected by the alienating effects of 'the book'. There is ample evidence in Caribbean writing, and in Rhys's writing, of the ways in which European books, disseminated via colonial educational systems, erased or distorted the lived reality of Caribbean experiences. Rhys's 'real' but precarious attachment to 'Christophine's world' results, in *Wide Sargasso Sea*, in an overemphasis on the *difference* of that alter/native culture. This overemphasis of difference is reminiscent of some of the Caribbeanist arguments cited above.

The contestation over the reception of Rhys's books, particularly *Wide Sargasso Sea*, which Hulme and Brathwaite engage in is interestingly related to the issues raised above. In a sense what is at stake in this discussion might also be seen to cohere around the kind of meanings they

respectively invest in the word 'Creole'. Hulme concludes his essay by
suggesting that:

> *Wide Sargasso Sea* belongs in all of these places [in English, West
> Indian, Caribbean and post-colonial literary/teaching contexts]: the
> pedagogical imperative is to make it readable in circumstances very
> different from those which produced it, and yet to remain responsible
> to its moorings in a very particular locality. (Hulme 1994, 10)

In the body of the essay, however, with its careful exposure of the reliance
on 'racial derivation' in earlier West Indian readings of the novel,
particularly that of Brathwaite, Hulme's approach seems to exclude 'race'
from the constitution of that 'particular locality' altogether; 'race' appears
to be discarded as a relic of a more naïve reading practice. Instead,
Hulme's reading of Rhys's work and its multiple literary designations
emphasizes her in-between status and liminality in a manoeuvre which
makes her comfortably hybrid. Brathwaite, on the other hand, emphasizes the importance of race and the difference it makes to both the
writing and reading of a text such as *Wide Sargasso Sea*: 'Above all, can we
treat a race-founded & race foundered society as if it – looking back at its
future – didn't exist?' (Brathwaite 1995, 74). Further, Brathwaite reads
Hulme's intervention as part of a broader global picture in which he
(Brathwaite) and other Third World critics are spoken *about* and *for* in
ways which appear to consign them (again) to the periphery, '– in fact, as
is so often the case in much/most of this "post-colonial" writing, we hear
about the natives but we still don't hear them' (Brathwaite 1995, 70). I
am reminded here, too, of Carolyn Cooper's comments, 'Despite the
egalitarian neologism, most of us "post-colonials" know that not all post-
colonials are created equal. Some post-colonials are more out-posted
than others' (Cooper 1993, 15). Brathwaite voices this concern in
passionately unequivocal terms:

> What I continue to maintain is that too many nonCalibans* & now
> 'post-colonialist' critics are trying to shift Rhys's 'figment & guilt' onto
> Tia & 'me' & I RESENT this. I also resent the notion of 'post-colonial'
> applied so easily to our **neo-colonial** condition, its false premises of
> FIGMENT strategically (re)designed to continue the OLD STORY.
> One wonders where all these now 'post-colonial' voices were during
> the period of colonialism . . . why in 1994 shd I still be reading obvi-
> ouses, obliviouses & heavy-handed snides such as Hulme p7 col 2
> 'treating' Ramchand & then mwe each other in this manner.
> (Brathwaite 1995, 74)

In turn, Hulme, in *his* reply, recognizes the structural inequalities within the academe and laments that 'there are too few opportunities for voices from West Indian yards and English gardens to speak to each other' (Hulme 1996, 50). The *voices* in which Brathwaite and Hulme conduct their respective contributions are pertinent to my broader argument. Hulme uses a mild-mannered tone and a measured critical discourse and offers evidence of a wide coverage of 'the field'. Brathwaite's tone, by contrast, is passionate, overtly committed to a 'position' and he inserts the personal without apology into his argument. He makes use of Creole in several places and of the typographical virtuosity of the computer to further estrange his mode of writing from the dubious (as he would see it) objectivity of postcolonial critical discourse. It is part of the larger argument I am making to suggest that *voice* is as crucial to discussions *in* postcolonial critical discourse as it is to those *about* 'postcolonial' literary texts. Brathwaite's reply is partly propelled by the need to challenge the authoritative tone of Hulme's critical voice and to refuse the tendency, which Hulme's focus on Rhys endorses, for Rhys to eclipse consideration of other West Indian writers. In what follows, I discuss Rhys alongside other West Indian women writers, with regard to her use of Creole, in an attempt to resist isolating her in her representative postcolonial role.

I begin by mentioning the novel *Crick Crack, Monkey*, by the Trinidadian writer, Merle Hodge, which has a secure place in the canon of West Indian fiction. In the novel, Hodge makes use of the Creole/English binary to structure the narrative and to explore a 'nationalist/feminist' agenda. Following the death of her mother, and her father's departure for England, the young protagonist, Cynthia ('Tee'), is left with her Tantie in the country. When Tee wins a scholarship to go to 'big-school', however, she is forced to leave behind the noisy warmth and affection of Tantie's world for the sterile order and primness of her Auntie Beatrice's home in town. By contrast to the formidably voluble, volcanic figure of Tantie, Beatrice is presented as lonely and forlorn in her dogged determination for upward social mobility. Beatrice devotes her attention to 'hauling' Tee out of the 'ordinaryness and niggeryness' associated with Tantie's Creole world. One of the most effective ways in which Hodge dramatizes the difference between Tantie's and Beatrice's worlds is in their respective use of words; where Tantie's Creole is expressive and loud,

> Well she [Beatrice] know big-shot, yu know, big-shot in all kinda government office, Father-priest and thing – so she get this paper. But we wipe we backside with she paper – we send the chirren to get some town-breeze an' in that time I get a statement from Selwyn – yu

shoulda see the bitch face in the Courthouse! Eh! She look like she
panty fall-down!   (Hodge 1970, 39)

Beatrice's use of language is mincingly contorted as she attempts to 'speak
properly'; hearing that Tantie is arriving to visit Tee, Beatrice responds:

'Oh my good Heavens, and father is coming today!' she made for the
telephone. . . . Auntie Beatrice was saying on the phone that something *rorther* unexpected had turned up and couldn't Forther please
come another day.   (Hodge 1970, 106)

The novel ends with the mortified Tee watching the spectacle of Tantie
and 'Uncle' Sylvester contaminating the pristine domain of Beatrice's
living room with their greasy bags of 'coolie' food. The novel's rootedness
in Creole culture and its direct critique of the alien values disseminated
via colonial educational systems have secured its place in most 'canons' of
Caribbean writing. Despite being published only four years after Rhys's
Wide Sargasso Sea, it is not usual for the two texts to be discussed together.
Rather than proving Brathwaite's point, that 'Antoinette' and 'Tia'
cannot speak to each other, I would argue that the 'incompatibility' of the
novels may require more nuanced and varied readings of the ways Creole
is inscripted in texts.

    Phyllis Shand Allfrey's *The Orchid House* is a much more familiar –
even routine – point of comparison for Rhys's *Wide Sargasso Sea*. Like
Rhys, Allfrey is a white Dominican Creole whose ancestors included
plantation owners, and her novel similarly conveys the lushness of the
Dominican landscape alongside the decaying prosperity of the white
Creole elite. Unlike Rhys, Allfrey lived for most of her life in Dominica
where she died, impoverished, in 1986. Allfrey's active involvement in
Dominica's political life is well known, first in the Dominica Trade Union
and then as a founding member of the Dominica Labour Party (1955); she
was the first woman minister in the short-lived West Indian Federation
(1958–1961). Allfrey also started and ran the *Dominica Star* for which she
wrote many political editorials. Allfrey's claims to West Indian status
have seldom been questioned because of her lived commitment to the
region; a recent biography of Allfrey, by Lizabeth Paravisini-Gebert,
asserts this sense of belonging in its title, *Phyllis Shand Allfrey: A Caribbean Life*. In *literary* discussions, however, Allfrey's name is invariably
prefaced by the label 'Creole' or 'white'; the following quote from
Paravisini-Gebert conveys some of the ambivalence which marked
Allfrey's perception of her own place in the West Indies:

Now for the first time in her life [after reviewing the current issue of *Caribbean Quarterly*, in February 1979, which emphasized black contributions to West Indian identity] she began to acknowledge her whiteness as a problem. 'I sigh, thinking how during Federal days I believed that the West Indies could be the best small nation of *mixed* people in the world. After all, I have been here for 356 years (since Thomas Warner came). *Then* I strolled to the Trinidad Library and found my one novel on a shelf for "white people's fiction" '.

(Paravisini-Gebert 1996, 255)

Earlier in the biography, Paravisini-Gebert describes the illicit means by which Allfrey learnt to speak patois/Creole by eavesdropping on the private conversations amongst the domestic staff employed by the Allfreys:

Her father had been adamantly against the girls learning patois; he was a member of the League for the Suppression of French-Patois, and considered its use a 'deterrant to progress in the community'. But patois was everywhere around them.   (Paravisini-Gebert 1996, 22)

In her adult life, Allfrey seldom made use of patois/Creole in her writing but *did* frequently use it in her political speeches and, occasionally, in the column she wrote for *The Star* using the pen-name, 'Rose-O'. Adversaries accused her of manipulating a rather *frenchified* patois for strategic political ends but Allfrey tartly responded to one journalist by saying, 'Do you think I could ever conduct a political meeting here without knowing patois?' (Paravisini-Gebert 1996, 117), while, in an interview with Polly Pattullo, Allfrey said, 'I found that patois is a very useful thing. I would never have won the federal elections without it' (Pattullo 1988, 231). The context in which Allfrey learnt patois (eavesdropping on the servants) and her very partial use of it in her writing are very suggestive. The parental taboo confirms the importance of speech as a marker of social class (and, of course, in the West Indies class and race are structurally intertwined) and the preservation of the privilege associated with being part of the small West Indian Creole (in its older sense) elite has a long history. Kenneth Ramchand includes a wonderfully telling extract from *Lady Nugent's Journal* (1839) in his *The West Indian Novel and Its Background*:

The Creole Language is not confined to the negroes. Many of the ladies, who have not been educated in England, speak a sort of broken English, with an indolent drawling out of their words, that is very tiresome if not disgusting. I stood next to a lady one night near a window, and, by way of saying something, remarked that the air was much cooler than usual; to which she answered, 'Yes, ma-am, him rail-y too fra-ish.'   (Ramchand 1970, 86–7)

The 'drawling' Jamaican vowels undermine the Creole woman's claims to 'full ladyhood'; in a similar vein, Brathwaite argued that in the perform-ance of their poems, the accent and pronunciation of some West Indian writers betrayed their full claims to 'English poetry'. The image of the young Allfrey eavesdropping on the servants to learn the patois they spoke and to take in their 'gossip' recalls one of her own narrative crea-tions, Lally, the nanny used as the narrator in *The Orchid House*. In the novel, Lally is presented in the role of devoted and loving nanny and this, along with her unquestioning attitude to the kinds of political change Joan (whom she looked after as a child) later advocates, consolidates her in the 'Mammy' role. The fact that Lally narrates events in Standard English, rather than Creole, and that she has to be placed strategically, in several unlikely locations, to 'overhear' the conversations of the Creole family, on whom the text focuses and to which she is, for the most part, peripheral, begs questions about Allfrey's choice of her as a narrator.[4] Does Lally provide Allfrey with a convenient device for displaying black conservatism (and the necessity of Joan's radical politics)? Is Lally the most convenient way to ground the text and make it recognizably Dominican? Or is Lally, 'accidentally', a more ambivalent figure in that Allfrey's decision to *speak through* her is motivated by Allfrey's personal experience of the centrality of such figures in her own upbringing and, simultaneously, their *difference*? Allfrey seldom makes use of identifiably black speakers in her poetry but in the poem 'The White Lady' (sub-titled 'Martinique'), she uses a black speaker who is observing the white ladies ('the untarnished ones, the wives of officials') promenading between the trees in 'precious gowns, imported from Paris'. The speaker claims a collective voice: 'We are the trees, we are the silent spies' and continues:

> we know that they conceive their children in rooms
> with the jalousie blinds drawn, the mosquito net tucked in.
> We are not jealous of that love-making:
> happy we are to dig our roots firm into the earth,
> happy we are to be brown and strong and lissome.

---

4   There are also places in which an 'omniscient narration' takes place but the text is narrated largely by Lally.

> Our children are multiple, and all have beauty:
> we fear not dirt, nor age. There was but one we feared,
> and she was a queen. (Allfrey 1940, 4)

The poem then describes the mesmerizing beauty of Napoleon's Creole wife, Josephine, whose beauty eclipses that of the black/brown women and with whose statuesque image the poem concludes.[5] As in Allfrey's use of Lally, the Standard English register which the speaker uses and the unequivocal celebration of Josephine's beauty suggest that the black woman is a convenient *mouthpiece*, rather than having any intrinsic value. At times, then, Allfrey's own romance with her past,[6] alluded to above in her claim to a connection with Dominica which goes back to Thomas Warner, sits uneasily with her political beliefs in cross-race, cross-class political values.

Jean Rhys's interest in, and use of, a black Creole-speaker in 'Let Them Call It Jazz' provides a telling comparison. The story is narrated by Selina and Rhys uses a 'stylized patois'[7] throughout her narration, as Selina recounts the circumstances in which she finds herself homeless in London:

> Don't talk to me about London. Plenty people there have heart like stone. Any complaint – the answer is 'prove it'. But if nobody see and bear witness for me, how to prove anything? So I pack up and leave, I think better not have dealings with that woman. She too cunning, and Satan don't lie worse.   (Rhys 1968, 47)

That Selina is a *black* Creole-speaker is made clear when her new, hostile, neighbour says, 'At least the other tarts that crook installed here were *white* girls'[8] (Rhys 1968, 57). Selina is eventually taken to court on a 'drunk and disorderly' charge and then sent to Holloway prison where she overhears one of the women singing 'the Holloway song'. It is this song

---

5   Paravisini-Gebert argues that the poem was inspired by the statue of Josephine which Allfrey had visited in Martinique.
6   See Paravisini-Gebert 1996, pp. 11–29, for further detailing of this strand in Allfrey's thinking.
7   In a letter to Francis Wyndham, Rhys wrote, 'I've finished the Holloway story long ago. It's "stylized patois" – how true!', suggesting that the term 'stylized patois' was Wyndham's.
8   Given the careful detailing of Selina's racial 'mix' which Rhys gives within the story (white father and 'fair-coloured' mother), Selina's designation *within the West Indies* would more likely be 'coloured' than 'black'.

which, when she hums it at a party following her release, is taken and 'jazzed up' by a man who sells the song and pays her five pounds. Selina's first reaction is despair, 'Now I've let them play it wrong, and it will go from me like all the other songs – like everything. Nothing left for me at all' (Rhys 1968, 67), but she consoles herself with the uncontaminated memory *she* carries of the song:[9]

> So let them call it jazz, I think, and let them play it wrong. That won't make no difference to the song I heard. I buy myself a dusty pink dress with the money.   (Rhys 1968, 67)

While the bulk of the story dramatizes the difficulties Selina experiences in being recognized and *heard* in the context of an increasingly racist (1950s) London, the story's conclusion is unequivocal in asserting her ability to survive it. Creole speech is used economically and effectively throughout the story; it is crucial to Rhys's construction of Selina as a 'survivor' in that her use of it signals her sharp insight and perception of her place and circumstances. At the same time, Selina also recognizes that her Creole speech, with its associated body language, compounds the perception of her racial difference:

> I want to say all I do is sing in that old garden, and I want to say this in decent quiet voice. But I hear myself talking loud and I see my hands wave in the air. Too besides it's no use, they won't believe me, so I don't finish. I stop, and I feel the tears on my face. 'Prove it.' That's all they will say.   (Rhys 1968, 60–1)

When Selina breaks the neighbours' window, she throws her head back and laughs loudly, 'like my grandmother, with my hands on my hips and my head back. (When she laugh like that you can hear her to the end of our street.)' (Rhys 1968, 58). At other times, Rhys's use of Creole is expressive and comic in ways reminiscent of Sam Selvon; here Selina describes the policewoman's entry into the house:

---

[9] In a letter to Francis Wyndham on 6 December 1960, Rhys expresses concern about Selina's language because she had 'not read any of the "West Indian" people. It's by ear and memory' (Wyndham and Melly 1984, 197). Here, memory appears 'to do the trick', whatever Rhys' doubts. Selina's memory of song and its function as a survival strategy can also be very productively compared to Jean 'Binta' Breeze's poem, 'Riddim Ravings', in which the supposedly 'mad' speaker describes 'the DJ in her head' whose music helps her survive her impoverished circumstances.

As soon as I open the door the woman put her foot in it. She wear
sandals and thick stockings and I never see a foot so big or so bad. It
look like it want to mash up the whole world. Then she come in after
the foot, and her face not so pretty either.   (Rhys 1968, 59)

The calypsos Selina sings, along with the 'stylized patois' which Rhys
'gives' her, function together to affirm the values of West Indian culture as
an alternative cultural centre for Selina in her travels in 'the' centre. If
Allfrey, as I have argued, speaks *through* her black characters, Rhys is more
successful in speaking *as* a black woman because her choice appears to be
prompted by aesthetic *and* political considerations, which, when meshed
together, convey 'authenticity' in terms established by and within the
narrative, but which also resonate beyond the text by utilizing well a
recognizable currency of representation – Creole. The experiences
described in the story were drawn from Rhys's own experience of being
charged and imprisoned in Holloway on an 'assault' charge and her letters
make it clear that maintaining privacy was a concern, but it is significant
that Rhys chose to mediate these experiences through a character whose
voice and circumstances would be *recognized* as *black* Creole. Sue Thomas
argues that Rhys's use of patois 'functions as the principle sign of the
authenticity of Caribbean difference' (Thomas 1994, 186). This does not
demonstrate a cynical manipulation of linguistic registers on Rhys's part
but an awareness of the political and aesthetic implications of voice. It
may also indicate Rhys's penchant for a dubious dichotomized reading of
white and black: 'I wanted to be black, I always wanted to be black. . . .
Being black is warm and gay, being white is cold and sad' (Rhys 1967,
32–3). But it also testifies to her desire – and need – to make a claim to
that world and that voice.

I will turn now to look at two contemporary Caribbean women writers
by way of 'updating' Rhys's Caribbean literary context. The first, Jamaica
Kincaid, is Antiguan and has published three novels, a collection of
stories and, recently, an autobiographical work; unlike other users of
Creole, Kincaid eschews Creole in an explicit and strategic way. The
second, Erna Brodber, is Jamaican and has published three novels which
each, in different ways, affirm the centrality of Creole – language and
culture – to her work.

Jamaica Kincaid's texts convey an ambivalent attitude to Creole
language and to Creole culture. In Kincaid's first novel, *Annie John*, there
are several moments in which Creole cultural practices are endorsed
(Annie and her mother's herbal baths, the grandmother's obeah reme-
dies, for example) while the violence and stupidity of the English colo-

nizers are exposed (the English girl Ruth regularly wearing the dunce's cap, for example). The most dramatic evocation of this collision between cultures takes place in the chapter entitled 'Columbus in Chains'. Here, the young Annie remembers something her mother had laughed and said upon hearing that her father was ill and bed-ridden, 'So the great man can no longer just get up and go. How I would love to see his face now!' (Kincaid 1985, 78). Annie then inscribes 'The Great Man Can No Longer Just Get Up and Go' ('in Old English lettering – a script I had recently mastered') beneath the picture in her history book of the disgraced Columbus about to be shipped back to Spain. Kincaid seldom represents 'direct speech' in her texts but clearly, here, the mother's words and, by association, 'orality' are given a symbolic power. But Creole/patois is not presented as the specific source of that power, for the mother's words are not represented in Creole speech. Patois is avoided more explicitly, and referred to but not represented, in another moment later on in the text, when Annie's mother sees her talking in the street with a group of boys:

> She went on to say that . . . it had pained her to see me behave in the manner of a slut (only she used the French-patois word for it) in the street and that just to see me had caused her shame. The word 'slut' (in patois) was repeated over and over again until suddenly I felt as if I were drowning.   (Kincaid 1985, 102)

Rather than amplitude and 'slackness', the patois word here is associated with cruelty. There is a similar association when, in *The Autobiography of My Mother*, the protagonist is punished by her father for contradicting his lie to Lazarus (who has come to ask for nails) that he has no nails, by dragging her through the house and pushing her facedown into the barrel of nails, 'at the same time saying in French patois, "Now you know where the nails are, now you really know where the nails are" ' (Kincaid 1996, 190). The bracketing of patois words also features in an autobiographical work, *My Brother*, which Kincaid wrote about her brother's death from AIDS. In this text, Kincaid frequently reports things her mother or brother have said and then includes a 'translation' in brackets which conveys the patois in which the words were spoken. So, for example, her brother tells her, 'that he had made worthlessness of his life ("Me mek wutlessness ah me life , man")' or, later, 'and my mother was sorry about his absence ("Me miss he, you know, me miss he")' (Kincaid 1998, 29, 151). In an interview, Kincaid was asked why she doesn't make use of Creole in her work and her response conveys some of the nuances about the worlds of the printed and spoken word which are the subject of this essay:

> it's hard to know just what to do. Then you'd have to learn a new language, it doesn't really take in your past, the new language, it takes in what you're learning now. . . . there are no books written in these languages . . . I don't even know how to speak English patois any more.
>
> (Kincaid 1992, 22)

Kincaid's argument, that patois/Creole is a language which, for her, symbolizes the degradations of colonial history, is one which she makes many times, in different ways, in her texts; it is also a position which stubbornly resists the seductive orthodoxy of Creole as a marker of dynamic and authentic West Indianness, as 'the real thing'. So, when her brother bids her farewell after a tense visit, she reports:

> and he said, So this is it, no hug, no nothing? (and he said it in that way, in conventional English, not in the English that instantly reveals the humiliation of history, the humiliations of the past not remade into art) . . .   (Kincaid 1998, 108)

In the novel *The Autobiography of My Mother*, Kincaid uses the relationship between Xuela (whose African/Carib mother died at her birth) and Philip, an Englishman, as a device for exploring History. Xuela's narration is punctuated with reminders of her own position as one of 'the defeated' and that, as such, she is 'not in a position to make [her] feeling have any meaning' (Kincaid 1996, 137). Language is crucial to this exploration and Kincaid foregrounds the way in which both colonizer and colonized take refuge in the *noise* of speech; the former, as represented by Philip, is described below:

> Philip belonged to that restless people unable to leave the world alone, unable to look at anything for too long without becoming troubled by its very existence; *silence is alien to them*.
>
> (Kincaid 1996, 209, my italics)

Describing her first sight of the town, Roseau (the novel is set in Dominica), 'outposts of despair; for conqueror and conquered alike these places were capitals of nothing but despair', the narrator concludes:

> In this sort of house lived people whose skins glistened with exhaustion and whose faces were sad even when they had a reason to be happy, people for whom history had been a big, dark room, *which made them hate silence*.   (Kincaid 1996, 61–2, my italics)

The novel concludes with an account of Philip and Xuela's marriage in their home high up in the mountains, away from Roseau, 'He and I lived in this spell, the spell of history. . . . He spoke to me, I spoke to him; he spoke to me in English, I spoke to him in patois' (Kincaid 1996, 218–19); in other places in the novel, Kincaid suggests that this lack of 'a common language' encapsulates the mutually exclusive worlds – and words – of colonizer and colonized and, by implication, the impossibility of translating between those worlds.

Kincaid's strategy for writing herself out of the subject position designated her by colonial history is to insist on speaking from *within* the tradition in which those stories were told, rather than constructing a voice which claims its origins and power from an alter/native cultural mode. So, Kincaid's writing voice is one in which authorial control is always manifestly obvious – there is little room for the reader to indulge in sympathy for characters, for instance – and events are narrated in deceptively 'simple' sentence structures which, together with the almost 'mincingly correct' English, combine to consolidate the effect Kincaid achieves of 'this is how it happened'. The anger concerning colonial history which Kincaid describes in *A Small Place*, 'But nothing can erase my rage – not an apology, not a large sum of money, not the death of the criminal – for this wrong can never be made right' (Kincaid 1988, 31) is the force which is evident in all of her texts and which she harnesses into shape using, exclusively, 'the master's language'. In the process, Kincaid refuses 'the lure of the folk' and the associated claims made in the name of 'the oral' and insists on a literary voice which is relentlessly spare – and solitary.

Erna Brodber's first novel, *Jane and Louisa Will Soon Come Home*, dramatizes the process by which Nellie, who is from a family who were 'brown, intellectual, better and apart' (Brodber 1980, 7), manages to reconnect with her local community after studying abroad. Central to this process is Nellie's debunking of some of her 'book-learning' and the dry fixity of ideological positions associated with this, by learning how to use her Creole voice again. Her catharsis comes when she finally vents her anger in the company of her rasta mentor, Baba:

> You understand this r. . .-c. . .t of a hungry man from nowhere who is to watch and observe me. What the hell he think he is. Man don't let me . . . I had been talking aloud. Is that me? With such expressions. Am I a fishwife?   (Brodber 1980, 71)

Baba replies, 'You have found your language, Ma'am' and it is then her receptiveness to various voices of her community that allows her to 'get ready' for her future. In her second novel, *Myal*, Brodber focuses even more explicitly on the *zombifying* effects of texts, particularly as they are disseminated via colonial education and Christian religions. The story focuses on Ella, the mixed race child of Irish-Jamaican parentage, whose racial indeterminacy – she is called 'ginger', 'raw', 'Salt pork', 'Red Ants Abundance' and 'Alabaster baby' (Brodber 1988, 9) by her peers – makes her a misfit in Grove Town. At school she remains 'unrecognized', hovering always at the threshold of, but never *in*, the classroom and takes refuge in the world of books. This sense of 'in-betweenness' is reminiscent of Antoinette in *Wide Sargasso Sea* explaining the significance of Amelie's song about 'white cockroach' to her husband:

> I've heard English women call us white niggers. So between you I often wonder who I am and where is my country and where do I belong and why was I ever born at all.   (Rhys 1966, 85)

Ella is offered a way out of this racial limbo by marrying an American, Selwyn Langley, who takes her to live with him in America where he makes 'the making of Ella' his project:

> It was Selwyn who explained to her in simple terms that she was coloured, mulatto and what that meant, taking her innocence with her hymen in return for guidance through the confusing fair that was America.   (Brodber 1988, 43)

Under his guidance, Ella shaves, powders and straightens any traces of her 'black self' out so that she can 'pass' respectably for white. Selwyn's interest lures Ella into telling stories about the people she grew up with in Grove Town, Jamaica; in the process of this story-telling Ella becomes aware of the artificial way in which she has divided her 'self':

> With her hymen and a couple of months of marriage gone, there was a clean, clear passage from Ella's head through her middle and right down to outside. Poisons drained out of her body. . . . For years there had been something like gauze in her head where she supposed her mind to be. It stretched flat across her head, separating one section of her mind from the other – the top of the head from the bottom of the head. In there were Peter Pan and Lucy Gray and dairy Maid and at one time Selwyn – the top section. At the bottom were Mammy Mary and them Grove Town people.   (Brodber 1988, 80)

Selwyn takes Ella's stories and transforms them into a play, 'Caribbean

Nights and Days', in which the Ella figure is white with flowing blond hair (like Antoinette, the husband attempts to manoeuvre her like a 'marionette') and all the Grove Town people are reduced to minstrels with boot-black, shiny faces and chalk-white mouths. Ella whispers, 'It didn't go so', before 'tripping out' in a nervous breakdown which Brodber presents as a dramatic phantom pregnancy; it is not until Ella is returned to Grove Town that the healing can begin as the foreign poisons symbolically drain from her. Like Selina, whose song is taken and commodified, Ella's stories are commodified by Selwyn – he plans to make a film of the play and sees its potential as 'the biggest coon show ever' (Brodber 1988, 80). In the process of this trafficking in stories, despite the distortions along the way, Brodber emphasizes that stories can always be retold and that meanings *can* be transformed, just as Selina insists on retaining the 'original' song in her memory. This is underscored by another narrative strand in *Myal* involving the animal characters in a farmyard story; their activities and rebellions have punctuated the 'main' narrative and towards the end of the novel they make a powerful assertion of their refusal to remain in their 'storybook' designations:

> My people have been separated from themselves White Hen, by several means, one of them being the printed word and the ideas it carries. . . . Now, White Hen, now, we have people who can and are willing to correct images from the inside, destroy what should be destroyed, replace it with what it should be replaced and put us back together, give us back ourselves.   (Brodber 1988, 109–10)

This strategy for manipulating texts so that more empowering meanings are produced is one which Reverend Simpson advises Ella to adopt in her new role as a teacher:

> – Now listen, – he said to her. – You have a quarrel with the writer. He wrote you think without an awareness of certain things. But does he force you to teach without this awareness? *Need your voice say what his says?*   (Brodber 1988, 107, my italics)

Brodber re-places Ella in Grove Town where she refuses the 'privileges' of her 'lightskin' and the novel ends with the suggestion that Ella's teaching of the written word will be conducted in dialogue with the community. The novel itself demonstrates this dialogic approach in the dense plethora of voices which interrupt, disrupt and punctuate the text, so that the story of Ella is embedded within this weave of voices. The emphasis on dialogue between 'book' and 'spoken word' at a thematic level is matched, in formal terms, in the seamless shifting between the multiple registers available in the standard English/Creole continuum. In places in her texts, Brodber's representation of Creole is almost 'hyper-real' in the detailed intimacy of its use but, because it is always placed in dialogue with other discourses, Creole does not signal 'native' essence or authenticity but is used strategically to suggest ways in which it might provide a powerful medium for dialogue with other words and other worlds.

In discussing these Caribbean women writers together, it is not my intention to 'rank' them in order of the success of their use of Creole. Rather, I want to emphasize the very varied ways in which they deploy – or avoid – Creole-use and the very different agendas which underlie this. Rather than Creole, and by association, 'the oral', *automatically* signalling resistance and native authenticity, as many Caribbean and postcolonial critics might suggest, the discussion above suggests a much more nuanced manipulation of Creole for strategic literary ends. As a consequence, questions about 'cultural belonging' appear more subtle and *hearing* 'the natives', rather than hearing *about* them, may require more patient listening. Given the complex and ambivalent realities of writing and reading Creole, Jean Rhys appears perfectly 'at home' when aligned with Caribbean women writers. By way of conclusion, a brief extract from a poem by Olive Senior, in memory of Jean Rhys, 'Meditation on Red', conveys some of the ways in which Rhys's voice has enabled other Caribbean women's voices:

> Right now
> I'm as divided
> as you were
> by that sea.
>
> but I'll
> be able to
> find my way
> home again
>
> for that craft
> you launched
> is so seaworthy
> tighter
> than you'd ever been
>
> dark voyagers
> like me
> can feel free
> to sail.   (Senior 1994, 51–2)

Works Cited

Allfrey, P.S. 1940. *In Circles*, Harrow Weald: Raven Press.
———— 1982. *The Orchid House*, London: Virago.
Allsopp, R. 1996. *Dictionary of Caribbean English Usage*, Oxford: Oxford University Press.
Ashcroft, B., Griffiths, G.and Tiffin, H. eds 1989. *The Empire Writes Back: Theory and Practice in Post-colonial Literatures*, London: Routledge.
Bennett, L. 1982. *Louise Bennett: Selected Poems*, Kingston: Sangster's.
Brathwaite, K. 1973. *The Arrivants*, Oxford: Oxford University Press.
———— 1993. 'A History of the Voice', in *Roots*, Ann Arbor: University of Michigan Press, 259–304.
———— 1995. 'A post-cautionary tale of the Helen of our wars', *Wasafiri*, 21 (Spring), 69–78.
Breeze, J.B. 1988. *Riddym Ravings and Other Poems*, London: Race Today Publications.
Brodber, E. 1980. *Jane and Louisa Will Soon Come Home*, London: New Beacon Books.
———— 1988. *Myal*, London: New Beacon Books.
———— 1994. *Louisiana*, London: New Beacon Books.
Cooper, C. 1993. *Noises in the Blood: Orality, Gender and the 'Vulgar' Body of Jamaican Popular Culture*, London: Macmillan.
Gregg, V. 1995. *Jean Rhys's Historical Imagination: Reading and Writing the Creole*, Chapel Hill and London: University of North Carolina Press.
Habekost, C. 1986. *Dub Poetry: 19 Poets from England and Jamaica*, Neustadt: Michael Swinn.
Hodge, M. 1970. *Crick Crack, Monkey*, London: Heinemann.
Hulme, P. 1994. 'The Place of Wide Sargasso Sea', *Wasafiri*, No. 20 (Autumn), 5–11.
———— 1996. 'A Response to Kaman Braithwaite', *Wasafiri*, No. 23 (Spring), 49–50.
Katrak, K. 1989. 'Decolonizing Culture: toward a theory for postcolonial women's texts', *Modern Fiction Studies*, Vol. 35, No. 1 (Spring), 157–80.
Kincaid, J. 1985. *Annie John*, London: Pan Books.
———— 1988. *A Small Place*, London: Virago.
———— 1991. *Lucy*, London: Plume.
———— 1992. 'I Use a Cut and Slash Policy of Writing: Jamaica Kincaid Talks to Gerhard Dilger', *Wasafiri*, No. 16 (Autumn), 21–5.
———— 1996. *The Autobiography of My Mother*, London: Virago.
———— 1998. *My Brother*, London: Virago.
Paravisini-Gebert, L. 1996. *Phyllis Shand Allfrey: A Caribbean Life*, New Brunswick: Rutger's University Press.
Parry, B. 1987. 'Problems in current theories of colonial discourse', *Oxford Literary Review*, 9, 1–2, 27–58.
Pattullo, P. 1988. 'Phyllis Shand Allfrey Talking with Polly Pattullo', in M. Chamberlain (ed.) *Writing Lives: Conversations Between Women Writers*, London: Virago, 224–34.

Ramchand, K. 1970. *The West Indian Novel and Its Background*. London: Faber.

Rand, J. 1984. 'Talk, talk: nigger talk' in Berry, J. ed. *News for Babylon: The Chatto Book of West Indian British Poetry*, London: Chatto & Windus, 112–14.

Rhys, J. 1966. *Wide Sargasso Sea*, London: Penguin.

—— 1967. *Voyage in the Dark*, London: Andre Deutsch.

—— 1968. *Tigers Are Better Looking*, London: Andre Deutsch.

Senior, O. 1994. *Gardening in the Tropics*, Toronto: McClelland and Stewart.

Spivak, G.C. 1985. 'Three women's texts and a critique of imperialism', in H.L. Gates (ed.) *'Race', Writing and Difference*, Chicago: University of Chicago Press.

Thomas, S. 1994. 'Let them call it jazz', in C. Tiffin and A. Lawson (eds) *De-scribing Empire*, London: Routledge.

Wyndham, F. and Melly, D. eds 1984. *Jean Rhys letters 1931–1966*, London: Andre Deutsch.

Shamanism in Oceania:
The Poetry of Albert Wendt

BRIAR WOOD

Mr. C: Keep Comin On you know you keep Comin On
With a Vibe that is laced with Consciousness, inspiration,
Love, Dedication, Keep Comin Yes,
Re-evolution in Progress
Reality Changing Moving Shifting Higher
Into connection with Gia
Running on a rhythm you know that we're Comin On Strong
('cos we keep Comin On)[1]

Shaman of Visions, when we die disperse
every particle of our dust into the dawn
which gave birth to the first word.

('Shaman of Visions' Wendt 1984, 59)

THIS ESSAY FOCUSES on a number of ongoing questions about the relationship between the physical, literary and imagined concerns of Pacific
literature, as they emerge in the poetry of Albert Wendt. This involves
some of the historicizing of the retrospective approach, but it is also an
attempt to think about how a reading of Wendt's poetry might inform an
understanding of the present – not to sound too portentous – a present
poised at the edge of a new millennium. The significance of the growth of
Pacific literatures in English since the 1960s, in which Wendt has been a
crucial figure, has yet to register in its diversity and complexity on European and American debates about postcolonial literature, 'new literatures' and literary theory.

Pacific literatures make significant contributions to debates in
contemporary theory about how creative and imaginary spaces are represented across the in-betweenness of postcolonial and postmodern, global,
local and borderline spaces. Reading the poetry in the context of this
volume involves an engagement with the working verities of the study of
new literatures and postcolonial theory. This essay will trace a course in

---

[1] 'Comin On' by The Shamen, taken from the LP *Boss Drum*, 1992. Written by
Angus/West. Published by Warner Chappell Music.

which the identification and deconstruction of the centrality of binary
structures gives way to more diverse and indigenous based models of
reading and writing. The reading takes place in the context of a recognition that local and international readings are in many ways inextricably
connected, and debates about how to situate and interpret the relationship between these discourses in the Pacific will no doubt continue for a
long time yet.

In *South Pacific Literature: From Myth To Fabulation*, the first specialist
critical study of Pacific literature written in English, Subramani argued
that both Wendt's fiction and his poetry 'assume a fragmented traditional
culture' (Subramani 1985, 61). Subramani's study indicates that shifts
between prose and poetry have long been a feature of Pacific oral traditions and that the poetry of Wendt's first poetry collection *Inside Us the
Dead* (1976a) is linked closely in terms of motif and symbol to his prose
writing. The fiction has been more widely read than his poetry, yet the
poetry offers the reader much to consider in its own right. The purpose of
this reading is not primarily to promote the study of Wendt's singular
career, but to point out the ways in which his poetic output has been
shaped by the social, linguistic and political forces informing it; including
a shamanic heritage. Wendt's writing uniquely links a number of influences – life in Sāmoa, New Zealand, Fiji, international travel and a long-
standing interaction with 'world literature'.

Throughout his career, which spans from the 1960s to the present,
Albert Wendt has been aware of the discourses and disciplines of the
physical and social sciences in the Pacific. He has warned against
attempts to read his writing as sociological data. His writing has consistently been concerned with the relationship between an Oceania of the
imagination and the intersection of popular/academic representations of
the Pacific. Where European literature had so often imagined Oceania as
an empty space to be written on by Europeans, and the Pacific as a world
of nature to be tamed and cultivated, Wendt has represented the Pacific
as place and Oceania as space in terms of endless diversity. This understanding of the Pacific as multiple and various is fundamental in the work
of indigenous writers of the region and informs their representations of
geography and history. Paul Sharrad has described Wendt's model of
indigenous literature in the Pacific as one of the 'antagonistic overthrow
of the misrepresentations and erasures of white writers' (Sharrad 1994,
123). While this struggle against the legacy of colonial authority is
undoubtedly an important aspect of the writing, it is sometimes modified
in the poetry by the implied speaker's wry understanding of his own role
as a critical participant in the state institutions of education. 'Dad', the

internalized voice of the young daughter asks in the poem 'No Islands in the Sun, Just Misters' towards the end of *Inside Us the Dead*, 'how come you're a Mister?' (Wendt 1976a, 51). In the reference to the title of the popular song 'Islands in the Sun', made internationally famous in a version by Harry Belafonte, the poet refers to a relationship of similarity and difference between the islands of the Pacific and the Caribbean. It is also a comment on the relationship of poetry to popular song, folk and calypso music, to the promotion of singers' careers (with some similarities to those of the poet/writer) through the structures of commercialization and internationalization, and the subsequent shift in the specificity of the local.

Wendt's writing has become increasingly significant not only because he writes about Sāmoa – in his own mythology, and in the history of the Samoan nation – as 'sacred centre' of the Pacific[2] but also because his writing is pivotal in terms of recent and long term histories of Pacific migration. Engaging with pre-contact, colonial and contemporary histories, the poetry spans a number of shifts in the way the globalization of Pacific literature has been unfolding. It addresses issues of global, communal and individual identity, questioning Pacific Way ideology[3] where it assumes too great a homogeneity between Pacific cultures or individuals, the colonizing impetus of theories such as 'the fatal impact' version of contact and binarist Māori/Pakeha models of culture in Aotearoa/New Zealand.

In an influential essay 'Towards a New Oceania', first published in *Mana Review*, journal of the South Pacific Arts Society, Wendt listed the many metaphors produced to describe Oceania, and added a few of his own. Colonial literary myths have portrayed the Pacific as paradise, new Eden, home to Noble Savagery. For Wendt, in this 1976 essay, Oceania was multidimensional, feminine, and ultimately unknowable; 'only the imagination in free flight can hope – if not to contain her – to grasp some of her shape, plumage, and pain'. Colonial economics, racism and education systems had 'castrated' Oceanic cultures. 'The quest', he wrote 'should be for a new Oceania' (Wendt 1976b).

Twenty years later, Wendt's introduction to *Nuanua*, a new anthology

---

[2] There are many interpretations of the word Samoa – one of which is 'sacred centre'.

[3] For an account of the 'The Pacific Way' see Mara 1997, 117. 'I had coined the phrase "The Pacific Way" and felt we could speak from our own experience, insofar as Fiji was recommending continuing dialogue as a means of resolving differences on a basis of mutual understanding.'

of Pacific writing, was focused through the term 'Pacific', which is now widely used to refer to an area that corresponds to the geographical area occupied by the Pacific Ocean, the islands and inhabitants of sea, land and air. The writing selected for *Nuanua* represents particular regions united by social, political, geographical and historical ties. In the introduction Wendt describes Pacific literature 'for the purposes of this anthology' as 'that written or composed by Pacific Islands peoples, especially the indigenous peoples' (Wendt 1995b, 2). The introduction frames Pacific writing so defined in a relationship to international culture, but foregrounds issues of indigenization of language and literary form, as well as those of local histories.

Epeli Hau'ofa, Professor of Sociology at the University of the South Pacific, novelist and leading figure in the academic and literary debates about Pacific cultures, has expressed views that seem compatible with Albert Wendt's; Oceania co-exists and intersects with a drive in the Pacific for a 'much stronger and a genuinely independent regionalism' (Hau'ofa 1997, 132). The occupants of Oceania are, he argues, everyone who comes in contact with the Pacific: 'human beings with a common heritage and commitment . . . a world of people, connected to each other' (Hau'ofa 1997, 137). Reinforcing Wendt's description of Oceania as an imaginary location, Hau'ofa reminds the reader that these terms – Pacific and Oceania – signify both separate and interlocking areas. Representations of the Pacific and Oceania have local and global dimensions, though in Hau'ofa's terms, it is the idea of Oceania which lends itself most readily to global structures since it is not as closely bound by the realism of regional or linguistic boundaries as ideas of the Pacific. Though Subramani used the terms 'South Pacific' and 'Oceania' interchangeably in *South Pacific Literature* (1985), Hau'ofa's recent discussion makes them separable, though frequently linked.

Homi Bhabha writes of a 'third space' in which boundary tensions between the global and the national make it a site for the production of new forms, some of which may challenge existing versions of the community (Bhabha 1994, 218). 'Cultural globality is figured in the *in-between* spaces of double-frames: its historical originality marked by a cognitive obscurity; its decentered "subject" signified in the nervous temporality of the transitional, or the emergent provisionality of the "present" ' (Bhabha 1994, 216). By intervening in global educational discourses, as I am suggesting Pacific literatures will increasingly do in the new millennium, they negotiate and insist on more widespread recognition of the importance of Pacific cultures both in their own right and in terms of the contributions they make on the international scene through, for example, migrant work forces and attempts to protect the environment. Oceania functions as an imaginative space/location that can help to support the impetus and the sociopolitical communications made in Pacific literature across local and global trajectories. Wendt has mobilized into literary discourse a concept that facilitates the description of existence and identity not simply as either/or, but as a mediated or transitional state, a crossing, the Samoan word *vā*:

> the concept of *va*, which means the space that relates all things. For example the *va* between you and me is our relationship – a space, but also our relationship as human beings, an emotional relationship. And we must cherish and nourish and nurture that *va*. The concept of *va* is also related to outer space; our name for outer space is Va-nimo-nimo, 'the space that appears and disappears' – and gives meaning to all of us as individuals. It defines us.   (Alley and Williams 1992, 182)

Although Wendt dismissed the idea of 'a return to an imaginary pre-papalagi Golden Age or utopian womb' (the word papālagi has been translated as 'white man, European') in 'Towards a New Oceania' (1976b) my reading of this phrase interprets it as the refusal to return to previous and failed attempts to represent Pacific cultures, rather than the idea of abandoning the fantasy of achieving ideals all together. Wilson Harris' notion of 'the womb of space' as the locus of 'the cross-cultural imagination', in which space is the primal category where ambivalences dissolve and realign can be compared with Wendt's concept of the importance of vā (Harris 1983). Harris perceives the potential for the creative fusion in the cross-cultural imagination to operate as a counter force against the pull towards nihilism, which is so often one of the lingering effects of colonialism. Through its fusion of shamanic, Samoan and modernist influences, Wendt's poetry crosses through the domain of post-colonial nihilism in which individuals confront their fears and communities engage with life threatening ideologies.

A Poetics of Shamanism

Shamanism, a term derived through Russian, from the Tungus word saman, has been described as an ancient and universal form of religion. The use of the term 'shaman' came into widespread use in the 1920s through anthropological and ethnographic discourses. Mircea Eliade described shamanism as a 'technique of ecstasy' (Eliade 1964, 4). Eliade's studies focus on the common features of shamanistic practice, but also recognise the importance of cultural difference in shamanic performance and discourse. They identified the existence of cross-cultural structural features, such as the shaman's initiatory illness and possession by spirits or gods, the faculty of ascension or magical flight and access to the three cosmic zones. Nicholas Thomas and Caroline Humphrey describe shamanism as 'more of an exotic essence, a romanticized inversion of Western rationalism, than a scholarly category that can stand up to any sustained interrogation' (Thomas and Humphrey 1994, 2). Peter Furst favours the term 'shamanistic worldview' (Furst 1994). Among the recognizable cross-cultural features of shamanism, he has identified the belief in the equal importance of all (natural) things, transformation as origin, reciprocity as the principle of relations between humans, spirits and gods and emphasis on the importance of ecological awareness.

Albert Wendt's mobilization of the term 'shaman' can be read as postcolonial autoethnography (Pratt 1992, 7) which redefines hegemonically determined terms of colonization by recontexualizing them. Wendt's second collection titled *Shaman of Visions* (1984) draws the reader's attention overtly to the shamanic role, the poet's success and failure in this role and Pacific/Oceanic histories of shamanism, such as the prophetic role of taulāitu in Samoan culture. The word taulaitu is translated in Allardice (1985) as 'spirit medium'. Eliade pointed out that in Polynesian shamanism, definition is complicated by the functional division of social groups for religious purposes: 'the divine chiefs [ariki], the prophets [taula] and the priests [tohunga], but to these we must add healers, sorcerers, necromancers, and the spontaneously "possessed" ' (Eliade 1964, 366). Thomas argues for the existence of a broad historical 'counterpoint or conflict between a variety of forms of inspirational or shamanic agency and the centralizing force of chieftainship or kingship' (Thomas and Humphrey 1994, 15). Wendt's generalized use of the term shamanism allows for a wide variety of participants in shamanistic practice, from those who have chiefly and perhaps archaic connections to shamanistic rites/rights to those whose possession and insight may be critical of custom and 'traditional' social order. As Eliade noted, Christianity tended to attempt to suppress pre-European shamanistic practices and in Wendt's poetry this suppression is sometimes linked to colonization through Christianity.

In Samoan cosmology Pulotu (the spirit world) is a cosmic zone which co-exists with the human world, and which human spirits may enter after death. Niel Gunson, writing about Tongan history, situated shamanism in 'the dead tradition' of 'traditional material examined or analysed in its own right and not in the context of modern Tonga' (Gunson 1996, 13). However, as both historian and poet, the implied speaker of Wendt's poems understands the taulāitu's messages, interpreting and translating them into new poetic forms. The shaman's role is that of a spirit medium – communicating with spirits and the natural world, moving between heaven, earth and the underworld, past, present and future. In the poem 'Shaman of Visions' the shaman seems to be a separate entity, to whom the poet addresses questions. The taulāitu 'drinks the silence of the bush' in 'The Season of the Moon' and is represented through images of the natural and the pre-papālagi worlds:

> The taulāitu is the season's vessel.
> His flesh bone blood
> are a chart back
> into the light's source.
> ('The Season of the Moon' Wendt 1984, 12)

In *Shamanism, Colonialism and the Wild Man* Michael Taussig describes shamanistic journeys as those which travel 'the space of death . . . a threshold that allows for illumination as well as extinction' (Taussig 1986, 4). His focus on shamanism in the Putumayo region of Colombia leads him to describe the way a 'space of death' has been shaped by the terrors of colonialism, capitalism and dictatorship; a space which is then traversed by the shamanistic journey. The shaman, Taussig argues, is a 'strategic zone of vacuity' – a person who undergoes extreme physical and emotional deprivation, evoked to some degree by drug taking (yage in most of his examples) in order to attain a visionary experience. Shamanism is understood as contemporary practice in Taussig's study, rather than only a historical phenomenon which belongs to an anthropo-logical past or a Europeanized concept of primitivism. Writing and the process of publication, as distinct from the oral performance of shamanism, situates the poet differently to the shaman, though there are important elements of continuity. Ted R. Spivey traces shamanism in modernist poetry through W.B. Yeats and T.S. Eliot – though he argues that because of a modernist loss of faith, they were both shamens manqué (Spivey 1988). Like Wendt, both poets experienced forms of exile from their homelands and according to Spivey, this gave their shamanistic poetry a particular edge, and perhaps precipitated or exacerbated crises of separation and maturation. There is also a parallel to the hollowness Eliot located at the centre of identity in the idea of the shaman as a performer, charlatan or 'sham man'. While Eliot's poetry approached and described the achieved calmness of the meditative state characteristic of shamanism, Yeats' poetry continued to reference a vivid consciousness of desire. Wendt's writing falls somewhere between these two – since at times it sharply evokes the pangs of desire – for love, sex and possessions while at others it evokes tranquillity and the relinquishing of earthly pleasure.

Many of the sacred discourses of shamanism have not been passed on in the printed medium, and if they have, they may remain difficult, if not impossible, to understand or interpret. The aspect of religious ritual is a vital one in shamanism, though for Eliade shamanism is primarily a tech-nique rather than a religion. Modernity's record of the fragmentation and loss of faith(s) is documented in the contemporary poetry of postmod-ernism, a preoccupation Wendt's writing shares. On the other hand, the construction of shamanistic discourse may often have involved the shat-tering and reconstruction of boundaries or taboos. As poetry is preserved, anthologized and canonized for future generations it can become, to some extent, reinvested as relic. Performances may approximate some of the effects of the shamanistic rituals and chanting, which may even include archaic language that cannot be understood by the speaker or audience.

The use of the term shaman in the 1984 collection, rather than the Samoan language term taulāitu, could be said to privilege the inter-national and the postcolonial over the specifically Pacific, Samoan language term. If it does, then it is by way of recognizing the power of the international. While the titles of the collections may suggest writing that is accessible to an international English language audience, there are layers of interpretation and contextual aspects of the poetry that would be more readily available to a Pacific readership.

In some poems the poet/implied speaker seems to be possessed by a discourse that has shamanistic features, such as the esoteric language and fragmentary structure of the title poem of 'Inside Us the Dead'. Since contact, there have been taulāitu who combined Samoan and European belief systems. Freeman's study of the cult of Siovili in 1830 describes him as

> a taula aitu or spirit medium . . . proclaiming that he held intercourse with Jehovah, declaring himself to be possessed by Jesus Christ, claiming sway over spirits, the divine powers of healing the sick and restoring the dead to life, and prophesying with fervour the immi-nence of a better world.   (Freeman 1958, 7)

The study also points to the existence of many mediums in the Siovilian cult, some of whom were 'women and transvestites', locating shamanism as a skill that crosses gender boundaries.

Wendt's fiction has been criticized for its stereotypical representations of women and he has indicated that the course of his writing has been affected by feminist critiques. Many attitudes towards women are explored in the poems – desire, tenderness and love – as well as resentment and aggression. Wendt's work has appeared at a productive time in the history of Pacific literature, a time during which multiple viewpoints have appeared in print. By the 1980s, substantial poetry collections by women such as Konai Helu Thaman, Momoe Malietoa von Reiche, Jully Sipolo and Grace Mera Molisa were circulating. Though special places are often set aside for gender specific activities which become highly significant in literary texts, representations of national, cultural and individual identities in the writing space can often be ambivalent, or in-between, in gender terms. Two poems about a daughter in *Inside Us the Dead* – 'For Sina' and 'Conversation' – represent the fusion of present, past and future. Sina is both the name of the daughter described as 'playing all morning', sleeping then waking to 'breathe the scent/of the falling sky' (Wendt 1976a, 21/28) – and a legendary, mythical name. At times, 'Sina' functions in Samoan cultures as a signifier for woman in general, and at others, as a figure in specific local beliefs, sometimes representing woman in various symbolic forms across Polynesian culture.

Mixed Images and Spatial Metaphors

Many possible descriptions exist in the polylogues of postcoloniality for the spaces encountered in the process of communication: The third space, the space of death, the gap, the womb of space, vā, the lava fields, Vaipe, Oceania, the Void, the abyss, the sublime – locus of ends and beginnings, the point at which languages fail at the edge of meaning, where differends become impossibly manifest. Jonathan Lamb interprets this term of Lyotard's 'différend' as marking 'that point in the investigation of a wrong when the victims find that they are bereft of any phrases of complaint that their opponents would understand or a tribunal admit' (Lamb 1990, 666). The anxiety of New Zealand's cultural history during the 1980s is described as a situation marked by the différend – 'an abyss in language and law, a moment when neither words nor rules operate to arrive at a cognitive judgement' (Lamb 1990, 666). Lamb discusses the way this abyss marks some of the most problematic issues in postcolonial relations between Māori and Pākehā (a person of predominantly

European descent) such as land rights, political structures, legal and linguistic rights, all of which involve the reinterpretation of historical narratives.

Albert Wendt arrived in New Zealand at the age of thirteen and was educated in a system that, although undergoing rapid changes, was still marked by the hierarchies of colonial ideology. The 1960s saw an increase in Māori demands for cultural and economic revival along with a resurgence of anti-colonialist politics and intellectual attitudes shared by Wendt. He studied history at Victoria University in Wellington and worked in the education system in Sāmoa and Fiji and is now Professor of English at the University of Auckland, New Zealand. This mobile life has made him both an insider and an outsider in all three places, a journey the poems reflect and mark. In the collection *Inside Us the Dead* Wendt's periods of residence in Aotearoa/New Zealand, a country that is both homely and uncanny for migrants from other Pacific Islands, are contrasted and reconciled with life in Sāmoa and Fiji. The title of the first collection, dated from 1961 to 1974, refers to the ambivalent relation between the living and the dead and to the way the dead continue to influence the living. In a situation of postcolonization (which includes an awareness of neocolonialism) the dead and living must mutually protect each other since their continuity is under threat not only from the erosions of time but also from the malevolence or at best the negligence of the dominant culture.

Rereading *Inside Us the Dead* in the late 1990s it is apparent that the subject matter of the poems anticipated many of the theoretical concerns of postcolonial and postmodern theory. The poems are marked by the impact of mechanization and modernity. The death of an older brother who has 'a mathematical universe wired/to his computer fingertips' (Wendt 1976a, 12) disrupts and enters the living consciousness of the poet. Japan is set up at the beginning of the collection as the model of a nation that mixes ancient beliefs with a contemporary technological warrior model of masculinity. The young poet/teacher speaker in 'A History Lesson About Japan' rejects binarist logic in favour of Zen Buddhism, identifying also as a nominal Christian but 'by right a pagan' (Wendt 1976a, 2). The suggestion that the speaker identifies with militant defence of paganism is modified by the ironic reflection that 'Only the samurais are safe; they're in books.' Literacy and writing, by implication, become the weapons of the cultural warrior. Religion in the collection is a matter of adding and fusing beliefs rather than choosing one and refusing others.

Signifiers of death are turned back onto European culture while non-

European/indigenous Pacific images are revived and invested with energy. The poem 'Flying-Fox' from *Inside Us the Dead* associates the bat with the most abject of creatures in European culture – 'more rat than bird' (Wendt 1976a, 26). However, the association of the rat in European culture with death and disease is reversed. The bat's energy, its rising out of the darkness, as if from the dead, as though out of the repressed night-mares of colonial history, locate it as a trickster, a symbol of defiance, resistance and continuity. The poetry plays on the fact that the Samoan word for flying-fox is pe'a – a word also used for the tatau or tattoo which symbolizes a mature male sexuality.[4] The bat's upside-downness makes it interpretable as the surfacing of the carnivalesque, an uprising of the repressed of the 'post' of colonial culture.

According to Eliade an encounter with representatives of the under-world like the pe'a is a recurrent feature of shamanic initiation and prac-tice. Plants and animals also inhabit, cross and transform the boundaries of the life/death space. The banyan tree, the lava fields and the pe'a are perhaps the best known symbols in Wendt's writing and all have the effect of making connections across and beyond human concepts of time and space. In 'Lava Field and Road, Savaii' the imagery is apocalyptic. The juxtaposition of road, signifying human activity, and lava field, suggesting natural phenomenon, is extreme. The imaginative space of the poem is the post-nuclear death space, destruction on a grand scale: 'stripped/of the voice of birds', 'the mask/of Hiroshima's twisting from mountain/ ridge to sea'. Yet this desolate landscape, one sometimes read as existen-tialist, remains open to 'the world's/beginning' . . . 'the miracle/of resur-rection when lava decayed/and green fingers broke to su:1' (Wendt 1976a, 23).

In Eliade's terms, shamanic experience begins through a separation from society and a spiritual crisis, of which there are strong traces in *Inside Us the Dead*. The early loss of his mother and transportation to school in New Zealand at the crucial period of adolescence are noted by Wendt himself as having had a profound effect. Physical and psychic separation from the Samoan community took place at a significant age, a threshold period marking the transition between childhood and adulthood. In the most recent collection, *Photographs* (1995a), links are made to the impor-tant figure of the grandmother. She is viewed as a shamanistic connec-tion, story teller and medium of tutorship. Her photograph has been

---

4 For an extended account of the significance of pe'a (tatau, tattoo) see Wendt 1999.

'rephotographed and enlarged to suit the size/of Mele's mythic propor-
tions within our community' and 'she's eternally twenty something'
(Wendt 1995a, 81). In contrast with the implied speaker's consciousness
of ageing, the grandmother's photo remains as mythic mirror or icon,
inspiring devotion, hope and joy. Reminding the reader that photography
is composition and construct, the description of a gallery of family photographs evokes both presence and loss in its presentation of a fragmented
yet enduring version of family history or gafa (lineage, genealogy). Family
histories, genealogies with their multiple branches and origins disrupt
official, linear versions of history. The elements of gafa in the poems
zigzag across time periods, making connections between different generations and countries.

In *Photographs* Wendt made explicit a poetic method of image layering
he had been developing (in a photographic sense) throughout his career.

> Historial materialism wishes to retain that image of the past which
> unexpectedly appears to man as it flashes up at a moment of danger.
> The danger affects both the content of the tradition and its receivers.
> The same threat hangs over both: that of becoming a tool of the ruling
> classes.   (Benjamin 1969, 255)

In order to explore the historical function of shamanism (what he calls
'sorcery as history') Taussig evokes Roland Barthes' distinction between
signs and images, 'obvious' and 'obtuse' meaning. In the latter, images
seem 'to open the field of meaning totally, that is infinitely' (Taussig 1986,
366). Taussig then steers his study of shamanism and colonialism through
Walter Benjamin's discussion of the importance of images in historical
memory. Taking Benjamin's description of the suspended image: a
'magically empowered image flashing forth in a moment of danger'
(the 'magically' is Taussig's) (Taussig 1986, 367) Taussig moves on to
suggest that montage, an artistic characteristic of the technological age, is
capable of representing, like dream imagery, a series of dialectical images
that can evoke and represent the repressed. In this way he assembles an
explanation for the way shamanic practice, with its dream-like evocation
of images and hallucinations which call up repressed elements of
historical discourse, disrupts the closure of historical narrative. Frac-
turing the fluency of historical accounts is a way of installing doubt, diversity and distance into narratives of colonization, inserting myth and
distance into the sequential logic of chronology.

Lamb argues in favour of the deployment of Nietzschean *wirkliche
Geschichte* or 'effective history' in which the aim is 'the typically

modernist derangement of the cognitive approach to the truths of historical process' (Lamb 1990, 669). 'Effective history' focuses on the most 'unique characteristic' of an event, an event as a 'reversal of a relationship of forces, the usurpation of power, the appropriation of a vocabulary turned against those who had once used it' (Foucault 1977, 154). It is precisely this 'uniqueness' of the event that the poet struggles to preserve. The poet is aware – like Benjamin's images 'frozen at a moment of danger' and his recognition of the importance of the loss of the aura of ritual in an age of 'mechanical reproduction' – that what is assembled in each rereading of a poem or viewing of a photograph is a representation of the moment/event. But for the moment of a reading or a viewing, the frozen images, the cliches, the stereotypes can be momentarily unfrozen, reanimated, rearranged so as to effect a different outcome.

Experienced in matters of cross-cultural trade and exchange, Wendt has consistently attempted in the poetry to negotiate between a refusal to regard tradition as unalterable and a recognition that (sometimes unavoidable) changes undertaken without due respect for custom may have dire and unpredictable effects. Writing across vā – a term which predates colonialism – or into a 'third space' means that the synthesized position will contain new ambivalences rather than a final and homogenized identity. An example from *Shaman of Visions* can show how the concept (vā) works in poetic practice. In 'Three Poems for Kenzaburo Oe', the second poem comments on the linguistic and historical connection between Samoan and Japanese: 'In Samoan your name means "You"' (Wendt 1984, 10). The poem is conversational, dialogic; Oe replies 'No wonder/I have always considered myself/ an alienated man –'. The second poem in the triptych focuses on the split consciousness of the individual (never 'I' but always 'You') and opens out into the third term/third person through paternal relations, a meditation on the relationship between Oe and his son in the third poem.

Wendt's poetry recognizes the openness of the trajectory of individual lives; the poem 'Inside Us the Dead' 'ends' or is suspended with lines that suggest the impossibility of knowing what the future will hold, but maintaining the necessity of gambling on the future in any case: 'the wheel spinning/spun the white dew/of prophecy: the ball/coming down/to stone,/(breaking)' (Wendt 1976a, 14). This reference to a modernist recognition of fragmentation can equally be read as a gesture towards the Samoan local mythology, in which legendary figures or evidence of their passing are said to have been turned to stone. It can also be read as signifying a return to origins in which the first act of Tagaloaalagi (translated in *Shaman of Visions* as 'Supreme God') was to create rock. Eliade

mentions instances in Siberia when the gods' choice of shaman was indicated by stones falling from the sky. (Eliade 1964, 19).

The function of the 'ava (kava, a shrub or drink) ceremony as a form of
social release and control can be compared with the use of hallucinogenic
drugs in many forms of shamanism. Shamanistic ceremonies in Taussig's
account are rituals that can involve small or large numbers of participants
and they are an event where the outcome cannot be predicted. As such,
they constitute a break in the narrative held together by ideology and can
cause a reordering or reconsideration of the dominant discourse, though
most commonly they signify at least a gap or failure of the logic and order
of the dominant. Significantly, the 'ava ceremony has become an oblique
reference in Wendt's poetry rather than a unifying symbol, since the
poet's position as insider/outsider means that concepts of social unity are
constantly questioned. In poems such as 'A History Lesson about Japan'
and 'Why Can't They Stop' the implied speaker critiques established
histories and ideologies – both those of Western culture and of the fa'a
Sāmoa (Samoan Way).

The sinnet symbolizes the bond between leaders and people, gods,
humans, the past and the present. In *Inside Us the Dead* it is 'the sinnet of
myth' ('Inside Us the Dead'), in the hands of the decrepit 'Old men, in
fale, spin/death out of words,/angels they weave from sinnet' ('The
Pastor'). It can also signify a substance which links objects, people and
places to each other in the present: 'Once, in the time of omens, this
conch shell/dangled from a sinnet thread/in the miraculous light of a
palm grove' ('Conch Shell'). The calling up of the spirits by blowing the
pū or conch is done at the daughter's request by the papalagi wife. The
sound conjures up awe and fear for the implied speaker, because the aitu
(spirits) are a powerful present absence. He must cross the space of death,
the womb of space or 'the Void' as it is called in the poem. Alcohol –
whisky, cocktails – consumed individually or in groups substitutes (inade-
quately) for the collective function of the rituals in which 'ava is
produced and consumed. In 'The Faa-Samoa is Perfect, They Sd' neither
the intoxicated speaker accused of being 'too fiapalagi' (i.e. too like a
European) whose social critique is refused and can only tell his accusers to
'fuck off' (though this might be called an achievement in itself), nor the
representatives of tradition the poetic 'I' finds smothering, can speak on
behalf of a united Samoan community. The significance of the poem lies
in the (drunken?) dialectic, into which antagonism, envy, dissatisfaction
and desire can intervene to disrupt the platitudinous ideologies of nationalism, alofa (love) and righteous living.

Taussig locates some of the explanation for the overwhelming emotions of fear and envy in those who seek shamanic assistance in the shift from feudalism to capitalism: a shift produced through the exigencies of colonialism, marked by stark inequalities, social and political unease. The colonialism in Sāmoa and New Zealand experienced and described by Wendt has some significant parallels with Taussig's account. As a collection, *Inside Us the Dead* can be read as an attempt to exorcise and understand the injustices and inequalities perpetuated into the so called postcolonial era. Some poems attempt to reconcile anger at the legacy of colonial systems with the love for papālagi individuals and the acceptance of some of the more desirable aspects of European cultures. Marriage in *Inside Us the Dead* has personal, public and symbolic dimensions, as does divorce and falling in love with a new partner in *Photographs*.

Illness, which can be understood as the wound the shaman carries – the external evidence of crossing the space of death – has many possible explanations, among them the material. Physical excess and the demands of a modern life style are recognized as potentially destructive at both personal and public level. In 'God's Road For the Middle Aged', an aunt tells the speaker, hospitalized with an ulcer, 'if living means/eating up the mileage of God's road/ahead then you've been driving too fast' (Wendt 1984, 30). Beside Jesus as the Christian prototype of prophet and perhaps shaman, the poem lists the damaged cultural heroes of the times – Mao, Nkrumah, Sukarno, Ho Chi Minh, Che, Bob Dylan and Elvis. Another poem 'Where the Mind Is, or, A Conversation with My Mind' consists of lists of popular icons, a confessional which mixes brand names with politicians' names, academic degrees with Tarzan and Mickey Mouse, exploring the mind as a shopping mall or waste heap piled up with the stored junk products of modern life. Shamanism as esoteric language here is not an example of the retention of archaic elements, but an outpouring of cultural signifiers severed from their signifieds so that they now appear archaic – elements of a twentieth-century lifestyle which is already worn out.

Awesome

'How do you split a lifetime's imagery?' asks the poem 'Photographs' (Wendt 1995a, 78). The split images are not only of the broken marriage, though it is a recurrent theme in the collection; there are also the divisions and distances of diasporic families, of divided national and cultural loyalties, and the losses that inevitably occur over time. Snapshots in family albums, publicity shots, the movies, paintings; all remind the viewer/implied speaker of the absence of those subjects who feature in them and the changes moving rapidly across life. *Photographs* preserves in verbal pictures, panoramas, snapshots and portraits the fragility and strength of 'aiga, family, love, agape and eros, landscapes in volcanic, city-scapes and sea-swept settings. It reveals the growth of extended narrative and epic forms and is the most self-conscious of the collections about a method of mixing the mythic with the documentary.

The collection *Photographs* plays on the etymology of the word 'album'. From the Latin *albus*, white, it is a book originally blank, used for preserving photographs, views, portraits. *Photographs* continues and extends the technique of montage and the shamanic metaphor:

> Since I started stepping out with Reina
> three years ago so to speak like the 1950s
> we've bought a Korean camera that needs no instructing
> and filled four fat albums with photographs.
> ('In Reina's Albums' Wendt 1995a, 83)

The book's title suggests a combination of writing and light to produce images – a kind of picture writing – and also suggests the 'moving pictures' of film. Thematically, the collection balances the continuity of legend, myth and symbol against the recognition that life, and time, are unique and unrepeatable. Though the collection is peopled with names, experiences, flashing images of good times, it also explores absence, loss and the tensions of living in the present. What Jonathan Lamb has described as Lyotard's focus on 'a feeling of intense expectation, an exacting, vigilant awaiting' (Lamb 1990, 666) – in which awareness of the sublime – or the vā space – surfaces – is an essential element in a reading of Wendt's poetry.

The opening poem of *Photographs* – a collection recording the joy of love as well as the bitterness of divorce – is called 'Summer Wedding' and it describes the speaker's preparation for a daughter's wedding – the hot day, the pleasure of ice-cold beer. It is a poem of celebration and conciliation, referring to the wedding ritual as a tradition in a painterly layering of disparate images, 'an embryo cauled in fire a Van Gogh/ sunflower the succulent yellow of kina' (Wendt, 1995a, 3), combining a chant of sun worship with epithalamium. The poem celebrates the process of preparing for and awaiting the new. A personal dedication (for Sina and Johnny) provokes questions about what relationship the daughter has to the mythological Sina and the perceptive, enquiring child of earlier poems.

The trees in the garden can be read as symbolizing a cultural mixing, though each is represented in its separate space, linked by the creepers, which in Samoan belief and in shamanistic discourse are axis mundi, plants which connect the separate realms of earth, heaven and under-world: 'a peach tree/a gum tree creepers and ponga' and 'the young pohu-tukawa'.[5] Although it is barely referenced, the cosmogenic narrative reinforces the importance of the death/rebirth imagery of the shaman in the poem.

The poem 'Nightflight' consists of a sequence of twenty-two poems, linked by theme, image and symbol. The nightflight, a journey from Guangzhou to Sydney, becomes the metaphor for an extended medita-tion on history, language, (popular) culture and the body. 'Nightflight', like a dream, unfolds with its own internal logic, the spacing between words and phrases evoking geographical and historical distances trav-elled, the gap between signifier and signified, and what Benjamin calls the 'leap in the open air of history' – except that, characteristically, there is an ironic awareness in Wendt's poetry that this leap or flight takes place in the technologically controlled environment of an aircraft (Benjamin 1969, 261). Flight in the aircraft can also be recognised as, and contrasted with, the spiritual flight of the shaman.

In Taussig's account of shamanism, colonial views are frequently still dominant. The contemporary shaman is modelled on a European version of the native as spiritualized other. However, in the process of shamanic ceremony, the shaman can expose colonial versions of history to the critique of a more open-ended and open-universe model of discourse. Shamanism's links to oral tradition and performance disrupt monological concepts of chronology and identity. Wendt's collections acknowledge the power of the 'Capitalist mish-/mash of symbolic suffering/and Holly-wood stereotypes' (Wendt 1995b, 64). Each collection, like the single poem 'Nightflight', makes a montage out of the enormously varied stimuli experienced by the poet in the contemporary world. In 'Nightflight', contrasting elements such as the officially approved art of Chinese communism (the film *Backlight*), scenes and dialogue from a Hollywood

---

[5]   In the cosmogenic beliefs of Sāmoa, Fue, a creeper or vine, is the source of human life. When Fue was sent by Tagaloaalagi to weigh down the trees as they began to approach his heavenly domain too closely, the creeper grew so profusely that he crowded out the food-bearing trees and was in turn crowded out by another tree sent by Tagaloaalagi. Felled, Fue rotted, producing large worms/maggots which Tagaloaalagi's servant Gaio was sent down to earth to turn into humans (this version from Stuebel and Bro 1987, 101).

movie *Runaway Train* and identification with the traveller/translator
Xuanzang, whose cargo of sutras from India the Big Wild Goose Pagoda in
Xi'an was built to house, call attention to the poem's mixed bag of signs
and imagery. References to Borges and Calvino as (past) 'masters of the
calligraphy/of spells and magic' invite a comparison between the holistic
practice of the art of calligraphy and poetry writing. The view of Chinese
landscape and culture is of necessity that of an outsider, and recycles some
of the generalized global images/ideas about China:

> mountains that
> float in mist like opium . . .   (Wendt 1995a, 62)

Yet these repetitions function like the flashing images Benjamin
describes and the stereotype as Bhabha understands it in which it is
ambivalent: 'a form of knowledge and identification that vascillates
between what is always "in place" already known, and something that
must be anxiously repeated' (Bhabha 1994, 66). This record of an
encounter with Chinese culture works to undercut and sideline the
effects of dominant European colonial legacies, as do the continuing
revelations of proximity to Māori culture in the poems. The foregrounding of the non-European takes place in terms of content, symbol
and form. And, as Wendt himself has argued, in an on-going process of
decolonization, Pacific writers indigenize the English language.

The final poem of the *Photographs* collection 'Te-One-Roa-A-Tohe'
(the footsteps of Tohe) (Wendt 1995b, 88–9) depicts the poet and his
lover Reina in relation to the beach named in the title – the Pakeha name
being 'The Ninety Mile Beach'. The choice of the Māori name emphasizes the poet's commitment to Māori language and cultural values. The
beach in question has long been used as a road by the living, as it still is
today, and it is also the pathway taken by the spirits of the dead as they
move towards their resting place in the ancient homeland, Hawaiiki. In
the history of Pacific literature, the beach is an in-between zone, a
boundary space marking divisions, but also the crossing over between life
and death, the local and the foreign. The landscape is too broad, 'no
camera can take in one shot/the whole stretch' – just as no single perspective can capture the lives of the many communities whose dead leap from
land's end at the headland known as 'Te Rerenga Wairua'. The sublime
landscape of 'Te-One-Roa-A-Tohe' is contrasted with that of 'the Fafa at
Falealupo/where the La sets and the Po begins' (the sun sets and the night
begins). In this juxtapositioning of images, Wendt brings together
Aotearoa/New Zealand and Sāmoa and closes the collection with a salute

to the power of the goddess Nafanua, whose temple offers a space to the people of Falealupo in times of trouble, consolation and hope:

> They leave one row of blinds facing the west raised
> for Nafanua to enter for the inventive consultation
> Her direct descendant is now Cardinal of Polynesia
> Outlawed atua have surprising ways of conquering the present
> (Wendt 1995a)

Note

Samoan language terms according to R.W. Allardice, 1985, *A Simplified Dictionary of Modern Samoan* (Auckland: Polynesian Press).

Works Cited

Allardice, R.W. 1985. *A Simplified Dictionary of Modern Samoan*, Auckland: Polynesian Press.

Alley, Elizabeth and Williams, Mark eds 1992. 'Albert Wendt interviewed by Michael Neill', *In the Same Room*, Auckland: Auckland University Press.

Benjamin, Walter 1969. *Illuminations*, New York: Schocken.

Bhabha, Homi 1994. *The Location of Culture*, London: Routledge.

Eliade, Mircea 1964. *Shamanism*, Princeton, NJ: Princeton University Press.

Foucault, Michel 1977. 'Nietszche, Genealogy, History', in D.F. Bouchard (ed.) *Language, Counter-Memory, Practice*, Ithaca: Cornell University Press.

Freeman, J.D. 1958. 'The Joe Gimlet, or Siovili Cult: An Episode in the Religious History of Early Samoa', Department of Anthropology and Sociology, Australian National University, Canberra.

Furst, Peter 1994. 'Introduction: An Overview of Shamanism', in Gary Seaman and Jane Day (eds) *Ancient Traditions*, Colorado: University of Colorado and Denver Museum of Natural History.

Gunson, Neil 1996. 'Tongan Historiography: Shamanic Views of Time and History', in J. Herd, J. Terrell, Niel Gunson (eds) *Tongan Culture and History*, Canberra: Australian National University, 12–20.

Harris, Wilson 1983. *The Womb of Space*, London: Greenwood Press.

Hau'ofa, Epeli 1997. 'The Ocean In Us', *Dreadlocks in Oceania* Vol. 1. Suva: University of the South Pacific, 124–48.

Lamb, Jonathan 1990. 'The New Zealand Sublime', *Meanjin*, Vol. 49, No. 4, 597–606.

Mara, Ratu Sir Kamisese 1997. *The Pacific Way*, Honolulu: University of Hawai'i Press.

Ministry for Youth, Sports and Cultural Affairs 1994. *Samoa Ne'i Galo*, Vol. 1, Auckland, NZ.

Pratt, M.L. 1992. *Imperial Eyes*, London: Routledge.

Sharrad, Paul 1994. 'Making Beginnings: Johnny Frisbie and Pacific Literature', *New Literary History*, Vol. 25, No.1, 121–36.

Spivey, Ted R. 1988. *Beyond Modernism*, London: University Press of London.

Steubel, C. and Bro, Herman 1987. *Tala o le Vavau*, Auckland: Polynesian Press.

Subramani 1985. *South Pacific Literature*, Suva: University of the South Pacific.

Taussig, Michael 1986. *Shamanism, Colonialism, and the Wild Man*, Chicago: University of Chicago Press.

Thomas, Nicholas and Humphries, Caroline 1994. *Shamanism, History and the State* (Ann Arbor: University of Michigan Press.

Wendt, Albert 1976a. *Inside Us The Dead*, Auckland: Longman Paul.

——— 1976b.'Towards A New Oceania', *Mana Review* Vol. 1, No. 1, 49–60.

——— 1984. *Shaman of Visions*, Auckland: Auckland University Press.

——— 1995a. *Photographs*, Auckland: Auckland University Press.

——— ed. 1995b. *Nuanua*, Auckland: Auckland University Press.

——— 1999. 'Afterword: Tatauing the Post-Colonial Body', Vilsoni Hereniko and Rob Wilson (eds) *Inside Out*, Maryland: Rowman and Littlefield, 399–412.

The Necessity of Error:
Memory and Representation
in the New Literatures

DENNIS WALDER

ONE OF THE WAYS in which the 'new literatures' may be thought of as new is in the prominence they give to the politics of the present. Literatures, like societies, from time to time seek legitimation; and the new literatures, like many of the societies out of which they have emerged, are interested in finding new ideas about the relation between the present and the past, the individual and the community, truth and reality. Literary and cultural criticism in recent years has been steadily drawn towards an exploration of boundaries, which has allowed an expansion of what has been validated as counting in the study of literature without however always taking into account the implications of that expansion. In what follows, I want to seek out some of the implications of reading the new literatures in the present – a present defined to some extent in terms of my personal history, interests and concerns as a South African academic long resident in Britain.

If it seems indecorous to refer to myself, my defence is that it is worse than indecorous, indeed culpable, to pretend to be objective when what I am writing about has an obvious and specific claim upon former colonials like myself, hovering between detachment and complicity, and provoked by the political impotence and historical amnesia of postmodernist criticism. In what follows, I want to tease out some implications of reading texts with various claims upon the rubric of 'new literatures' in the context of the anti-foundationalist assumptions which most commonly underlie the politics of representation and memory – a politics of acute interest in particular places today, from Cape Town to Sarajevo. Our lives are not just inextricably bound up with signs and texts, but with signs and texts of power, as Nietzsche saw. This is something to remember not to forget. Hence, in claiming to read the new literatures today we cannot avoid certain implications to do with the position of the reader, as well as the nature of the read(ing). For a start, it is impossible to avoid asking who 'we' are. That is to say, the position of the speaker needs to be articulated, if not at once, then at least in the course of production. These metaphors suggest the nearness of my interest to the theatrical mode, a mode present as performance, while also always having already existed as a text, or preceding script, of some kind. But if I can say I wish to focus on what is variously defined as drama, theatre, and performance, this is because of what this cultural mode of representation means as a critical force in the present, in South Africa; but also, by analogy, in many other countries struggling to redefine themselves in moments of striking transformation or crisis.

Now that South Africa is bent on a new course, as a multiracial democracy, questions have arisen about the continuing role of the theatre, as part of a questioning of the role of the arts and culture in society generally. This questioning, in the context of the struggle to deal with the country's recent past, is what provides the context in which I want to address the reading of new literatures. I make no excuse for focusing upon South African theatrical production (although I will touch on other matters and other texts), while being aware of the tendency towards special pleading or parochialism which such a specific focus often attracts; on the contrary, it is precisely because of my own sense of the need to acknowledge my inevitable errors, that I wish to address what is familiar to me – if distanced to some extent by my exilic status and professional commitments, the result of my personal journey from Cape to Cairo, and beyond.

Many years ago, before anybody had heard of him, the South African playwright Athol Fugard found himself invited to define his position. The circumstances were these. He had dropped out of the University of Cape Town shortly after the start of his third year BA, and with his friend the poet Perseus Adams had set out to hitchhike from Cape to Cairo, with about 30 pounds and ten tins of sardines between them. Why Cape to Cairo? There was a brand of cigarettes then on sale in Cape Town called 'C to C', Cape to Cairo. 'That seemed like a pretty good idea, so you can gather our imaginations weren't very fertile' (qtd Vandenbroucke 1985, 7). Like many aspiring writers of the early 1950s (and later), the two were acting out the cultural memory of Anglophone imperialism, still traceable in Rhodes's famous phrase embodying his dream of painting the map red from Cape to Cairo.

The two actually did reach Cairo, where colonial presumption met one of the boundaries established by the 'new' nations of Africa: they were arrested as illegal immigrants, and sent back to the Sudan. But Fugard was a slippery customer: he had already talked his way into one lift by saying he was the Pope's emissary in Africa; and while in the Sudanese capital Khartoum, he inveigled an invitation to address a group of students at Gordon University. Having just been studying philosophy,

Fugard thought he would talk about that. But his student audience were more interested in politics. 'They asked me the reasons for the white man's attitude in the Union and I gave in. I told them the situation was more complicated than they presumed. Bottles rained down on me from all sides, and the lecture devolved into a riot' (Vandenbroucke 1985, 7).

As Fugard's career proceeded, he was to learn how to negotiate more effectively with his audiences, drawing on their experiences so as to cross the race boundaries which, in his own country, had become deeply entrenched, however 'complicated' the situation. His chosen genre, theatre, had the potential to allow collaboration and exchange of a kind unique among the literary-cultural forms available then – and now. Moreover, as he was among the first in his country to demonstrate, its potential as a means of crossing boundaries, and resisting prevailing ideologies, was to become of great importance, as many groups arose to challenge the laws of the country as they challenged the cultural conventions which helped to underwrite them.

Fugard's Khartoum dodge did not succeed: neither philosophy nor politics would enable him to engage his audience. We now know that his *métier* was literature. Nor am I going to engage directly with either philosophy, or politics; rather, I want to address the space in between, because that is where I find literature, including the new literatures. That is to say, I am proposing a recognizable presence, which now seems to many critics either lacking or fragmented, or overtaken by the term 'postcolonial' – a term I have happily used myself, while attempting to suggest the advantages and disadvantages of doing so (Walder 1998). According to Bruce King, it is one of the ironies of recent literary history that 'the new national literatures had barely begun to find a place on the cultural map before they were shoved aside, or said to be oppressive and dominant, by the post-colonial deconstruction of national culture', with the result that 'the study of post-colonial theory replaced the study of post-colonial literature' (King 1996, 17).

This may seem a rather crude exaggeration, but perhaps there is some truth in it. In any case, I will not be addressing the issue of the status and authority of the term 'postcolonial', since although no thinking person can now take it up without unease, I see no reason to avoid engaging with the literary or cultural artefacts, and the approaches they invite, which the term may still evoke. 'New literatures' has the advantage of evoking the literary dimension of cultural activity, as well as foregrounding the issue of (national) identity, without obliging us to adopt a predominantly theoretical posture; although of course theoretical considerations come with the territory. But the formulaic way in which attending to the new literatures has emerged within academic discourse must give pause for thought to all of us who belong to academic institutions which, while long considered a source of values, traditions and authority on the one hand, and critically new truths on the other, seem to many to no longer exert real authority or autonomy (see e.g., Clark and Royle 1995).

I want to return to the space I have rather loosely identified, between philosophy and politics, as the space where you may find or at least recognise the new literatures; and where the role of theatre can suggest the larger role(s) of literature. I am going to refer to plays (although not exclusively plays) for reasons I have already given, but also because I am assuming that my reader is not like, say, Cassius in *Julius Caesar* who, as Caesar points out in Act One, scene 2, is dangerous because he 'loves no plays'. Cassius is a late sixteenth-century English puritan in Roman disguise, and the puritans, of course, wanted to close the theatres. They still do. Why? Because the theatre is conspicuously where you enjoy yourself, where you play; where there is beauty and sensuality, where taboos are broken, and boundaries crossed; where you do not find 'truth' – indeed, where you are more likely to find 'error'. When the Cape education authority instructed schools to burn copies of Athol Fugard's *Boesman and Lena* (1969) in 1984, they did so because of the use in that play by the desperate Cape Coloured couple at its centre, of words like 'kak' ('shit') and 'moer' ('cunt'), words in everyday use among Cape schoolchildren of all languages and races, but which, by their appearance in a set text, challenged the boundary between the familiar reality of children's lives, and the narrow world of their education (the words are now available in the new *Dictionary of South African English on Historical Principles* 1996). And when the South African Publications Board first banned *'Master Harold'* . . . *and the Boys* (1982), four months before it was due to open in Johannesburg, it was ostensibly for the use of similar words, although I suspect more likely because one of the black performer's reaction to a racist joke is to expose his bare backside to the audience – thus crossing an even more profound and entrenched boundary. The gesture was an error, which would, and did (the play when it was eventually allowed to appear, caused a furore) remind audiences of a truth.

I will come back to these terms, which I am recalling from Nietzsche. My point here is that puritans and Calvinists alike prefer to keep things within definable boundaries, they prefer their Bottoms in trousers – in the United Kingdom in 1999 a version of *Midsummer Night's Dream* in which Bottom was rampant with Titania caused a fuss, and demand for a ban on school parties going to the production. Whereas plays are typically in-between things. So, too, are literary works more generally, as cultural and linguistic products which share a family resemblance with many other forms of communication. But it is the in-betweenness of literary works, their hovering between what we often blithely call truth and forget we also call error, with the result that they have no *final* meaning, that I want to emphasize; and I want to use some examples, especially of plays, to suggest what I mean.

After all, plays by generic definition cross the boundaries of writer, text, performer and audience in order to reach completion, even momentarily. Their existence is contingent – but not therefore ephemeral, as Shakespeare has proved: 'So long as men can breathe and eyes can see/So long lives this, and this gives life to thee' (sonnet 18). So far in South Africa, perhaps only the San oral performance art can compete with the longevity of those lines from 400 years ago. I'm thinking of the San song which was rendered by the nineteenth-century German philologist W.H.I. Bleek as 'The Broken String', and then more recently by Cape poet Stephen Watson as 'Xaa-ttin's Lament' (Watson 1991, 61). If such thin echoes of the long past can survive, there is hope for the survival of other works, their listeners and rememberers.

One of the most important boundaries crossed by artworks in general, by literary works in particular, and, most strikingly by the specific phenomenon of theatre, is that between the past and the present (Gadamer 1995, 3–53). Theatre pre-eminently among cultural products designated as literary exists in the present, as an event, as a specific performance in time; but the event, the performance itself, depends upon a pre-existing text or work of some kind. We are all aware on some level of the past in the present: otherwise we couldn't begin to understand what we see. Memory makes us who we are, and enables us to think, as the sad cases of amnesiacs documented by neurologist Oliver Sacks may remind us (1986). But there is also a continuity of past and present on another level, a continuity made visible by more than self-reflection, by the collective memory, by what one might call *historical* awareness. Hegel said that the historical spirit consists not in the *restoration* of the past, but in the *thoughtful mediation* of the past in the present. Without memory, individual and collective, that mediation is impossible. As Jay Naidoo puts it: 'The past lives on in the present, through genes and culture, through ideas and traditions; and the present, because the past has to be filtered through a temporal present, lives on in the past' (1989, 9–10). It is the *way* we remember the past in the present, I would add, that enables us to re-member ourselves in the present. This is as true of critics and teachers, as it is of 'normal' human beings.

As the St Lucian poet Derek Walcott reminds us, there is a sense in which 'history is fiction, subject to a fitful muse, memory' (1998, 37). Servitude to the muse of memory in the new societies of the Caribbean, Walcott says, has produced 'a literature of recrimination and despair, a literature of revenge written by the descendants of slaves or a literature of remorse written by the descendants of masters' (Walcott 1998, 37). There has been a parallel trend in the literary production of South Africa, another 'new' society, where, as a result of the modern form of enslavement known as apartheid, there has also been what may be called a literature of revenge and a literature of remorse: a binary or polarised rhetoric which has developed over the decades since 1960, a rhetoric which registered on the one hand, how badly people had been treated as victims of the system, or, on the other, how remorseful or at least guilty those felt who belonged to the ruling groups. The South African writer and critic Njabulo Ndebele's remarks along these lines in his influential essay 'Redefining Relevance', which appeared at the height of the crisis in apartheid in 1986 (1991, 58–73), retain their potency, as does his argument that there must be more open ways of imagining the present in relation to the past than has commonly been the case in South African writings, at least until the 1980s. Yet there were exceptions to this gloomy account, even among South African writers, evidenced, for example, in the more self-critical and exploratory work of Fugard, for instance his maligned and neglected play *Dimetos* (1975) – maligned and neglected for its focus upon the inner torments of the semi-mythical artist-figure of the title, rather than any kind of explicit reaction to the external disasters then overtaking the country.

What we need now might be a stronger sense of the relevance of representing interiority, of the inner life of memory and reflection which, it has long been felt among South African critics, if not more widely, should be downplayed, if it should be acknowledged at all, so as not to interfere with the progressive agenda. This aspect of literary, and particularly theatrical production, has commonly been identified with the dissenting, guilty and remorseful figure of the descendants of the masters, a figure once represented by the so-called 'white liberal' writer, such as Fugard (or Nadine Gordimer), but which in post-1990 South Africa has become more widespread. What both Walcott and Ndebele have identified in their different societies, linked however by the common experiences of colonialism, is the way present agendas, agendas of revenge or despair, dominance or remorse, have shaped the past to serve our present ends.

Whereas, in Walcott's words, 'The truly tough aesthetic of the New World neither explains nor forgives history' (1998, 37). This seems to imply that history is after all a monolithic construct, which we must be tough enough to face without complaint or guilt, as we clamber over it with the grappling hooks of our individual memories, like tiny figures trying to tie down a Gulliver. As my imagery suggests, while there may be something deeply attractive about developing the tough aesthetic recommended by Walcott, an aesthetic which transcends our present rewritings of the past by attempting neither to explain nor forgive history, it is nonetheless difficult to look calmly upon the past, when that past involves, amongst other things, South African memories – memories which cry out for explanation and, yes, remorse and maybe even forgiveness. I stress 'maybe' and 'even'; I wonder if resolution is not a better word – some things cannot be forgiven, torture and the abuse of children, for example.

Perhaps I am not alone in having an obsession with disembodied truth, created in my case by futile attempts to hold together the wildly different and contradictory versions of my own family history fed to me by my parents before I could distinguish fantasy and reality – not that I am sure I can now. But families rely on constructing fictions for survival. The past cannot be put together like a jigsaw puzzle, but always involves shifting memories, experiences and interpretations, a merging of truth and error, as Proust above all other writers reminds his readers, from the first sentence of A la recherche du temps perdu, where the involuntary associations of the past bring barely tangible, fleeting experiences to produce the reality of the self in the present. As Paul de Man suggests, in a characteristically nuanced reading of Proust's figurative language, from the start we have to deal with 'light and dark, truth and error, wake and sleep, perception and dream . . . As a writer, Proust is the one who knows that the hour of truth, like the hour of death, never arrives on time, since what we call time is precisely truth's inability to coincide with itself' (de Man 1979, 60, 78). Involuntary, unwilled remembering is perhaps what has made me feel, after almost all the actors in my family drama have died, that some things cannot be forgotten, although maybe they should be, maybe they will be. Maybe life cannot continue without forgetting. After all, as a well-known Borges story reminds us, memory is always also forgetting.

That Borges story, 'Funes the Memorious', is the story of a man who never forgot anything. Through Funes, Borges shows how if everything is retained in its fullest detail, everything is unique, and there can be no way one thing can signify for any other. Without the abbreviation essential to a symbolic communication system, you would have to have a linguistic model of the world precisely equal in size and detail to the world. There is a nice illustration of this point in Borges's sample of seventeenth-century scientific, truth-telling discourse, taken, apparently, from a book entitled Travels of Praiseworthy Men, by a certain J.A. Suarez Miranda. The excerpt is headed 'Of Exactitude in Science', and it is about cartography, or mapping, a form of knowledge which developed alongside, as it helped to ensure, the rise of the European empires, including the Spanish empire in South America, Borges'own place. Cartography is crucial for exploration, exploitation and control of territory. Here is the entire piece:

> In that Empire, the craft of Cartography attained such Perfection that the Map of a single Province covered the space of an entire City, and the Map of the Empire itself an entire Province. In the course of Time, these extensive Maps were found somehow wanting, and so the College of Cartographers evolved a Map of the Empire that was of the same Scale as the Empire and that coincided with it point for point. Less attentive to the Study of Cartography, succeeding Generations came to judge a map of such magnitude Cumbersome, and, not without Irreverence, they abandoned it to the Rigours of sun and Rain. In the western Deserts, tattered Fragments of the Map are still to be found, Sheltering an occasional Beast or beggar; in the whole Nation, no other relic is left of the Discipline of Geography.
> (Borges 1975, 131)

Because the map takes up all the room there is, there is no margin between sign and signified, for signification to occur. In the same way, the kind of language needed by a memory incapable of forgetting would use up all the space, the internal space of consciousness, of thinking – which in the end amounts to the loss of all significance, and meaninglessness. For thought, for language to function, there has to be a partial forgetting, creating as it were an empty background for figuration.

But figuration, that is, the metaphoric articulation of language, is, as Nietzsche pointed out, continually undermining sense. Not only does memory always involve forgetting, it doesn't bring the truth; being partial, memory also brings error. You cannot have truth without error, the one defines the other, as Western philosophy has been saying since at least the seventeenth century, the time of the scientific revolution and Descartes, who created the central paradox of enlightened, humanist thought: the paradox that in the search for universal truths, we find there is nothing we can know finally and without doubt – and even when the very capacity to doubt presupposes the fact of existence or self-consciousness, we find ourselves wondering at the circularity of the Cartesian logic which insists upon that fact. Of course I am simplifying complex philosophical developments here, but I am doing so in order to highlight the explosive and lasting effect which Nietzsche's words had and still have – an explosive effect which set off the tremors undermining traditional humanist discipline areas like English studies for some time now, through the speculations of 'theorists', many of whom rely on Nietzsche without knowing it.

One of Nietzsche's most explosive contributions to the West's understanding of itself may be found in the so-called 'Attempt at Self-Criticism' he added to his first book, *The Birth of Tragedy* (1872) in 1886. Here, in an extreme version of the characteristic self-doubt which was coming to unhinge many Western thinkers during the nineteenth century, Nietzsche casually concluded that 'all life is based on appearance, art, deception, point of view, the necessity of perspective and error' (Nietzsche 1993, 8).

All life depends on 'the necessity of perspective and error'. Like Borges, Nietzsche takes us beyond the deep-seated presuppositions of what conventionally passes for truth. He is undermining the very idea of truth itself, anticipating the postmodern project of undermining the foundations of modernism, and all traditional, post-Enlightenment distinctions between disciplines, logic and thought, the disciplines which have shaped the idea of the university, as they have helped create the power-structures expressed in such institutions. The collapse of the traditional Western framework of thought signalled by Nietzsche, sweeps away foundational ways of thinking, according to which, for example, there is an objective order of values which we can discern through the use of universal reason, and which teachers can pass down to their students. The kind of art this postmodern project produces is characterised by a plurality of perspectives, by pastiche and collage, since it is derived (consciously or not) from the Nietzschean idea that art does not belong to any fixed or unitary frame of reference, but is part of a flow of experience both arbitrary and fragmentary. Styles and genres are juxtaposed with effects both fascinating and shocking, trivial and boring. Elements from different periods and epochs are torn from their contexts to be recycled and put together, creating ironic and cynical effects. This is the stuff of Western experimental art and its followers worldwide since the early 1960s, celebrated by postmodern gurus such as Jean-Francois Lyotard, and Jean Baudrillard, for whom postmodernist culture is a culture of the present made with fragments of an exploded past.

The only South African writer who seemed to me until recently to display postmodern credentials, has been the short story writer Ivan Vladislavic, whose work is not a million miles away from Borges' (depending on the size of your map), and who similarly collapses distinctions between the fantastic and the everyday and, I would say, between truth and error (Vladislavic 1996). But the most telling example in contemporary South Africa that I know of, and one worth contemplating as a distinctive, highly-charged attempt to mediate the recent past in the present in the new literatures, is provided by the theatrical work called *Ubu and the Truth Commission*. I would like now to turn to this work, which, like the phenomenon to which it alludes, the South African Truth and Reconciliation Commission, not only aspires towards truthfulness, but indicates the problems such an aspiration raises.

Ubu and the Truth Commission was a collaborative production, scripted by writer-academic Jane Taylor, directed and illustrated by artist-filmmaker William Kentridge, and performed by the Handspring Trust Puppeteers, Basil Jones and Adrian Kohler, with actors Louis Seboko, Busi Zokufa, and Dawid Minnaar (Taylor 1998). The production uses a given play-text, Alfred Jarry's outrageous 1890s parody of *Oedipus Rex*, *Ubu Roi*, as its source (Jarry 1993). The original *Ubu Roi*, which caused riots in the Paris theatre when it first appeared, began, it is worth remembering, within an educational institution, as a schoolboy satire on Jarry's physics master, a certain Monsieur Hébert, whom he transformed into the marionette king of an imaginary Poland. Elements of this schoolboy original survive in the South African version, from the opening word 'Shit!' to its emphasis on farting. The aim was to provide a timely mediation of the first hearings of the Truth and Reconciliation Commission – still hearing evidence in 1997, when the first production was showcased at the Market Theatre Upstairs in Johannesburg, before it went to Germany, France and North America – and then finally in 1999, for the last performances (there have been 184 in all), to London. The technique of *Ubu and the Truth Commission* is that of a multitude of techniques; its point of view a multitude of viewpoints. In that sense, it represents quite well the postmodern project initiated by the sense of crisis in European values identified over a hundred years ago by Nietzsche, using texts and images to refer to other texts and images, which themselves refer to others, in a receding series of allusions and illusions.

This reflexivity signals a gap or break in the relation between sign and signified which it is typical of such works to promote, on the assumption that there can be no direct or even indirect relation between sign and signified. The multimedia production gave us a live Pa and Ma Ubu, excellently played by Dawid Minnaar as an underpanted Afrikaner and Busi Zokufa as a nightgowned black mama, accompanied by a puppet crocodile called Niles and a three-headed dog called Brutus, as well as a talking vulture on a swing, against a backdrop of animated drawings, documentary film footage, and a dense soundscore. The production acknowledged as it disrupted generic, aesthetic, cultural, political and historical categories, to occupy a liminal space and time, neither here nor there, neither then nor now, but somewhere in-between, thereby suggesting a postmodern inflection upon contemporary events. The problem is: in what sense, if at all, can it be taken to represent anything, conjuring as this suggests a sort of spell in the space between different pasts and the present?

If we consider some of the elements which contribute to this spell, we may find something more concrete. Elements such as the recreation of the character of Jarry's insane despot Pa Ubu as a cowardly, brutal government agent from the apartheid era who has committed appalling crimes, but who, through a mixture of fake remorse and low cunning, manages to escape punishment; and the recreation of his accomplice Ma Ubu as a grossly self-satisfied black matriarch, a kind of puffed-up Winnie Mandela, who tries to match her partner's misdemeanours (which at first she thinks are merely marital infidelities) by betraying his crimes on national TV. The narrative of Pa and Ma Ubu's grotesque and farcical relationship – according to Kentridge, based on the marriage of government killer Dirk Coetzee – this narrative is interrupted by extracts from actual witness statements delivered at the Truth Commission. The witness statements are delivered in dignified tones by Busi Zokufa and Louis Seboko, in the original language used by the witnesses before the Commission, but made to appear as if uttered by semi-life-size puppets, whose words are then simultaneously translated by an actor standing in a transparent booth on one side of the stage. The black-and-white documentary footage, on a massive projection screen behind the performers, reminds viewers of familiar, historic moments of atrocity from the apartheid era. Kentridge's charcoal animations, reminiscent of Goya's *Horrors of War*, fill the gaps between film and stills with flickering, dark images, which create a kind of running commentary involving three main motifs: the figure of the balloon-like Ubu strutting about like a playground bully; a tripod-shaped camera machine which sets up scenes of torture and murder; and a repeated close-up of a huge staring eye, challenging us to keep watching, while implying voyeuristic overtones.

These complex elements, mixing the fantastic and the historical, the documentary and the surreal, suggest how far *Ubu and the Truth Commission* represents a complete break from the straightforward, predominantly naturalistic and didactic work that drove South Africa's oppositional theatre during the apartheid era. The first impact of a production is almost overwhelming in its intensity: pain, guilt, laughter, sorrow and fear are all evoked, and I recall at the Paris production in December 1998 (Maison des Arts, Creteil) overhearing spectators reacting with shock –

'*Quelle horreur! Quelle horreur!*' a woman behind me kept muttering. Many were in tears. The addition of sur-titles in French for that production, translating the dialogue and the witness statements, as well as the visual appearance of the moustachio'd Dawid Minnaar as Pa Ubu, had the additional effect of recalling France's recent colonial past, the torture, killings, and betrayals, and the cynical manipulation of truth so brilliantly represented, for example, in Gillo Pontecorvo's *Battle of Algiers* (1966), a film originally banned in France, where the authorities did not want to face what was done in their name, before they withdrew from their nearest and largest colony. When I mentioned this to members of the *Ubu* group afterwards, they said: 'Wherever we do this work, skeletons fall out of cupboards.'

The great strength of *Ubu and the Truth Commission* is that it crosses national, cultural and linguistic frontiers in remembering the past, re-membering or bringing together fragments in the present. It does this with immediate and shattering effect, forcefully registering the claim to be remembered of the anonymous and therefore all-too-forgettable victims, urging us to realise that every single act, every single name before the Commission, like that before other tribunals, carries its truth. And yet – what are those truths? 'Our Reign of Terror was no Reign of Error', proclaims the underpanted Ubu; 'We knew what we did, and still we did it' (17). The truths of the perpetrators are not the same as the truths of the victims: there are errors fundamental to the truth-telling process, it seems. But surely that is inevitable, since, as Jane Taylor points out, what we are hearing in and through the play are individual testimonies, 'the private patterns of language and thought that structure memory and mourning', rather than the larger, more public narratives which marked the decades of protest. Developing a representation of interiority, of multiple subjectivities, necessarily involves the development of an art of multiple viewpoints, multiple perspectives – hence, too, necessarily, of error.

Kentridge has remarked that people expect the truth in South African theatre; although of course theatre is a fiction. 'That kind of political theatre which we had so much of in South Africa does not tell "the truth" ', he said in a *Guardian* interview which coincided with the final appearances of *Ubu* in London (Jones 1999, 14). Does not now, perhaps – but did it, then? As Nietzsche reminds us, it is an error to search for truth in art, in drama. However, if he is right, is it not then a *necessary* error? For Nietzsche, the effect of Greek tragedy was to lead him to ponder the relation between our experience of suffering in life and our experience of suffering in art. How to cope with the pain of others was a central question in Nietzsche's work; a question which, it seems to me, is raised in an acute form by *Ubu and the Truth Commission*, a question of deep importance in any consideration of the value of art or literature, but especially the art or literature of countries or communities who have experienced oppression.

This is not to say that *Ubu and the Truth Commission* is a work without weaknesses: the banality of its script, the tendency towards stridency and excess, were particularly striking in the London production at the cramped little Tricycle Theatre in Kilburn in June 1999. This was the venue which had recently witnessed shows on the Stephen Lawrence inquiry and the Nuremberg Trials, shows whose effectiveness sprang from their documentary simplicity, rather than the battery of devices, the anthology of theatrical techniques, required by the South African production of *Ubu*. And compared with the openness, the freedom for the spectator of differing, even contradictory views, set up by Pontecorvo's film, the South African *Ubu* came across as an harangue – ironically, given its postmodernist aspirations. It came across as finally more monolithic and less multifarious and multiperspectival than it seemed at first, and more tied to its historic moment, than other and I suspect more lasting works.

Nevertheless, the play encourages thought about how literary and dramatic productions may be able to carry worthwhile meanings for us today, how the attempted mediation of what we might provisionally call truths, which we *can* only call provisional truths, within the uncertain, shifting but irresistible present, can operate. As representations, theatrical events rely on audience foreknowledge, in order to work: but then, work they do in this case, although that foreknowledge, or set of memories, varies a lot among audience members, and between audiences, with the result that the sum of our experiences becomes what Nietzsche described: a multitude of perspectives, necessarily erroneous. I want to come back to this, in relation to another example of relatively recent theatrical work concerned with truth and error in the decolonising moment – Ariel Dorfman's *Death and the Maiden*, which engaged with the model for the South African Truth Commission, the Rettig Commission on Human Rights set up in post-Pinochet Chile.

But first I want to say that the texts (in the broad sense of cultural productions) that I am talking about, texts such as the *Ubu* play, are recent, uncanonical works: for two reasons. Firstly, to make a point about the importance for anybody interested in the world we live in as we enter the millennium, of literary work, specifically in its theatrical form, because that is where we find one immediate and sympathetically accessible shaping of our most pressing concerns at the millenium; but also, secondly, to explore the importance of work specifically addressing the concerns of countries engaged in unshackling themselves from the long colonial inheritance – countries such as, but not exclusively, South Africa. In the new millennium, such countries must realise that they are, for better or worse, part of the larger world: a world in which they are one of many nation-states striving to overcome a past which is being intermittently recalled in the present, a present almost exploding under the pressures of deprivation, poverty and crime. With new freedoms, come new oppressions. The freedom to speak, but not necessarily to be heard; the freedom to desire, but not necessarily to be satisfied.

Another problem with *Ubu and the Truth Commission* is its cynicism, not just the cynicism of the postmodern, fiddling with techniques while the world burns; but a cynical take on the workings of the Commission, before even the words of the perpetrators had been heard, much less the Commission's final deliberations and the report which came out on 29 October 1998. If audiences were familiar with the original Jarry play, they might have expected Pa and Ma Ubu to sail off into the sunset, as they do in the Handspring Kentridge version; life carrying on as before, it seems to be saying. This message upset some of the early South African audiences, committed to the success of the Truth and Reconciliation process. But, unfortunately, *one* of the truths which have since emerged, is that many of the perpetrators *have* sailed off, receiving, for what we understand are 'political' reasons, i.e., so as not to rock the boat of the rainbow republic, receiving golden handshakes and retiring to their farms to sip Marula on the stoep until the end of their days.

So: why revisit the *Ubu* play? Well, because it poses at least one real continuing issue, a reaction raised by the memories of apartheid in the present: the issue of how you satisfy the desire for objective truth, when truths are always accompanied by error. This desire is reflected in Chairperson Archbishop Tutu's Foreword to the Report of the TRC, where he recorded that:

> A Dutch visitor to the Commission observed that the Truth and Reconciliation Commission must fail. Its task is simply too demanding. Yet, she argued, 'even as it fails, it has already succeeded beyond any rational expectations'. She quoted Emily Dickinson: 'the truth must dazzle gradually . . . or all the world would be blind'.
>
> (1999, 4)

Dickinson's poem ('Tell all the truth but tell it slant') is apt, even when misquoted: 'the Truth must dazzle gradually/Or every man be blind', it concludes (Johnson 1975, 507). Tutu went on to say that the way the stories of the past are told and the way they are heard change as the years go by. 'The spotlight gyrates, exposing old lies and illuminating new truths . . . The report of the Commission will now take its place in the historical landscape of which future generations will make sense – searching for the clues that lead, endlessly, to a truth that will, in the very nature of things, never be fully revealed' (4).

The Archbishop Emeritus expresses the Christian view, according to which there is an absolute truth, even if it is only revealed to us through a glass darkly; and I am not sure that Nietzsche's position is as far from it as he would like it to be. According to Antjie Krog's account of the Commission in her book *Country of My Skull* (1998), the truths she heard included obvious lies, but these, too, were revealing. Captain Jacques Hechter's testimony, for example. By day he was just a cop, working in an office; by night he became, in his own words, 'a white Afrikaner terrorist', as he went out in balaclava and gloves to kill scores of people in the townships and rural areas. The judge asked him about his memories: 'Are you able to remember that on a certain day in 1987 on a farm near Pienaarsrivier you electrocuted three people?' Answer: 'I can remember the path . . . it was a white chalky road . . . and there were guinea fowl. I can remember things like that, but the really . . . the worse deeds . . . those I do not remember' (Krog 1998, 94). Like certain Nazi operatives before him, Hechter remembers the trivia, the irrelevancies, not the killings. But it is his memory of the trivia that persuades us that he carried out those deeds in fact. Truths operate in strange ways, especially in oral narrative forms; but they may carry an aura of conviction, even if, as is the case with the TRC, they are not being used to convict (although the evidence revealed may lead to some convictions, of people who did not come before the Commission). Krog says that before, white people denied these things happened; after this, they deny they knew about them.

As I have remarked, the producers of *Ubu* have been criticised for complicating and obscuring the simple and devastating truths of the witnesses' testimony: 'Why does it need to be performed by puppets and spiced up with animated images?' asked the *Guardian* (Billington 1999, 25). Kentridge's answer was that he did not want us to listen and say 'Poor people': he wants the audience to experience 'what it is like to have your reality destroyed'. He compared *Ubu* with *The Story I'm About To Tell* (*Indaba Engizoxoxa*), an unpublished theatrical work which accompanied *Ubu* at the 1999 LIFT season in London, and which subsequently appeared at the Grahamstown Festival in South Africa in July 1999. *The Story* was created by journalist/activist Bobby Rodwell, writer Lesego Rampolokeng and director Robert Colman, in collaboration with three professional actors and three survivors from the Khulumani Support Group, set up to help people who had come before the Commission with their stories of atrocity. Like *Ubu* in attempting a representation of witness statements on stage, but using the witnesses themselves, who are referred to somewhat comically to begin with as the 'real people', *The Story I'm About To Tell* harked back to the radical storytelling techniques of Athol Fugard's early 1970s plays *Sizwe Bansi* and *The Island*, which mixed fictional drama with the remembered truths of the black performers' personal experiences to offer an added claim on truth, working popular storytelling motifs and memories into oppositional theatre.

These works represented a transgressive, culturally hybrid urge which it was the unique potential of theatre in South Africa to provide during the darkest days of repression. The continuity of the collaborative work between Fugard and the Serpent Players from the New Brighton township, bringing together into a creative new synthesis Western European and African traditions of representing the everyday was reiterated in the figure of the presenter in *The Story I'm About To Tell*, reminiscent for example of Serpent Players' most Brechtian piece *The Coat* (1966), itself directly derived from the court appearance and statements of Player Norman Ntshinga – whose written accounts of his experiences on Robben Island also provided the material for *The Island*. *The Story I'm About To Tell* used a presenter to mediate between the stage and the audience, a technique taken further by concluding every performance with about twenty minutes of invited audience participation and discussion.

A strange thing happened during one of the performances of this production that Kentridge attended: 'At some point one of the performers forgot his own words. It was his own experience he was talking about, but he forgot his words. It was when he looked like an amateur that you got closest to truth' (Jones 1999, 15). Forgetting created an experience of truth. This truth is the truth of an experience remembered – in the given example, the experience of three years on death row in Pretoria for a crime he didn't commit, by Duma Kumalo. Kumalo's memories take us further into the dark depths of the past than perhaps any of the others, into that region identified by Primo Levi, as the region of the drowned, not the saved. According to Levi, one of a handful of Italian Jewish holocaust survivors, only those who died in the camps could really tell us the truth. That final truth will elude us, as it eluded Levi. In his witness statement, Kumalo recalls hearing the chains of a group of condemned men rattling a final farewell to him as they went to the gallows in Pretoria: theirs is a truth he does not know and cannot even always remember, insofar as he glimpsed it; nonetheless, his representation of it on stage gives audiences an inkling of their reality.

For as Nietzsche says, reality is necessarily somebody's, although it is also necessarily multiform, perceptible only in part and temporarily. For Nietzsche, to glorify an artwork as if it were the way to discover truth is perverse; at the same time, though, his reflections upon the birth of tragedy lead us to think about the relation between our experiences of suffering, memory and drama in a profound and intense way. He focuses upon extremes, and his language is correspondingly extreme. But we live in extreme times, too, although not all the time, of course, that would be intolerable, to those of us lucky enough to be in receipt of regular salaries and some security. However, this security brings a responsibility: to attend to the stories which are being told in our societies, and the ways in which those stories are being told, so as to remember them, and thereby re-member ourselves in our societies and institutions. Bearing witness, it might be called, although that is a phrase which, if it goes deep, should be handled with care.

I would like now finally to turn to Ariel Dorfman's play *Death and the Maiden*, first performed in London in 1991, and a work the author has claimed touches upon tragedy 'in an almost Aristotelian sense, a work of art that might help a collective to purge itself, through pity and terror, in other words to force the spectators to confront those predicaments that, if not brought into the light of day, could lead to their ruin'(Dorfman 1998, 147). What are or were those predicaments? Dorfman was prompted by the events marking the transition to democracy of Chile in 1990, when he returned from exile, and in particular the Rettig Commission, set up to investigate crimes that had ended in death, but without naming or judging the perpetrators. Dorfman was prompted to ask questions which are very familiar to South Africans and others (for example, in the north of Ireland) today: such as, 'how do you reach the truth if lying has become a habit? How do we keep the past alive without becoming its prisoner? How do we forget it without risking its repetition in the future? Is it legitimate to sacrifice the truth to ensure peace?' (Dorfman 1998, 146).

The play which emerged from these questions does not attempt to resolve them, indeed it concludes in a strikingly ambivalent way, facing both characters and audience with a mirror, in which they and we see ourselves, as Schubert's piercingly sad music shifts the moral issues onto some indefinable and enigmatic level. I say enigmatic, although I found it myself a question-begging, even perhaps somewhat glib ending to an enormously powerful and timely play, in which – as many people now know, since the play has run in many countries, including South Africa and the USA, as well as being made into a Hollywood film – a woman kidnaps at gunpoint the doctor her lawyer-husband brings home, and forces him to confess to complicity in her torture as a political prisoner. What we don't know is whether he has lied about being her torturer to save his skin, or whether he has been forced into telling the truth about his past. He sounds convincing as he records his confession:

> ROBERTO: I would put on Schubert because it was a way of gaining the prisoners' trust. But I also knew it was a way of alleviating their suffering. You've got to believe it was a way of alleviating the prisoners' suffering. Not only the music, but everything else I did. That's how they approached me, at first . . . The prisoners were dying on them, they told me, they needed someone to help care for them . . . The real, real truth, it was for humanitarian reasons. We're at war, I thought, they want to kill me and my family, they want to install a totalitarian dictatorship, but even so, they still have the right to some form of medical attention. It was slowly, without realising how, that I became involved in more delicate operations.   (Act 3, 1998, 135)

This is chillingly convincing, although somehow I can't imagine the doctors who saw the dying Steve Biko putting on Schubert to gain his trust. But I suppose Dorfman's play is aimed at the consciously cultured elite, who might enjoy Schubert after watching images of atrocities from around the world on their TV screens. Or am I being too cynical? Perhaps there is here also a little reminder of those Nazi commandants who listened to Schubert for some light relief after a heavy day's work in the camps. In that sense, there is here a truth in the recognition of what struggles another formerly dark, totalitarian state is going through as it moves into a democratic present, but a present still haunted by the past.

The strength of *Death and the Maiden* is that it engages with the personal, even domestic, intimate level of this struggle from the past into the present, and future. The relationship between Gerardo, the husband, and his wife Paulina is damaged, by strains they impose upon each other, from both within and outside themselves. This is demonstrated by the moment when we are encouraged to believe with him that Roberto the doctor will now be forgiven, he has created the conditions for reconciliation – a belief Paulina encourages, until her husband leaves them alone. She then turns on Roberto, saying now she will shoot him, since she cannot live in peace with herself if he lives. Is this the urge of the vigilante? Or the urge for justice? 'Don't do it' the man cries, 'I'm innocent.' 'I made it up. We made it up . . . Your husband told me what to write . . . most of it was what he got from you . . . he convinced me that it was the only way that you wouldn't kill me and I had to.' What is farce in *Ubu* is tragedy here; husband and wife are ensnared in the larger evil of their society. Paulina says she fed her husband some lies, too, which Roberto has inadvertently corrected, so he *must* be guilty. Now all she wants is for him to admit the truth. He continues to protest his innocence, saying that if she kills him because of what was done to her, his children will want vengeance, and so the killing will continue. Her last words ask why it is always people like *her* who have to make a sacrifice. Then the mirror descends, obscuring the two protagonists and facing us with ourselves. A kind of coda is provided by a brief scene in which we see the couple at a Schubert concert, and the image of the doctor watching the woman appears, but it is unclear whether we should take it as a memory, or a dramatic reality. The couple, like the audience, look at themselves in the mirror. (In Barney Simon's 1992 Market Production in South Africa, the audience faced each other from opposite sides of the stage, and Gerardo was cast as black.)

As a reviewer of the first production of *Death and the Maiden* at the Royal Court in London put it in the *Times Literary Supplement*, 'the audience is caught in a neat moral trap and is made to confront choices that most would presumably rather leave to the inhabitants of remote and less favoured countries' (Butt 1992, 22). The reviewer's position is self-consciously that of the well-meaning, self-aware liberal West. This may explain how quickly and easily the play became a Hollywood commodity, although not a success. The commodification of such work is part of its problem, imposed by a globally determined arena of cultural production.

But Dorfman also put his play on in Chile, a year after the democratic government took over, and two days after their Commission on Human Rights published its report. The response is instructive.

> In the forums we held afterwards, those in the audience who were themselves victims said they had found the play liberating. But many who had been against the dictatorship, and were now part of the ruling group trying to take the country forward, felt that I had been irresponsible. Some of them said this was not the time, that it was too soon, that I was dwelling on the past. Others refused to see it. These were people in government who could have helped it tour schools and trade unions, so that it could be seen widely. Some of these people were my friends. (Dorfman 1992, 25)

In Chile, then, the play was understood to have the potential to intervene, on a public as well as on a personal level. The same assumption has led Bobby Rodwell to try and take *The Story I'm About To tell* around South African schools. But as this shows, intervention depends upon the circumstances, the time and place, of production. Dorfman remarked in 1998, that 'the story on that stage has not yet, in fact, ended . . . [and] how it really ends will depend on how we, who are watching, act out our own lives' (Foreword, viii).

Ironically, it is the theatre's potential to intervene – or, as I put it earlier, to cross boundaries, to invoke taboos – which makes it more susceptible to repression, and more likely to face censorship, official or unofficial. And, it also makes it more susceptible to error, if error it is when, for example, during the 1998 US production of *Ubu*, audiences laughed ecstatically at the antics of Pa Ubu, whom they saw as a reflection upon Bill Clinton, whose misdemeanours then dominated the public media. Is that identification an error, or does it touch on a truth? Or what about the effect upon members of the South African audiences who walked out in disgust at the same antics, when the underpanted Afrikaner cringed below his black mistress? Well, insofar as this play-production exists in a present moment and location, insofar as it recalls the unverifiable past – including the Truth Commission's deliberations, the events which led to them, and now, the debates which follow – it surely has a claim on all of us.

This is why I would argue for the continuing role of the theatre, as potentially a critical cultural force, even after postmodernism, and the rejection of the meta-narrative of truth. It is also why I would take issue with the puritans, or those who assume there are truths to be found, but that these are absolute and given truths. Even if we reject the extreme position, according to which reality cannot be captured, we can and should accept that all art, all history, is to some degree illusory, created from a multitude of viewpoints. In other words, we should accept the necessity of error. To do so, may enable us to begin re-membering ourselves in our many positions, always already caught up by the dismembering past, as we are by the dismembering, globalizing economics and politics of the present.

Note

This essay is a revised version of a 'key-note' paper given to the Association of University English Teachers of South Africa, Pretoria, 12 July 1999.

Works Cited

Billington, M. 1999. 'It matters, too much', *Guardian* (12 June), 25.

Borges, J.L. 1964. 'Funes the Memorious' (1956), trans. James E. Irby in Donald A. Yates and James E. Irby (eds) *Labyrinths*, Harmondsworth: Penguin Books.

——— 1975. 'Of Exactitude in Science' (1946), in Norman Thomas di Giovanni (trans.) *A Universal History of Infamy*, Harmondsworth: Penguin Books.

Butt, J. 1992. 'Guilty Conscience?' *Times Literary Supplement* (28 February), 22.

Clark, T. and Royle, N. eds 1995. 'The University in Ruins: Essays on the crisis in the concept of the modern university', *The Oxford Literary Review*, 17, 1–2.

de Man, P. 1979. *Allegories of Reading*, New Haven and London: Yale University Press.

Dorfman, A. 1998. *Death and the Maiden*, transl. and intro. by the author in *The Resistance Trilogy*, London: Nick Hern Books.

——— 1992. 'Silence is the enemy of a free press', *Observer* (3 May), 25.

Gadamer, H-G. 1995 'The relevance of the beautiful', in Nicholas Walker (trans.) and Robert Bernasconi (ed.) *The Relevance of the Beautiful and Other Essays*, Cambridge: Cambridge University Press, 3–53.

Jarry, A. 1993. *Ubu Rex*, in Cyril Connolly and Simon Watson Taylor (trans.) *The Ubu Plays*, London: Methuen World Classics.

Johnson, T.H. ed. 1975. *The Complete Poems of Emily Dickinson*, London: Faber and Faber.

Jones, J. 1999. 'Pulling the strings' (interview with William Kentridge), *Guardian* (9 June), 14–15.

King, B. ed. 1996. *New National and Post-Colonial Literatures: An Introduction*, Oxford: Clarendon Press.

Krog, A. 1998. *Country of My Skull*, London: Jonathan Cape.

Naidoo, J. 1989. *Tracking Down Historical Myths*, Johannesburg: Ad Donker.

Ndebele, N. 1991. 'Redefining Relevance' (1986), in *Rediscovery of the Ordinary: Essays on South African Literature and Culture*, Fordsburg, Johannesburg: COSAW, 58–73.

Nietzsche, F. 1993. *The Birth Of Tragedy*, 1872, 1886, trans. Shaun Whiteside, ed. Michael Tanner, Harmondsworth: Penguin Books.

Sacks, O. 1986. *The Man Who Mistook His Wife for a Hat*, London and Basingstoke: Picador.

Taylor J. 1998. *Ubu and the Truth Commission*, Cape Town: University of Cape Town Press.

Truth and Reconciliation Commission of South Africa Report 1999. London, Basingstoke and Oxford: Macmillan Reference Ltd., vol. 1.

Vandenbroucke, R. 1985. *Truths the Hand Can Touch: The Theatre of Athol Fugard*, New York: Theatre Communications Group.

Vladislavic, I. 1996. *Propaganda by Monuments & other stories*, Cape Town and Johannesburg: David Philip.

Walcott, D. 1998. 'The Muse of History' (1974), in *What the Twilight Says: Essays*, London: Faber and Faber, 36–64.

Walder, D. 1998. *Post-Colonial Literatures in English: History: History, Language, Theory*, Oxford: Blackwell Publishers.

Watson, S. 1991. *Return of the Moon: Versions of the /Xam*, Cape Town: The Carrefour Press.

Notes on Contributors

Firdous Azim is Professor in the Department of English, University of Dhaka. She is the author of *The Colonial Rise of the Novel* (Routledge, 1993) and co-editor of *Other Englishes: Essays on Commonwealth Writing* (1991) and *Infinite Variety: Women Society and Literature* (Dhaka UPL Press, 1994). She is currently writing a book on the nineteenth-century Bengali poet, Toru Dutt.

Bryan Cheyette is Chair in Twentiet- Century Literature in the Department of English, University of Southampton. He has recently published a book on Muriel Spark for the British Council and is completing *Diasporas of the Mind: British-Jewish Writing and the Nightmare of History* for Yale University Press.

Denise De Caires Narain is Lecturer in English in the School of African and Asian Studies at the University of Sussex from 1991 to the present; she taught with the Open University from 1987 to 1991 and at the University of the West Indies from 1992 to 1993. She is currently completing a book on contemporary Caribbean women poets entitled *Making Style: Contemporary Caribbean Women's Poetry* which is to be published by Routledge.

Simon E. Gikandi is Professor of English Language and Literature at the University of Michigan. He is the author of many books in the area of African, Caribbean and postcolonial literatures, most recently *Writing in Limbo: Modernism and Caribbean Literature* and *Maps of Englishness: Writing Identity in the Culture of Colonialism*.

Dr Abdulrazak Gurnah teaches literature at the University of Kent and has published widely on African Literatures. He is also the author of five novels including *Paradise* (1994) and *Admiring Silence* (1996). His most recent novel, *By The Sea*, will be published in 2000.

Lyn Innes is Professor of Postcolonial Literatures at the University of Kent, Canterbury. She has published books and articles on Irish Literature, Chinua Achebe, and other African authors, and is currently working on a history of Black and South Asian Writing in Britain to be published by Cambridge University Press.

Susheila Nasta is currently Research Lecturer at the Open University where she is completing a book due to be published by Macmillan entitled *Home Truths: Fictions of the South Asian Diaspora in Britain*. Her previous teaching post was in the School of English & Drama at Queen Mary & Westfield College, University of London. Previous publications include work on Sam Selvon and women's writing from Africa, the Caribbean and South Asia. She is founding editor of *Wasafiri*.

Dennis Walder is Professor of Literature at the Open University (UK). Educated at the Universities of Cape Town and Edinburgh, he has published widely on nineteenth- and twentieth-century literature. His books include: *Athol Fugard* (1984), editions of Fugard's plays in three volumes, the best-selling edited volume *Literature in the Modern World*, and, most recently, *Post-Colonial Literatures in English* (1998). He is currently working on Narrative and Memory.

Briar Wood grew up in New Zealand where she studied at the University of Auckland. She is subject tutor in creative writing, new literatures and theories of postcolonialism at the University of North London. At present she is engaged in research for a book on poetry in the Pacific from the 1960s to the present. She has published poetry and short stories in journals and anthologies, mostly in New Zealand and the United Kingdom.